ASTRONUMEROLOGY

ASTRONUMEROLOGY

Your Key to
Empowerment
Using Stars
and Numbers

Pamela Hobs Bell and Jordan Simon

AVON BOOKS NEW YORK

AVON BOOKS, INC.
1350 Avenue of the Americas
New York, New York 10019

Copyright © 1998 by Pamela Hobs Bell and Jordan Simon
Published by arrangement with the authors
Visit our website at **http://www.AvonBooks.com**
ISBN: 0-380-79466-7

Library of Congress Cataloging in Publication Data:

Bell, Pamela.
  Astronumerology : your key to empowerment using stars and numbers / by Pamela
  Bell and Jordan Simon.
      p.   cm.
  1. Astrology and psychology. 2. Horoscopes. 3. Astrology.
4. Numerology. I. Simon, Jordan. II. Title.
BF1729.P8B47   1998   98-16524
133.5—dc21   CIP

First Avon Books Trade Printing: July 1998

AVON TRADEMARK REG. U.S. PAT. OFF. AND IN OTHER COUNTRIES, MARCA REGISTRADA, HECHO
EN U.S.A.

Printed in the U.S.A.

OPM   10 9 8 7 6 5 4 3 2 1

Dedicated to our families for their unconditional love and invaluable support.

Pam: To my wonderful parents who provided a magical childhood and ethical foundation that I could pass on to my own family.

Jordan: Barbara Simon, Rita Simon, Jerry Simon

Thanks for Everything!♥

ACKNOWLEDGMENTS

We would like to thank the fine folks at Avon Books for believing in our concept and to our editors, Ann McKay Thoroman and Kristen Cortright, for their direction and expertise in bringing our book about Astronumerology from concept to reality.

A special thanks goes to Barbara-J. Zitwer for the effort she has put forward on our behalf.

We extend a heartfelt thanks to those wonderful people who comprise our support network, whose encouragement and kindnesses are much appreciated.

Pam: Thanks to all my family, extended family, friends, mentors, and all of you who have inspired me to keep my own wagon hitched to a positive star.

Jordan: Hermann Lademann, David Rappoport, Cassandra Malaxa, Garth Christensen, Bill Curtis, Greg Lindeblom, Michael Stiles, Tracy Carns, Debbie Mills, Laurel Cardone, Barbara Tapp, Susan Fadem, Geri Bain, Michael Frank, and Karla Vermulen, Lisa Weinreb.

CONTENTS

Contents

Contents

INTRODUCTION

Let's admit it. We're all seeking the key to unlocking our potential to lead a more fulfilling life. We've learned "how to" and affirmed ourselves up the yin yang, searching for the shortcut to a better job, a better home, a better love life. And did you know that the secret to discovering your potential actually lies in your birthday?

Astrology and numerology are familiar tools used to learn more about ourselves and the people around us, thereby enabling us to lead happier, more productive lives. Both are ancient sciences dating back over twenty-five hundred years. Today astrophysicists confirm that the basis of the universe is mathematics. Astrology and numerology have always posited that very link between human beings and the cosmos.

Taken independently, each science provides revealing insights into our natural talents and behavior patterns. But put an individual's astrological and numerological birth charts side by side and you discover some amazing resonances and differences that paint a multidimensional personality portrait.

Certainly astrology and numerology stand alone as reliable self-help tools, but not only is a complete chart analysis enormously complex and time-consuming, it also requires expert, often expensive input. Combining the two into an entirely new science produces a more complete character analysis instantaneously. Your Sun Sign and Birth Number, both derived from your birthday, are the single most powerful aspects of the astrological and numerological charts. Sometimes the two seem utterly contradictory, and at other times they prove synchronous or complementary. Astronumerology™ can tell us whether our inner dialogue is harmonious or discordant. Most important, it identifies our strengths and challenges to help us work through deep-seated internal struggles, and maximize our potential to lead a more fulfilled and enriched life.

Astronumerology is user-friendly. Nearly everyone knows their Sun Sign. If you don't know yours, a chart is provided in this chapter, and a more detailed account in the chapter titled The Stars. Your Birth Number is easy to figure out: Just add the numbers in your birth date together and keep adding them until only a single digit remains. How to find your Birth Number is provided in this chapter, with additional information included in the chapter titled The Numbers.

Obviously there's much more to both sciences than the Sun Sign and Birth Number, such as the rising sign or ascendant, and the name number that is the numerical value of the letters in your birth name. But if we were to include *every* element of each science in this book, you'd need a Mack truck to cart it away! If you know these or other important chart influences such as the moon sign (your emotional life) or heart number (the total of vowels in your name, indicating your innermost desires), you can have fun and further enhance your self-awareness by reading them in combination with your sun sign or birth number. Keep an open mind, when reading your astronumerology combination. Astronumerology is an innovative, trail-blazing new science. Your sun sign and birth number don't exist in a vacuum: They interact in exciting, sometimes unpredictable ways! Understanding their disparate influences provides insights that will enrich your understanding of a special, singular individual: You.

With the twelve zodiac signs and nine primary numbers, there are 108 possible combinations or 108 unique personality types. For example, we have a Gemini client who forever protests that she doesn't fit the traditional Gemini mold. "I'm not a flirt," she sweetly insists. "And I may have a million and one ideas whirling round my brain, but I'm not scattered, I'm very, *very* focused." Oh, she's a Gemini, all right: glib, charming, and always doing at least three things at once. Yes, certain aspects of her astrological chart indicate why she's more practical and goal-oriented than the typical Gemini. Likewise, her numerological chart shows that this breezy, gracious chatterbox has what it takes to get things done. But while thoroughly interpreting either the astrology or numerology birth chart would take hours, a quick glance at her Sun Sign and Birth Number combination gives the answer in minutes. Our Gemini friend also has a 4 Birth Number, which adds balance, responsibility, order, and grounding to her profile. She can establish a stable foundation from which to operate, and quite smoothly, no doubt, thanks to the Gemini influence.

When this was explained to her, she asked, "Does this mean I'm limited to being a Gemini Four? Don't I have choices?"

YES! Your astronumerological profile is every bit as unique as your fingerprints. It indicates both the positive and negative polarities you were born with, but your stars and numbers are not fixed at either end of the spectrum. Think of them as the possibilities and challenges along a 180-degree line (or even a 360-degree continuum) and pick the point where you want to be.

You can choose to be whoever and whatever you want. There are successful entertainers, politicians, philosophers, scientists, teachers, writers, composers, explorers, designers, doctors, lawyers, ministers, businessmen, and bankers of EVERY sign and number. **You have the power to create the life you want. That power is free will.**

No matter what your number or sign, *you* decide whether to turn right or left at every crossroads; you're in charge of your life. Astronumerology provides a road map of your potential. It increases your self-awareness of natural strengths and talents, empowering you to make, if not always the right choices, then at least better-informed ones. And if you understand your challenges, you're already halfway to overcoming them.

Obstacles often furnish the needed energy, drive, and stamina to surmount them. You may be gifted with many abilities, but the quality of your life is up to you. Astronumerology not only identifies your positive traits, it helps you to reinforce them. Your stars and numbers are just the signposts on your road to happiness, but remember, you're the one firmly in the driver's seat.

Astronumerology: Your Key to Empowerment Using Stars and Numbers is not about predictions. It's about YOU and the people in your life: your parents, children, friends, siblings, fellow workers, and significant others. We hope you enjoy the book and use it to become the person you always knew you could be!

♥Love,
Pam and Jordan

HOW TO USE THIS BOOK

To find your unique astronumerology combination, locate your birthday under Find Your Sun Sign and figure your number under Find Your Birth Number. Put the two together and read the corresponding pages for that combination in the following text to learn more about yourself and your potential.

Find Your Birth Number

To calculate the Birth Number, convert the month, day, and year of your birth to numbers. Add the numbers together and keep adding them until only one digit remains. Example:

$$\text{March 31, 1968}$$
$$3 + 31 + 1968 = 3+3+1+1+9+6+8 = 31 = 3+1 = 4$$

or

$$\text{March} = 3$$
$$31$$
$$\underline{1968}$$
$$2002 = 2 +0 + 0 +2 = 4$$

In the example, 4 is the Birth Number. You may read about your Birth Number itself in "The Numbers" chapter on page 15.

Find Your Sun Sign

If Your birthday is:	Your Sun Sign is:
March 21–April 20	ARIES
April 21–May 21	TAURUS
May 22–June 21	GEMINI
June 22–July 23	CANCER
July 24–August 23	LEO
August 24–September 23	VIRGO
September 24–October 23	LIBRA

October 24–November 22	SCORPIO
November 23–December 21	SAGITTARIUS
December 22–January 20	CAPRICORN
January 21–February 19	AQUARIUS
February 20–March 20	PISCES

You may read about your Sun Sign by itself in The Stars chapter on page 1.

THE STARS

•

Astrology Sun Signs

All The Astrology You Need To Know For This Book

WHAT IS THE SUN SIGN, REALLY?

Forget the image of a cigar-chomping, tonsorially challenged, polyester-clad man shackled in gold chains sidling up to his prey in a bar, asking "Hey, baby, what's your sign?" Your astrological birth chart is unique and actually quite complex.

Consider your Sun Sign as merely a blueprint, or skeletal outline, of your personality; several factors flesh it out, painting a fully realized three-dimensional portrait of who—and where—you are as a human being. You can nevertheless glean a great deal of information about yourself and the people in your life by understanding each Sun Sign—but even that sign must be understood in the context of the zodiac as a whole.

THE ELEMENTS (OR TRIPLICITIES)

First, signs are grouped according to elements (Fire, Air, Water, and Earth); three signs in each element share certain

1

characteristics and approaches. Fire signs (Aries, Leo, Sagittarius) are zesty, lusty, outgoing, optimistic, and honorable. Think of them as life's spark plugs; their temperature runs from warm to hot-blooded. But like fire, they can burn themselves out quickly, both in love and business (occasionally singeing others in the process).

Air signs (Gemini, Libra, Aquarius) are intellectual, logical, inspired, and congenial. Because of their ability to be detached and see "the big picture," they play shrink to their many friends, but tend to rationalize their feelings in more intimate situations.

Water signs (Cancer, Scorpio, Pisces) are emotional, intuitive, compassionate, and sensitive. Just as the primordial sea gave birth to all life on earth and nothing can grow without rain, water signs are here to nourish and nurture; if they're not careful, they can drown in their own feelings.

Earth signs (Taurus, Virgo, Capricorn) are grounded, rooted, solid, and, well, earthy. The builders of the zodiac, they'll gladly put their noses to the grindstone to establish lasting foundations and comfortable surroundings. But they can be materialistic, stodgy, and, yes, boring: think trenches and ruts. . . .

THE QUALITIES (OR QUADRUPLICITIES)

The signs are also categorized as one of three qualities (fixed, cardinal, and mutable). Fixed signs (Taurus, Leo, Scorpio, Aquarius) are stable, loyal, and solid as the proverbial rock. Once they've settled into an opinion, place, situation, or relationship, they're nearly impossible to budge, which is their greatest strength—or weakness. They use the soapboxes as pulpits.

Cardinal signs (Aries, Cancer, Libra, Capricorn) are active and ambitious, purposeful and pushy. The movers, shakers, and self-starters, they build the soapboxes and send out invitations to life's lectures.

Mutable signs (Gemini, Virgo, Sagittarius, Pisces) are flexible, fluid, versatile, and tolerant. They seek solutions, weigh options, and hedge if necessary. They place the pulpit and microphone for maximum effect on the audience.

Don't worry, there's no such thing as duplicity in astrology—we have real life for that.

THE CUSPS

Astrologers fight like Siamese and Pekingese over the significance of cusps. According to Webster's, a cusp is a point or apex, defining it as anything from "the horn of a crescent moon" to "a point on the surface of a grinding tooth." If you're born within two to three days of the Sun Sign closest to your own, many astrologers claim you're "on the cusp." These starry-eyed seers swear that your basic personality is subtly colored by each adjacent sign. This isn't utter hogwash, but it is pretty sloppy astrology: wherever your sun happens to be, it shines brightly with equatorial heat. Your chart gives plenty of reasons why you might be a Scorpio yet behave at times like, say, a Sagittarius.

If you were born on the exact day the sun switched signs, you must consult an astrologer (or computer program) to determine whether you're a Taurus or a Gemini, a Pisces or an Aries. The following dates are generally accurate, but often change a day or two in either direction, depending on the year you were born. If you're in doubt, find out; if you're curious, you can always read both signs and decide which fits your description best. (Think of it as the turkey gravy spilling into the mashed potatoes: it may be messy, but it still tastes good.)

THE SUN SIGNS

Aries (March 21–April 20)
"The Grand Innovator"

The astrological glyph (or symbol) for Aries represents its horns, yet it also resembles a fountain. Both are apt descriptions. Rams love to butt heads; they rarely lack self-confidence, meeting everything and everyone in life head-on, and positively overflow with ideas. And yes, as the first sign of the zodiac, they're often teased by astrologers for being babies. Ariens are the original instant-gratification kids. They want what they want when they want it, no exceptions.

No wonder Ariens function best within a loosely structured work environment. They're dazzling initiators and go-getters: their alphabet begins with Adventurous, Bold, Creative, Dynamic, and Enterprising. Ariens aren't afraid to take risks when they believe in something; sure, they can come across as impatient, impulsive, pushy, selfish, even reckless. Still you can't help but admire their steamroller drive and enthusiasm. The problem is, they usually lack follow-through and staying power; no sooner have they pitched and sold one idea than ten—just as brilliant, mind you—take its place and they're off on the next adventure. If they're self-employed, they should have a loyal staff that can stack, process, and file the paperwork scattered in the Arien whirlwind.

The true Aries is utterly straightforward and unswervingly honest. Think of Dudley Do-Right in a flashier suit: totally gallant, guileless, and gullible in the extreme. See, Ariens don't cheat, and they're always shocked when someone else does.

Leo ignites your flames of passions and keeps them stoked. Bosom buddies Gemini and Sagittarius share your sense of adventure and questing intellect. Libra can help balance and ground you in both love and work.

Taurus (April 21–May 21)
"The Master Builder"

Remember *Ferdinand the Bull,* the classic children's book, whose hero wanted nothing more than to recline in a meadow, smelling the wildflowers? That's how Taureans see themselves: gentle, sensitive, peace-loving souls drawn to everything beautiful and artistic. They can't understand why people expect them to paw the ground, snort, and charge, let alone stampede the china shop. If anything, they'll order the newest Wedgewood pattern on consignment: no other sign so strongly equates material and emotional security. The wonderful thing is that Taureans are bullish on sharing the wealth.

As a Venus-ruled sign, Taureans like—no, *adore*—the finer things in life. They're usually as mellow as they seem, until riled; then you see the cartoonish steam gushing from the ears. Fortunately, this impressive display doesn't last long if you know where to stroke them, literally and ego-wise. (A nice candlelit dinner and bottle of wine won't hurt either.)

The other trait most associated with Taureans is stubbornness. Once a bull locks horns, goring can result. . . . To be fair, Taureans are often right to hold fast to their ideas and ideals; their insistence that others meekly capitulate waves a red cape at their opponents, who ironically appear far more steamed up than the placid bull. But that obstinacy (and serene self-confidence) gets things done. Taurus is here to build things, to plow ahead with amazing stamina. "Sow and ye shall reap" could well be this sign's motto.

Capricorn and Virgo share your material concerns and emotional stability. Cancer brings out your softer, protective side romantically. Scorpio provides a classic yin and yang yo-yo relationship with a torrid affair or tug-of-war.

Gemini (May 22–June 21)
"The Great Communicator"

Gemini is Latin for "twins," representing this quicksilver sign's duality. The glyph is the Roman numeral II, representing the clear choice confronting Geminis: should they be profoundly superficial or at least superficially profound? It also forms a column, suggesting Gemini's intellectual bedrock and surprising potential for underlying solidity.

Charming, eloquent, witty, and a born raconteur, a Gemini is everyone's idea of the perfect party guest. To the casual observer he or she might seem like the intellectual equivalent of a jack-of-all-trades, master of none. In fact, Geminis are haunted by that very fear of being essentially shallow. Let's put it this way, Gemini: If it worries you so much, you must have more emotional depth that you realize. Because they're fascinated by everything and everyone, Geminis also develop a reputation for being scattered. They simply enjoy going off on intriguing tangents and get sidetracked easily. Yet a fork in the road—literally or metaphorically—can drive them bonkers, since they love anything new. "If I take this road," asks poor Gemini, "what will I miss on the other?"

As a result of this curiosity and restlessness, Geminis often take longer to mature than other signs. They're eternally bubbling over with childlike enthusiasm about their latest project or amour, but can have a little difficulty facing reality and responsibilities. But growing up doesn't mean abandoning their inner child. Eventually, whatever their sex, the Gemini Peter Pan will get hooked by Wendy.

Aquarius will stimulate you intellectually as both friend and lover. Libra can gad about and throw parties, making you a perfect social match. Sagittarius can roam the world with you as your best pal. Leo shares your love of beauty and romance.

Cancer (June 22–July 23)
"The Universal Protector"

Crabby and *moody* are the two words many less sensitive souls associate with Cancer. Yes, those soft-shelled moon-ruled crustaceans ARE changeable and remarkably alert to their surroundings and themselves. Call the rest of humanity hunters and gatherers: Cancers collect everything from memories to people. They hate throwing anything away, even a moth-eaten varsity sweater or a destructive relationship. Just like their symbol, Cancers can be cautious and shy, but if their quarry threatens to elude them, they act with surprising speed and those pincers hold on for dear life.

Cancer is traditionally associated with home and hearth, and they do like comfortable surroundings. Cancerians know the value of a buck and are obsessed with quality; in fact, there are probably more millionaires born under Cancer than any other sign. Cancer men and women alike constantly fret whether they CAN have it all. It's just not good enough, as it is for Capricorn, to rationalize staying late at the office because you're putting bread on the table: Cancer has to SET that table, too.

Many astrologers claim that Cancers are as obsessed with their mothers as Anthony Perkins in *Psycho.* This is somewhat exaggerated; indeed, many Cancerians feel (s)mothered growing up. How ironic then that they repeat the pattern in their adult relationships, fussing like hens regardless of their sex. For their own happiness (and others'), Cancers must learn to retract those pincers and let go occasionally.

You'll feel safe and warm in the strong, silent arms of Taurus. Virgo can help you translate your career dreams into reality. Pisces will gladly indulge your nurturing side. Scorpio's intensity will both frighten and attract you like the tides.

Leo (July 24–August 23)
"A Star Is Born"

Leo is the King of the Beasts, ruled by the sun: when Lions aren't basking in the glow of the footlights, they shine like the sun itself, radiating life-giving warmth to everyone around them. If they had their druthers, Leos would spend their entire lives in three positions: standing in the spotlight, sitting on a throne, and lying on their backs getting their tummies tickled (then tucked). Leos are attracted to acclaim and fame like moths to a flame; once they're there, they don't flutter about, however, but know exactly what to do.

Lions are magnanimous, loyal, sincere, ardent, and generous to a fault—even their own. There's just one little catch: they require attention. Lots of it, bordering on fawning admiration. The flip side of this vanity is their deep-seated need for approval. This means that lions are more than usually susceptible to sycophants, yes-people, and hangers-on.

Despite their love of *la dolce vita,* Leos are rarely lazy; quite the contrary, since they recognize that living the good life requires both cash and cachet. As a fixed fire sign, Leos are able to harness their almost superhuman energy and ambition; once they've set a goal, they'll pursue it with passion. Leos are far too proud and independent to hang on to someone else's coattails; they'd need to receive credit where credit is due, even if it's not star billing. Lions may not entirely subscribe to the "there are no small roles, only small actors" adage, but they do believe in paying their dues.

The perfect friend, lover or business partner, Libra will know just how to stroke your mane. Gemini and Sagittarius keep you hopping socially. Aries plays the ardent suitor, though independence becomes an issue.

Virgo (August 24–September 23)
"The Idealistic Critic"

Let's put this virgin business to bed once and for all. Virgos do have libidos and they do obey them. But that virgin image makes sense when you consider that Virgos represent purity, dedication, service, even self-sacrifice. Remember how much the ancients believed in sacrificing virgins to appease the gods? Virgos do. They love to throw themselves with wild abandon into some higher cause.

No wonder Virgos are precise, private, fastidious to the point of Felix Unger obsession, critical (only because they CARE), and tremendously service-oriented, just like that nurse who fluffed up your pillows before jabbing you with a hypodermic.

Poor, sweet, misunderstood Virgo. You tell your friend she should join the gym, pick the lint off your lover's jacket, straighten the papers on your co-worker's desk—but does anyone ever appreciate your sterling advice and obvious concern for their welfare? No!!! The epitome of good taste and proper grooming, the dispenser of wise counsel: you're a perfectionist in an all-too-imperfect world. But as a result you hold yourself—and the people you love—to impossibly high standards.

Romantically, Virgos are equally fussy and precise (and yes, they like clean surroundings and showering before, after—and during—sex). If they love you, there's no end to the nagging and nitpicking. It's only because they see your potential and, like the army drill sergeant, want you to "be all that you can be."

Capricorn understands your perfectionism and you make an efficient team at home or the office. Taurus shares your need for security, both financially and emotionally. Cancer and Pisces can soften your analytical side and make sympathetic confidantes.

Libra (September 24–October 23)
"The Innate Diplomat"

Libra's is the only inanimate symbol in the zodiac: the scales of justice and balance. These natural-born diplomats know exactly how to pass the dip and stroke the ego. They are the judges, the politicians, the treaty makers, the arbitrators, the networkers. It's imperative that they see a situation from every side, play devil's advocate, be impartial: this is the source of that (in)famous Libran indecision. These gentle souls crave partnership and exist to create harmony. Hence they require peaceful, pleasant, beauteous surroundings; sudden or loud noises bother them, as do crushing crowds—unless, of course, it's their own guest list.

Libras will run a marathon in record time from confrontation; but in so doing, they can let their anger slowly build until it's a seething cauldron. They actually LOATHE feeling that they have to put on their "Don't worry, be happy" face every morning. When this is carried to extremes, Librans may tell the expedient fib. They're not devious, but hate the thought of hurting anyone's feelings. Remember their symbol: at times the charm is mechanical—they can turn it on and off like a faucet.

In romance, Libras float on fluffy little clouds. They shower their loved ones with attention, flattery, and far-too-exorbitant gifts (all of which they expect in return, along with the requisite long-stemmed roses and Godiva chocolates). The trick for Libras and Libra-lovers alike is keeping their heads in the clouds and their feet firmly planted on the ground: a delicate balance indeed.

Gemini and Aquarius satisfy your need for intellectual stimulation. The ardor of Aries sweeps you off your feet, while Leo's passion and shared love of beauty keep your head in the clouds and your feet firmly planted in reality. Cancer's moods can vex you, but the deep feeling of companionship can be rewarding.

Scorpio (October 24–November 22)
"The Self-Control Artist"

Scorpios are darkly sexy, intense, and magnetic in true *Wuthering Heights* manner. And that fierce little creature with the fearsome stinger is a daunting symbol indeed. But unlike the other signs, Scorpio has a second symbol, the eagle, suggesting their powerful polarity. They can be self-interested, vindictive, and vengeful—or they can soar above mundane life, sharing their spiritual insights with the world. No sign better understands its inherent strengths and limitations; Scorpios are typically fanatic about reinforcing the former and overcoming the latter.

Just as blondes don't really have more fun, Scorpios aren't sex maniacs, despite their reputation. They're quite capable of subliminating the libido in favor of accomplishing other, more far-reaching goals with that single-minded intensity, willpower, and self-control. You're fiercely loyal to those you love, and demand the same in return. Incredibly secretive, you can exercise a double standard, poking about in everyone else's affairs. Not surprisingly, it often takes forever for you to trust. If people really cross you, you'll cross them off your list forever. If they've double-crossed you, they're ERASED from that list—and blacklisted elsewhere. The Scorpio penchant for revenge is no exaggeration. They'll patiently weave complex webs of intrigue, the more byzantine the better. But treat a Scorpio fairly and you've made not only a friend for life, but a fierce defender of your rights and beliefs.

Leo and Taurus provide roaring flames, but someone might end up burned. Cancer and Pisces elicit your caring nature. Virgo and Capricorn provide a groundwork for your career ambitions and, being less intense, a sound sounding board.

Sagittarius (November 23–December 21)
"The Fun-Loving Philosopher"

Sags are the roamers, dreamers, philosophers, eternal children, and all-around cockeyed optimists of the zodiac. Their symbol is the archer, twanging his or her arrows out into the world, not caring what, whom, or where they strike.

These irrepressible creatures are athletic, loving the outdoors and the entire animal kingdom, yet they can be endearingly klutzy around the house. That clumsiness extends to a notorious lack of tact. Sags are always putting their hooves in their mouths, unthinkingly blurting out well-meant yet unintentionally wounding comments. They're big clowns at heart; like Pagliacci, though, they cry for others and wax philosophic about Life without their enthusiasm ever waning. Sags espouse (and sell with evangelical fervor) more causes, principles, morals, and ethics than any other sign. They genuinely care about people, and not merely in the abstract. A Sag will give a friend in need that proverbial shirt off his or her back—and if necessary, rip off a strip as a tourniquet, then carry the wounded pal two miles to the nearest hospital.

Sags expect their mates to be their best friends to whom they can confide everything (including the occasional harmless peccadillo). Always give them a little free rein: "leash, chair, and whip" and "the old ball and chain" are synonymous in the Sagittarian lexicon. Just be sure to laugh at those dumb "knock knock" jokes and farts in bed, and be ready to take off at a moment's notice on a weekend jaunt.

Gemini and Aquarius share your love of life and enthusiasm for new experiences: you make wonderful friends, but may love freedom too much for marriage. Libra's diplomacy, charm, and intellect could keep the home fires burning, as could Leo's optimism and devotion. Virgo's precision is ideal for business ventures.

Capricorn (December 22–January 20)
"The Executive Par Excellence"

The Capricorn symbol isn't just any old billy goat scavenging for tin cans; it's the tough, tenacious, wily mountain goat replete with powerful hooves and sharp horns to compete in their harsh habitats and climb any mountain—or corporate ladder—they choose. You may have heard that Cappies are ambitious, even ruthless. Capricorns are merely realists; they seem to understand ours is a dog-eat-dog (or the far tastier goat) world from birth, and they must go it alone. They possess amazing resolve, determination, and a never-say-die survival instinct.

Caps are generally very proper and conservative, keeping up appearances, both physical and social, at any cost (no matter how considerable) because of their essential insecurity. Many Capricorns endured difficult childhoods, when they felt they had to meet impossibly high standards to gain any love at all. No matter what their circumstances, they always feel like an orphan: Oliver Twist begging, "Please, sir, can I have some more?" Thinks the goat, "Maybe Mom and Dad will appreciate my efforts, now that I've made my first half billion." At its worst, this can breed an end-justifies-the-means attitude. No surprise it isn't easy to gain a Capricorn's trust (let alone access to his or her trust fund).

They're so goal-oriented, Capricorns often forget to have fun. Yet as they begin to achieve their aims, they loosen up; they embody Ben Franklin's epigram that "youth is wasted on the young," because they shine with wisdom and a delightfully wicked gleam as they grow older and more confident.

Virgo shares your need for structure, while Taurus understands the need for stability: you make solid friends and lovers. Scorpio and Pisces can help you express the passion buried deep inside. Cancer can make an intriguing marital or business partner, bringing sensitivity to your sense.

Aquarius (January 21–February 19)
"The Free Thinker"

Despite their symbol, the water bearer, Aquarians are pure, cool air: intellectual, dotty, eccentric. But the water they bear quenches humankind's thirst for knowledge. Aquarians are the frizzy-haired inventors and humanitarians, electrifying the world with their discoveries. Keeping an open house and open mind are the Aquarian credos.

Aquarians agonize over where their ultimate responsibility lies: to themselves, their loved ones, or the world at large? All human beings both crave and fear intimacy, and

Aquarians are as disgustingly, deceptively human as the rest of us. But they worry if they give their heart to one person, they'll be so overwhelmed they won't have time to relate (a favorite Aquarian word) to others. So to gain their precious objectivity, they overintellectualize their emotions, placing them under a microscope, or worse, dissecting them to see how they work. An Aquarian is perfectly capable of asking—purely hypothetically, of course—whether serial killers experience true love.

But once they settle down, Aquarians are usually faithful; despite loathing routine, they're a fixed sign that resists change. Just give Mr. or Mrs. Aquarius a little space (another favorite word), share his or her visionary goals, and don't nag about such mundane matters as the phone bill or PTA meeting. Yet Aquarians need a secure, stable foundation from which to sally forth and play messiah. Though they'd never admit it, an oh-so-deeply buried part of them envisions a cozy Norman Rockwell home (to which, of course, they can drag a bunch of strays, lost souls, walking wounded, messy Marxists, and bizarro artists—con and otherwise).

Gemini appreciates your unconventionality and keen intellect; you're good bets for any relationship. Taurus won't understand your quirkiness but could help you establish a good business foundation. Libra could charm you into marriage if you both agree on the guest list for dinner parties.

Pisces (February 20–March 20)
"The Dream Weaver"

The Piscean symbol is the fish. Though it's tempting to assume Christian symbolism (martyr is a favorite Piscean role), they're actually swimming in opposite directions. And that's how tender, oft-misunderstood Pisces frequently feel: they want to go with the universal flow, but in which direction? At times that acute Piscean sensitivity can make it seem as if they're swimming upstream without even the reward of a good spawn at the end.

If we see the zodiac as a circle, each sign learning from and rebelling against the previous one, then Pisceans sup-

posedly represent both the end of one cycle and the beginning of the next. Because of their strongly spiritual side, few
Pisceans fear death; they truly are in touch with the cyclical
nature of all existence. Their dreams are as lovely, deep,
and vast as the very oceans, and tug at them like the tides
themselves. But Pisceans often lose themselves in their
dreamworld, becoming self-pitying, even self-destructive.

Perhaps that's why they tend to lean a great deal on their
mates and close friends, seeking motivation from without.
Pisceans can be the ultimate romantics, but inevitably, crude
reality intrudes. They need help grounding their dreams,
without wrecking them on the shoals of Life. It's no easy
task. There is a sneaky, slippery side to fish. When they
don't want to confront reality, they can be passive-aggressive
manipulators, adroitly playing victim victorious. Yet no sign
is as capable of self-sacrifice and unconditional love as
Pisces. Help them bulk up their faith in themselves—and
watch them swim purposefully, even against the strongest
current.

Cancer will make you feel protected and loved, whereas
Scorpio will help you stand on your own: both good marital
matches. Taurus can provide you with the creature comforts
you crave. Capricorn enables you to ground and focus your
ambitions, and achieve greater worldly and personal
success.

THE NUMBERS

•

Numerology Birth Numbers

All The Numerology You Need To Know For This Book

Numerology is a science that's been around in one form or another for as long as we've had numbers. Its roots go deep through various religious, mystic, and philosophical origins. About twenty-five hundred years ago, numerology and mathematics were studied as parts of the same science. Much later, the sciences were split into two separate topics because numerology dealt with human psychology and potential.

HISTORY

Pythagoras is considered the father of modern mathematics, engineering, geometry, astronomy, and numerology. Born in Phoenicia around 590 B.C., after traveling widely around the known world and studying the mysteries of the time in Egypt, Greece, and Babylon, he settled in southern Italy and formed a school. In addition to studying letters and numbers, he and his students also studied astronomy, geometry, music, and mathematics.

The charismatic philosopher was said to be the son of the god Apollo. He believed that all things in the universe were in harmony and order, and the relationship of everything to each other and the cosmos could be defined by numbers. Pythagoras is said to have been the first to put forth the theory that the earth was a sphere. He used math to chart the movements of the sun, the moon, and the stars. In addition, he determined formulas used in architecture to achieve proportional relationships. It was his geometric theorem (number forty-seven to be exact) that provided the Egyptians with the basis for the Great Pyramids. He developed the theory of opposites and polarity and the concept of odd and even numbers.

Pythagoras first made the association between tonal sounds, or music, and numbers. He coined the term *vibrations* and taught his students that everything in the universe emitted a particular vibration, including each planet. His idea that all the planets' vibrations together should produce a harmonious cosmic octave has become known as the "music of the spheres." He also discovered the musical octave, and musical intervals that are essential to scoring music.

Numbers hold the key to the mysteries of the cosmos, according the Pythagoras. The vibration or tone at the moment a person is born was thought to define his personality and the challenges of his journey through life.

POLARITY

In school we learn the concept of positive and negative numbers. The plus and the minus represent the opposing polarity of every number. Numerology helps us understand the possibilities of those polarities as they apply to our lives. Since we always have free will to choose our course of action or reaction, knowledge of the numbers and the fact that each has two sides (+ and −) heightens our awareness of those possibilities and allows us to make better choices.

The positive aspect shows the number at its best; and it is what we experience when we're true to our constructive nature. The negative polarity comes into play when we veer off course, or surrender our free will. The positive needs nurturing, reinforcement, and self-knowledge in order to become a happy habit. By knowing more about yourself, particularly the possible heights and common pitfalls of the numbers, you can minimize the down times and maximize the up times to lead a more empowered life.

NUMBER CHARACTERISTICS

The primary numbers one through nine are the basis of numerology. Each number is classified by a series of basic characteristics in addition to a more specific and complex definition.

NUMBER CHARACTERISTIC CHART

EXPRESSION	*Physical*	4, 5	*"Show me." Must see or touch the tangible.*
	Emotional	2, 3, 6	*"Love me." Wants to know what you feel.*
	Mental	1, 8	*"Tell me." Needs to understand everything.*
	Intuitive	7, 9	*"Don't explain." Knows human nature.*
APPROACH	*Masculine*	1, 3, 5, 7, 9	*Active and Creative*
	Feminine	2, 4, 6, 8	*Passive and Receptive*
MOTIVATION	*Begins*	1, 5, 7	*Inventive and Active*
	Completes	2, 4, 8	*Develops and Finishes*
	Takes	3, 6, 9	*Pursues Pleasure*
SOCIAL BEHAVIOR	*Introvert*	1, 3, 5, 7, 9	*Self-contained, likes to be alone.*
	Extrovert	2, 4, 6, 8	*Needs others, likes to be with another.*

THE BIRTH NUMBER

To use this book you must know your Birth Number in order to choose the correct astronumerology combination to read. Why the Birth Number? Because based on an individual's numerological chart, the Birth Number corresponds to the astrological Sun Sign.

A complete numerology chart contains several pages of numbers, and one of the dominant numbers is the Birth Number, just as the Sun Sign dominates an astrology chart. Numbers reveal a distinctly different type of information than astrology does, and just as valuable. Also, the Birth Number is numerology sets in motion major events for the individual and is the basis for forecasting the future. The same is true of the Sun Sign in astrology.

FIND YOUR BIRTH NUMBER

To read about yourself, your lover, parents, children, boss, friend, or sibling, calculate the Birth Number. (Combine this number with your astrological Sun Sign later to determine your astronumerology combination.)

To calculate the Birth Number, convert the month, day, and year of your birth to numbers. Add the numbers together and keep adding them until only one digit remains.

Example: March 31, 1968
            $3 + 31 + 1968 = 3+3+1+1+9+6+8 = 31 = 3+1 = 4$
    or
            March = 3
                    31
                    1968
            $2002 = 2 + 0 + 0 + 2 = 4$
        In the example, 4 is the Birth Number.

MASTER NUMBERS

Master Numbers carry the same meanings as their single-digit sum plus an amplified vibration of responsibility and unexpected challenges to advance spiritual growth. To have a Master Number doesn't mean you *are* a master of that particular number, but rather than you are handed master lessons, usually through cataclysmic events and lifestyle changes. A Master Number indicates life is more complex than for a primary number and carries with it the glare of the public opinion in some form or other in everything you do. If you have Master Numbers, you set an example for everyone else whether you want to or not. The trick to mastering the challenges is to find your footing quickly in new and evolving circumstances and "to thine own self be true"!

If the last two digits in your Birth Number before the final addition were 11, 22, or 33 and the final addition means you have a Birth Number of 2, 4, or 6 respectively, then read about your Birth Number, and as you do, keep in mind the major change and visibility influence that accompanies these Master Numbers.

COMPATIBILITY

Some relationships run smoothly from the start while others need constant attention to keep from crashing. Relationship Road is often rocky whether you're together for business, friendship, or pleasure, and the numbers can provide a beneficial tool to identify both the productive and the challenging ones.

Making a relationship work is the choice of the two people involved, excluding those based in purely negative, aberrant, or abusive behaviors. The question to ask yourself is how much effort do you want to expend to nurture an acquaintance into a successful and lasting relationship.

Different people draw out particular aspects of your personality. You display some characteristics to one person that you don't to another. You laugh more with this one, are more creative with that one, have money making ideas with another, and want to play romance games with someone else.

The ease, fun, and durability of a relationship can be found in comparing the Birth Numbers. First consider the nature of the numbers as described in the Number Characteristics Chart on page 17. Are both your Birth Numbers similar or do they have different types of Expression, Approach, Motivation, or Social Behavior? You don't have to have the exact same characteristics to be compatible. In fact, sometimes opposite characteristics can be complementary and enhance the chemistry. But, you do have to understand and accept the differences in each other's behavior.

After consulting the Characteristics Chart, read the description of each Birth Number, including the positive and negative traits, for both the people in the relationship. Finally, consult the Compatibility Chart below.

The chart offers a star rating system to give you a general snapshot of the combination of two Birth Numbers. Find your Birth Number along the top edge of the columns, and the other person's Birth Number along the rows on the side edge. Where the row and column intersect is the general star rating of the relationship. The range is from one to four stars. A four-star rating is a very good combination while a one-star combination is sure to present more complex challenges.

Suppose the rating is lower than you want. Does that mean you should ditch the idea of getting closer to this person and run along to seek a four-star relationship in a mythical greener pasture somewhere? No, of course not. Good relationships are forged by the people who are in them. If a particular combination of numbers has a low star rating, it may be more difficult for you two to find common ground or to understand how each other thinks or what motivates you, but it doesn't mean you should give up on the idea of being together in peace and harmony. It just may take a little more time and effort to get there than the couple with more stars. In the end, you have the same potential for happiness as anyone. Building a mutually supportive and beneficial relationship is always the choice of the two people in it.

COMPATIBILITY CHART

Birth Numbers		*Your Birth Number*								
		1	2	3	4	5	6	7	8	9
The	1	****	*	***	***	***	**	***	**	****
	2	*	****	**	***	*	****	*	***	**
Other	3	***	**	****	**	**	****	***	**	***
	4	***	***	**	****	**	****	**	****	*
Person's	5	***	*	**	**	****	**	***	**	***
	6	**	****	****	****	**	****	*	****	***
Birth	7	***	*	***	**	***	*	****	**	****
	8	**	***	**	****	**	****	**	****	**
Number	9	****	**	***	*	***	***	****	**	****

**** = Very Good *** = Good ** = Okay * = Challenging

The Birth Numbers

1 One
"The Inventor"

+ Positive: original, independent, focused, innovative, a leader, direct, courageous, bold.

- Negative: stubborn, selfish, inflexible, overbearing, myopic, dictatorial.

1: Mental, Masculine, Introvert, Begins.

Ones are strong-willed, a quality to see you over the rough spots. You are direct and stay focused on the objective, able to ignore tempting detours when the goal is important. Mentally driven, you appreciate being surrounded by intellectuals who inspire you with inventive ideas and expert knowledge. Whatever you do and wherever you go, you prefer to travel first-class. The best life has to offer is how you strive to live, and you choose mentors and friends accordingly to learn from those who are successful and respected.

A risk taker, you're smart enough to (usually) land on your feet. Sometimes opinionated and obstinate about your beliefs, you surprise people by taking constrictive criticism well and incorporating their ideas into your plans. Yes, you want to have your own way, but you also want to do it the best way and you want to win.

Love makes you vulnerable because logic doesn't work there, but you can slap together a romantic evening with lightning speed if the mental connection jibes with the chemistry. Since you prefer quality in every aspect of your life, it's no wonder you expect a classy sweetheart who's able to keep up with your mental gymnastics and let's-not-beat-around-the-bush style. Come to think of it, that's how you choose your friends, too!

2 Two
"The Diplomat"

+ Positive: gracious, patient, supportive, intuitive, considerate, conscientious, charming, persuasive.

- Negative: moody, gossipy, argumentative, timid, nervous, worrisome, extremist.

2: Emotional, Feminine, Extrovert, Completes.

Companionship is the top priority, and it's that characteristic that makes you an excellent diplomat and an attractive catch as a lover, friend, partner, or spouse. Intuitive and sensitive, you often defer your own needs to the wishes and wants of others in order to preserve the relationship. You will make radical change at the drop of a hat when you believe it's necessary, but prefer to have the support of others. Tact and arbitration are the primary tools in your arsenal, and in addition to smoothing ruffled feathers, they've opened many doors for you.

Modest about your talents, you don't ask for constant praise, but do require honest appreciation for your unswerving support and patient pursuit of the part you play in making things come together. You perform best in the framework of a stimulating, complementary partnership, and and since you are so influenced by those around you, choose any partner—professional or personal—very carefully. Match more than preferences and skill; it's essential to know that the two of you care about each other's feelings as well.

Charming and friendly, though somewhat shy, you're se-

lective about friends and how you live your own life. You
know what you want, though you may not go after it without encouragement. And when you do go after your dreams,
you pull out all the stops, leaving a trail of dust in your
wake.

3 Three
"The Social Butterfly"

+ Positive: imaginative, creative, sociable, optimistic, super
shopper, self-expressive, story-teller, artistic, romantic.
- Negative: extravagant, verbose, scattered, cynical, boast-
ful, easily distracted.

3: Emotional, Masculine, Introvert, Taker.

Without you, there wouldn't be much laughter in the
world. You cast your happy, imaginative spell wherever you
roam. You are a creative jack-of-all-trades, and your mind
continually churns with new ideas and romantic plots. Always juggling three or more projects at a time, you are able
to do the same juggling act with people and relationships,
too. You get so caught up in a magnificent creative whirl
that you sometimes find it difficult to connect with the real
world. From the constant conjuring of dreams and fantasies,
you find extra doses of optimism to share with the rest of
the world.

Always generous with your time, money, and resources,
you also think about a thousand things before breakfast and
can accomplish more than the average human thinks is possible. Occasionally you try to do too much for too many with
too little and spend more money than you have, (always just
a temporary setback). Undeniably, you are a wonderful
friend with lively chatter and a quick wit.

A natural flirt, you keep falling in love with love until the
right dreamy swashbuckler sweeps you off your feet. You
view the world through rose-colored glasses, which means
your vision in the romance department isn't exactly twenty/
twenty. Before walking down the aisle, make sure you see
your betrothed in the harsh light of reality at least once.

4 Four
"The Builder"

+ Positive: enthusiastic, practical, persistent, ethical, constructive, works hard, thorough, organized, traditional, good-hearted.

- Negative: too busy, slow to change, lazy, needs proof, contrary, undemonstrative.

4: Physical, Feminine, Extrovert, Completes.

Fours are the planners and visionaries in the world; you envision what you want and work hard to turn the dream into reality. Practical and persistent, you quietly get the job done after others get discouraged and walk away. Sometimes you win simply because no one else sticks with it. You gained this choice bit of wisdom as a child and it's given you the needed confidence to recover from life's inevitable setbacks.

Because you are so tenacious, sometimes it's difficult to break off the pursuit of one dream to pour your energy into something new. Common sense makes the final decision. You're sensible about everything, committed, and fiercely loyal. The enormity of a project doesn't overwhelm you. Out comes the notebook and calendar to sketch out a plan. Once you decide where to start ("What can I do today to move in that direction?"), you chip away, one task at a time, going over, around, or through obstacles. You refuse to get bogged down and keep your eye on the finish line as it moves closer and closer.

You like upholding traditions, or starting a few of your own, but surprise people when you have a "rebel attack" and start swimming upstream. Doing the right thing and being appropriate are, in your opinion, essential qualities for a peaceful civilization, and logic usually, but not always, prevails. There are those times when the status quo needs a good shake to get back on track or to change direction. Being the You Can Count on Me character, who better to stand up for change?

5 Five
"The Adventurer"

+Positive: curious, adventurous, good communicator, progressive, resourceful, versatile, prizes freedom, energetic, networker.

- Negative: impulsive, fickle, sharp-tongued, reckless, self-indulgent, restless.

5: Physical, Masculine, Introvert, Begins.

Five is the number of motion and progress. Curious and adventuresome, you juggle friends and family with hobbies and career yet manage to regularly zip to and fro, hither and yon, in various quests. Sometimes you stick your nose out just a little too far and land in sticky situations. That's when your flexibility and smooth silver tongue come in to save the day.

You think personal freedom is a fundamental right and have little patience with those who would take away a single smidgen. In your book, all the "free" concepts—free press, free will, free thought, free love—are the right attitude. Besides, you want to hear what everyone has to say. It might inspire you to make another change or quench your insatiable thirst to know and experience everything.

Networking and change are a joy. You know that "no matter where you go, there you are," so it doesn't make sense to stay in one place collecting moss. As you wander and explore the nooks and crannies of life (solo or with the family entourage in tow), you gather an enormous network of friends. Check the addresses in your book and you see you know someone almost everywhere on the planet. "So many people, so many places, so little time." Warp speed was invented for you, but you know how to downshift to impulse power. Besides the springtime flowers, there are also magic moments that come around only once, and you have no intention of missing them, do you?

6 Six
"The Idealist"

+Positive: responsible, loyal, loving, idealistic, conventional, nurturing, loves home, caretaker, artistic, musical.

- Negative: idealistic, self-righteous, self-sacrificing, domineering, jealous, moody.

6: Emotional, Feminine, Extrovert, Taker.
"Love makes the world go round." You know all about
the cosmic glue that holds the universe together and do your
part to spread the word. Love isn't a convenience or a game
to you; it's an everyday necessity. You're a little more idealistic than the rest of us and that's why we need you. You
strive to find the good in everyone and extend your care
and concern beyond family and friends to co-workers, and
neighbors, even to the man in line behind you in the grocery store.
Joining your extended family is easy. The original good
Samaritan had to have been a Six. You don't give up on
people, and that durable quality has saved many a grateful
friend from falling over the edge. You go to considerable
lengths to ensure the right thing is done for all concerned,
but you know people make mistakes. You don't expect anyone to be perfect, but you do expect them to learn and
make improvements.
Home is where your heart is, and guests feel the welcom-
ing warmth the moment they step over your threshold. Each
room reflects your life priorities; good music, good food,
and comfortable surroundings to relax or entertain family
and friends. Marriage is the happiest lifestyle for you, but
you may hesitate to take the plunge because finding the
right partner seems overwhelming. Just spread the magic of
selfless love wherever you go, and eventually true love will
find you.

7 Seven
"The Scholar"

+ Positive: analytical, perfectionist, private, psychic, intellectual, seeks truth, technical, educated, scientific, logical,
researcher, solitary.
- Negative: aloof, secretive, suspicious, stingy, repressed,
argumentative.

7: Intuitive, Masculine, Introvert, Begins.

You have a knack for sizing up a situation in the blink of and an eye, and even though you know your first impression is usually correct, you still make a considerable effort to back up that initial take with cold, hard facts. Above all, you want to be taken seriously and pride yourself on being well informed. Friends think you're downright psychic! Your insight works with your finely tuned analytical mind to tie the data together to form the unerring first impression.

Knowledge is power. Secrets are safe with you—partly because you don't want the information flow to dry up and partly because you know all about secrets because you have quite a few of them yourself. You share Five's curiosity, but take it one step further by sometimes experimenting outside the mainstream norms when it suits you (hence your own secrets).

Friends and lovers must be bright and must love you as much for your intellect as for your smile, plus understand about the space you need. You enjoy your solitude and prize your privacy. Only those who understand this will ever get close to you. Marriage is a surprising adventure for you and more rewarding than you expected when you finally pop the question. When? When you find a sexy sweetie on the same wavelength who can discuss quantum physics as intelligently as choosing a restaurant for dinner and is willing to step into your private world.

8 Eight
"The Politician"

+ Positive: poised, authoritative, ambitious, open-minded, objective, professional, global view, understands money, capable, has endurance.

- Negative: Indecisive, aggressive, workaholic, materialistic, overreacts, shows off.

8: Mental, Feminine, Extrovert. CompLetes.

You've got expensive tastes and big plans. Luckily you have the fine business sense that enables you to realize your dreams. Because of your innate sense of fair play (the basis of your character), you are bewildered when others play dirty. When there's a decision to be made, others ask your opinion because people know you use a wide-angle lens to view the big picture and include all the possible scenarios.

As skilled as you are at guiding other people to make good decisions, you have considerable difficulty figuring out your own. Hopefully your parents taught you how to add up the personal pros and cons. Otherwise, your choices in life, even the big ones, are based more on what *others* want, which is something the Eight somehow always instinctively knows. A natural workaholic, you like to be in charge and can be tough as nails—with yourself. With your staff however, you can be a pushover, still professional but almost too understanding at times.

You're more than just the department executive, you're attractive and well groomed; you make a great friend and an exciting lover. Who could ask for anything more? Well, frankly, you do when looking for that Someone Special. You may meet the love of your life through the work you do, but in addition to looking good standing next to you, he also needs a mind that clicks on several different tracks at the same time, just as yours does. To win your heart, not only does a lover need to keep up with you, but to take the leads sometimes, too.

9 Nine
"The Entertainer"

+Positive: attractive, creative, a performer, artistic, impartial, spiritual, worldly, impressionable, compassionate, charitable, charismatic.

- Negative: impersonal, critical, demanding, egotistical, careless, self-absorbed.

9: Intuitive, Masculine, Introvert, Taker.

One busy day follows another until you start to wonder if the blur of car pools and appointments will ever end. Of course, it won't, and you don't really want all the activity to stop anyway. There are too many places to go and fascinating people to meet; there are adventures out there you simply don't want to miss! Because you take your obligations seriously, and squeeze in the want-tos and have-tos, your life becomes a carefully choreographed dance to fit everything in.

A nine never meets a stranger. However fleeting or casual contact with someone new may be, the connection has a sense of importance when it happens. Nine is a karmic number that doesn't let you stand still for very long. Life presents events and circumstances that push you through new doors even as you wail, "I'm not ready!" Stay positive and there's nothing you can't do, no mountain you can't climb, with the 9 Birth Number as a springboard. You can touch the hearts of a zillion strangers—entertain and uplift others even when your own personal life is at loose ends.

You are attractive—if not because of your physical appearance (which you change regularly anyway), then because of your talent and ability to inspire. Relationships are challenging—in business and in your personal life. With your chameleon tendencies, you must be careful who you hook up with. It's natural for you to become a mirror for the other person, so be certain you like what you see before making any long-term commitment. ♥

ARIES

●

♈ • 1
Aries One
"The Courageous Champion"

♈ +	1 +	♈ -	1 -
Assertive	Bold	Blunt	Dictatorial
Courageous	Direct	Domineering	Inflexible
Dynamic	Independent	Headstrong	Myopic View
Pioneering	Focused		

You aren't exactly antiestablishment, but don't have much use for the tried and true either. The usual channels take too long and you simply don't have the time to waste, ah, wait. Let everyone else wait, you have a life to live here! You go places and meet people on your terms, with seldom a stumble unless someone pinches your Achilles' heel. What do you mean, "No, I can't"? You want me to "settle for" what I can get? Fling either of these comments in your direction and you pour on the steam to overcome outrageous odds.

You can hear the thwack of a glove hit the floor in challenge a mile away. Challenges don't rule your life; well, not *all* the time. But you do delight in proving the doom-and-gloom gang wrong. Besides, most of the battles you engage in aren't for yourself. Sure, you fight when you have to, and for the truth, for honor, and for those who don't know how to fight for themselves. You set things straight for those who ask for your help. Pity be the unwary bloke who railroads your sister into buying an overpriced used car! You have no problem setting him straight either!

Events happen in their own time. You repeat this mantra over and over while not missing a single step forward on life's adventurous journey. There's always the light of a goal to guide you onward. Even when you don't end up where you thought you were going, you have the knack of landing on your feet. The different drummer's beat that sets your pace also lets you seize the moment to capitalize on opportunities not visible to others.

A natural leader; your warriorlike confidence and self-direction wraps you in an attractive shimmering cloud. Others see you as a guiding light and depend on you, you like that role as long as you can do things your way and don't have to contend with useless suggestions or time-consuming restrictions.

Love, Sex, and Marriage

You're forever young at heart with a full-bodied fantasy life; love and games simply don't mix in your book. Intrigued by a novel approach, you're not interested in coy looks and mixed messages. A life partner is important, but you won't sacrifice everything to have one. When communication is direct, open, and honest, and the would-be betrothed is smart, sexy, and stylish with mountains of his own to climb, you take notice. Should that particular mountain happen to be on your list, too, you explore it together. If the physical chemistry matches the provocative mental mambo, marriage enters the equation.

To make it work, you must share dreams, drives, and directions in the quest for the best of everything. It's okay to have different professions, but do walk shoulder to shoulder in pursuit of the world's many wonders.

Children may or may not be part of the package. However, if you become a parent, you are a responsible one. A strong figure with a love of laughter, you instill in your off-spring the confidence, purpose, ethics, and independence to find their own niche.

Money and Career

The sky's the limit once you figure out how to play well with others. As the CEO, you can lead a company through one successful coup after another with ease, but managing and motivating the folks to make it happen take practice. You know how to get things done, but as a manager, must slow down to show others how to be just as effective. Since you walk a different walk, you don't expect anyone else to be out on the limb with you.

You do best as a professional or an expert in almost any field. Your innovative approach can spell sweet success or financial disaster, depending on how much freedom you have to flex your considerable mental prowess. The boss finds you weird or wonderful, and it may take several career changes before you claim a spot in the workplace at large. Once you do, there's no stopping you!

The ♈1 Potential

A natural loner, you have strong opinions and believe in your ideas and abilities. You prefer taking action and use the direct route to get things done. You make things happen that need to happen. Your gift is to enable people to shine. Though you might not stick around for the actual event, you share your concepts and charisma to get others on the right road.

Stay flexible and open-minded and there literally isn't any peak too tall for you to scale. Your ability to think fast on your feet and your unique problem-solving methods make you stand out from the rest. Be approachable; allow a little vulnerability to creep in; develop friendships that become a welcome diversion, and the triumphs will be sweeter by sharing the success.

FAMOUS ARIES ONES

Michael York	*3/27/1942*	*Liz Claiborne*	*3/31/1929*
Geraint Wyn-Davies	*4/20/1957*	*Maya Angelou*	*4/4/1928*
Paul Reiser	*3/30/1957*	*Sarah Vaughan*	*3/27/1924*

♈ • 2
Aries Two
"The Diplomatic Warrior"

♈ +	2 +	♈ -	2 -
Courageous	*Gregarious*	*Headstrong*	*Argumentative.*
Inspired	*Sensitive*	*Impatient*	*Touchy*
Passionate	*Diplomatic*	*Impulsive*	*Shy*
Bold	*Conscientious*		

Squinting through the looking glass, you search for something to be happy about. Some days you feel like the legendary Aries Two Captain James T. Kirk (said to be born 3/21/2228). Is there a place to boldly go? A civilization to save? A peacemaker to fight for? You're in! Aries Two is a complex combination; passion runs deep and makes you as willing to make war as to make love. Guided by a strict code of ethics and the desire to build a better world, you fill your life with accomplishments, the respect of peers, collected treasures, and true love. That doesn't mean you haven't gone to phasers when necessary to get things done the right way.

Okay, so you aren't piloting a starship across the neutral zone on a hunch, but even behind the wheel of a snappy blue Pathfinder, playing car-pool mom, you have rules for passengers and a strict schedule to be kept. Unless, of course, something more interesting comes up, like a whale call from uncharted space or a conference with fourth grader Steffie's teacher. Heck, you've been known to veer off course for a walk through the blooming heather when spring fever hits.

The mirror, like the looking glass, has more than two

faces, and what you see there makes you sally forth to conquer tough trails. Reality doesn't scare you and you aren't a
quitter, even when told to pick up your toys and go home.
And you never, ever, give up on people you believe in.

Never at a loss to dish out advice, you hesitate only a
heartbeat before speaking up. You aren't afraid to shake up
the status quo if the result is an improvement. The reason
you try to avoid confrontation is that you play to win, and
prefer that others recognize that your way is the best way
on their own. Though a fight with you appears to have
started on impulse, opponents are vanquished swiftly because you have all the facts and wouldn't engage in any
battle you don't think you can win. Besides, the battle isn't
what it's all about; it's about obtaining the objective. And if
the spat isn't settled honorably, you smoothly retreat to the
consummate diplomat's role.

Love, Sex, and Marriage

Though you're not necessarily the marrying kind, the romantic you is an affectionate lover who prefers to be with
someone rather than alone. If you are alone, it's by choice
because there's no lack of willing lovers to warm your bed.
Finding a cultured and educated mate who is a wild and
earthy lover isn't easy. You know, someone like yourself
with sensitive eyes, and hands that expertly know exactly
where, how, and how long to touch.

As much as you like to taste the different fruits at a buffet,
eventually you earnestly search for a permanent arrangement. It doesn't take long for potential candidates to appear.
You settle down only when you find someone who understands you completely, is utterly faithful, and doesn't step
on your lifestyle or impede your progress as you charge off
to explore the galaxy.

Money and Career

You fuss and worry about getting the work done while
racing to the finish line. A competent leader, you have the
insight and focus to ferret out facts and figures needed to
get things done. If you can't get an assignment as a starship

captain, you do well as CEO, government official, military officer, educator, or executive manager. You prefer to be the first or second in command. And those working for you can depend on you for advice, direction, and an empathetic hug whenever needed.

When it comes to personal spending, you are conservative but never tight. Money is a just reward for your efforts, and you pour as much of it into dream investments as into a personal bank account. There has to be a payoff, whether cash, personal growth, or an improvement for mankind, before you undertake any venture. You never lose sight of the results and never kid yourself: Winning the game is as important to you as choosing the appropriate one to play.

Aries ♈2 Potential

You believe all things are possible and are more assertive when championing a cause than pursuing personal gain or glory. A person of action, you do best in a position that lets you show off your ability and charming personality in an acceptable way such as helping others and working with groups.

Daring yet careful, you prefer action to research and have been known to take up many a banner on gut feeling alone. Try not to overwhelm people with too much at once and you come out on top every time.

FAMOUS ARIES TWOS

Hans Christian Andersen	*4/2/1805*	*Diana Ross*	*3/26/1944*
General Colin Powell	*4/5/1937*	*Mariah Carey*	*3/27/1970*
Jackie Chan	*4/7/1953*	*Lucy Lawless*	*3/29/1968*

♈ • 3
Aries Three
"The Practical Romantic"

♈ +	3 +	♈ -	3 -
Assertive	*Artistic*	*Arrogant*	*Cynical*
Courageous	*Imaginative*	*Excessive*	*Distracted*
Creative	*Romantic*	*Domineering*	*Extravagant*
Enterprising	*Sociable*		

The Aries Three combination is the DNA blueprint for Peter Pan, magic flute in hand. Your charisma and sense of humor are mythical. At six or sixty, you're young at heart, vital, vulnerable, and in demand socially. Your private circle includes every age and stage of life. The only valid criteria to be your friend are an enthusiasm for life and a joy in trying new things.

The romance in your soul and fundamental belief that we each control our own destiny drives you to reach for achievements that others believe unattainable. Spurred forward by Technicolor visions, you vanquish obstacles that pop in the path. There's a rainbow to catch, and you aim to be there when it touches earth. This isn't fluff talk either; you've got the skills to get what you want, if you can just stay focused.

A chivalrous character with a vivid imagination and force of will, you enjoy being in the spotlight and find it much more of a gas when you draw others into it with you. It's a kick to be recognized, and there are plenty of opportunities to spread the pixie dust around.

An ambidextrous juggler of various ideas and projects, no matter what your work, you manage to stay connected to those who matter and not miss Robert's trumpet recital or the much-anticipated birth of Jazzy's precious kittens.

Okay, so you know you can accomplish almost anything, unless, of course, you get sidetracked playing Don or Donna Juan or maybe scraping together the cash reserves to fill the office with flowers to celebrate May Day. Folks feel your charms the moment you walk into a room. Even when delivering somber news or squaring off to make a point, you can coax a smile from the lips of any crabby opponent.

Love, Sex, and Marriage

In love with being in love, you kiss a lot of frogs and find a lot of princes and princesses. If your true love isn't already at your side, it's not for lack of trying. You target the object of your affections with swift surety that comes from years of observation peppered with the voracious input of romantic stories, from *Ivanhoe* to *Sleepless in Seattle*. When your eyes rest on your heart's desire, you *know* this is the one. In the blink of an gnat's eye, you are working an enchantment to win the tender heart toying with your own.

On the other hand, unrequited love is boring and you lose interest if physical consummation appears to be out of the question. Determination plays its part, too. Once the hormones are churning, you hop through every imaginable hoop until every ploy in your considerable bag of tricks has been tried to bring the two of you together.

Money and Career

Jack-of-all-trades, yes; and also a master of many. While working on one assignment, there are others waiting on a long list of possibilities. Most opportunities come through the friendship network you've developed. It's easy to get folks to believe in your ideas and ability, so before starting a serious sales pitch, make sure you can deliver what you promise. And when it comes to putting the actual deal together, you want to be there to close it.

Money is important to you, and once you settle down to doing one thing at a time, you have no problem making as much of it as you want. This is good because you're a generous spender—and not just on yourself either. You take great pleasure in helping others and showering friends and lovers with generous gifts.

The ♈3 Potential

Your dedication to a particular goal surprises creative contacts, while business types are equally amazed by the multitude of innovative ideas and solutions you effortlessly pull out of your pocket. Naive enough to be duped, kindhearted and easy to distract, you never lose your rosy optimism and tend to gloss over disappointments as you pick yourself up and get moving again. You are a delightful storyteller, able to charm and cheer up everyone—even your would-be adversaries.

Keep fantasy and reality in two separate files, and vow to use the arts of bluff and persuasion as a positive force. Refuse to get bogged down in the nitty-gritty grind for long because the creative mover and shaker in you brings out your best qualities.

FAMOUS ARIES THREES

William Shatner	3/22/1931	Gloria Swanson	3/27/1899
Billy Dee Williams	4/6/1937	Ellen Barkin	4/16/1954
Steven Seagal	4/10/1951	Saundra Santiago	4/13/1957

♈ • 4
Aries Four
"The Animated Architect"

♈ +	4 +	♈ -	4 -
Creative	Practical	Impulsive	Lazy
Courageous	Persistent	Naive	Too Busy
Enthusiastic	Organized	Domineering	Undemonstrative
Passionate	Traditional		

An Aries with brilliant ideas who actually transforms them into reality is a rare breed indeed, and that is you, my dear—the Aries Four. Your behavior is a shock to anyone who's locked horns with an Aries before and was left standing with an inspired but sketchy idea as that other Aries disappeared into the mist. A grounded visionary, you know you're on this earth to make things happen and occasionally have an idea that just might actually work. When that happens, you intend to see it through from start to finish!

You think big, but are too practical to go after dreams that can't come true. It's a waste of valuable time with your busy schedule. Better to daydream about things that *are* possible—well, except for that Richard Gere thing, but then you *could* live out that fantasy with your own lover one day, so it's okay to let the imagination flow. "Nothing is ever wasted," you say, and mean it. If one idea doesn't work out, you use pieces of it to bring another plan to fruition. The possibilities are endless. You know that from experience because you've tried numerous variations on a theme to make things happen and have a respectable success rate for your efforts.

You honestly think you're run-of-the-mill conventional until someone gives you an incredulous sideways look as you rattle off the particulars of your last three-thousand-mile move driving a rented twenty-four-foot truck solo with two squalling Siamese cats in the cab. Your life doesn't sound remarkable to you, even though you never hesitate to seize the moment. At least you have fond memories to show for it!

The good and bad news is that mentally, you never grow old. At fifty you still have the same wide-eyed optimism and curiosity that you did at five. Friends may fall by the wayside when they can't keep up with your adventures but that doesn't stop you. You go anyway and send them postcards. Even when you know the next destination and how to get there, you don't know what's going to happen along the way, and that's what excites you about the trip.

Love, Sex, and Marriage

To live is to love, and you love romance—remember the Gere à la Lancelot fantasy? An attentive knight in shining armor with love in his heart and lust on his mind is a daydream that you never tire of. When a modern version with a dazzling smile on his lips arrives at your door with a bunch of wildflowers in hand, you invite him to stay and play, maybe forever.

Marriage makes sense to you, and yours must provide a stable haven, with a generous yes-you-can-still-be-independent clause. Because passion runs deep in an Aries Four, the spouse in residence has to be a capable lover who knows how to keep the chemistry volatile. Faithful by nature, you may contemplate affairs, but pause to act due to the complications. You never lack for companionship, but after the vows have been said, conversation is about as far as it goes with a sexy stranger.

Money and Career

Money is an important part of your plans from the day you can add up how much change it takes to make a dollar. It isn't the money itself that's important but the security and independence it represents. Even married, you need a separate bank account. You genuinely like to work and started earning money young. With your drive to achieve and ability to organize, you do well in almost any profession. Measurable success is important, such as a title or big bucks. Any job you take should let you make decisions and set procedures. You are a competent manager and use common sense with a dash of parenting to motivate the staff.

Work would be central to your life if it weren't for family. Usually you keep priorities straight, but there are times when work consumes you. At some point you try being your own boss, and it could be the best move you ever make. Because you worry about things like medical insurance for the kids, it may be later in life before you take such an enterprising plunge.

The ϓ4 Potential

It takes a lot of adversity for you to be discouraged, but it does happen, usually when you push your body beyond its limits. Balance your schedule to include downtime and let the sun's rays rejuvenate you while you walk and ponder the present and the future. Walking is meditation in motion and helps you keep a balanced outlook.

You know it takes inspiration plus persistence to make any dream come true. By your example and by sharing your own experiences with others, you help everyone believe that anything is possible. Divulging triumphs and fiascos keeps you and those around you motivated. Nothing pleases you more than doing what you set out to do.

FAMOUS ARIES FOURS

Leonardo da Vinci	4/15/1452	Linda Goodman	4/19/1925
Hugh Hefner	4/9/1926	Betty Ford	4/8/1918
Elton John	3/25/1947	Linda Bloodworth- Thomason	4/15/1947

♈ • 5

Aries Five
"The Creative Liberal"

♈ +	5 +	♈ -	5 -
Creative	Communicator	Headstrong	Fickle
Generous	Freedom-loving	Audacious	Careless
Bold	Energetic	Quarrelsome	Self-Indulgent
Pioneering	Resourceful		

Bounding from one mountain peak to another makes it tough to keep up with you, but others find the effort is worth it. You can tell a tale of how to create a better planet like no one else. If only everyone had your vision and took the risks you do, much positive progress could be made. No matter that eventually you reach a heady pinnacle that requires a platoon of forest rangers to rescue you. No matter, dear ram, you have another five equally daring ideas to try tomorrow.

The idea of a world without underdogs makes you a champion of personal freedom. Just a hint of oppression launches you into action. The crusade to make things right started in small ways when you were a young tot, and grew once you got those little sturdy legs underneath you. By the time you were tall enough to start fencing lessons, you persuaded friends, then strangers, to consider your ideas. As your knowledge has expanded with experience, you are always ready for almost anything, and at home with a wide variety of people and topics.

Curiosity fuels the search for more information about everything under the sun and brings you to more than one unlikely doorstep over the years. You intend to make this a well-lived life. Whether or not you believe in reincarnation, you focus on the present—not so much the before and after. Since you are results-oriented, any spiritual search must relate to the present, too.

A risk taker, you choose battles shrewdly and prefer to schmooze your way out of confrontation to avoid making enemies. You know that the wheel turns and today's enemy could be a valuable ally tomorrow. You take a few hard knocks along the way, mostly because you overlook important facts like the necessary expertise to accomplish your dream or to get where you want to go.

Your salvation is the routine leap of faith you take to get from here to there. That and the willingness to do whatever it takes to learn how to get there and how to be the person you were meant to be. There's never a dull moment around you. You crave variety and stimulation, and go after it. Amazingly romantic, you need more love and approval than others think. With a partner at your side, you seldom get discouraged for long.

Love, Sex, and Family

In marriage, you need a mate you can count on, who trusts you as you zip from place to place and gives you the illusion of freedom that you so desperately need. "The only way to hold you is to let you go." A lover with a wide array of interests or an absorbing career works best. Any clinging vine will be immediately cut loose and tossed as you move on.

You do better with marriage as a domestic haven to provide a retreat to lick your wounds and recharge your batteries. Like all Aries, your love can survive separation and dramatic change if you know your partner is faithful to you. In fact, sometimes you need those little breaks to keep the romance alive.

Money and Career

The brass ring doesn't have much appeal for its own sake—a ring is just a ring. However, when it represents position, recognition, and independence, it's worth reaching for. Money to you equals freedom, and you learn young how to make it. As a manager, hire people who can get the day to day work done to free you up to attend and conduct seminars, visit clients, and gather more contacts to add to your considerable network.

Choose a career that lets you make regular treks through exotic lands, collect art, meet people, and visit as many spots on the planet as possible. Since you adore new people, you do well as a journalist, bodybuilder, athlete, warrior, or dancer, or in communications, sales, and law.

The ♈5 Potential

A trailblazer from birth, you're on the go from the moment you can walk. Fame isn't your thing, but getting the truth out there is. Teaching others how to find the truth is a soul-satisfying endeavor, and you're a natural mentor, showing others how to break through stereotypes and how to open doors.

Strive for balance and never think your health will take care of itself. Self-discipline doesn't come easy, but improves the quality as well as quantity of days that comprise your life. You have the potential to be a powerful, positive force by giving hope and direction to the masses, as well as those lucky enough to call you family or friend. Use those talents wisely.

FAMOUS ARIES FIVES

President Thomas Jefferson	*4/13/1743*	*Doris Day*	*4/3/1924*
		Sonja Henie	*4/8/1910*
Kareem Abdul-Jabbar	*4/16/1947*	*Samantha Fox*	*4/15/1966*
Dudley Moore	*4/19/1935*		

♈ • 6
Aries Six
"The Intrepid Idealist"

♈ +	6 +	♈ -	6 -
Generous	Nurturing	Jealous	Self-Righteous
Ambitious	Responsible	Excitable	Nosy
Practical	Loyal	Sanctimonious	Obstinate
Constructive	Idealistic		

"Educate and encourage" is your motto as you strive to make improvements wherever you think essential. You see undeveloped potential in others and take action to help them improve themselves. No one could have a better cheerleader to prod them to success. You only get discouraged when the object of your efforts is unappreciative or snarls at you. Well, what did you expect when you didn't ask Jeff what he wanted before you signed him up for a computer course?

With a practical Renaissance-man view, your "to do" list starts with being an individual, includes romance, music, and the arts, and ends with being the best you can be. You intend to try everything, from parenthood to a corner office with a view on the ninth floor at work. In the process, you bend over backward to bring along anyone who wants to go along. You spend as much time helping others succeed as you do helping yourself.

Always aware of your reputation and appearance (be it stunning or frowsy), you expect everyone else to care about their own, too. You're tough on those you love, and though you might blurt out a cutting criticism, you recognize the blunder the second it happens. You would never intentionally hurt anyone—not even that harpy receptionist who continually mixes up your dental appointments.

That mischievous sense of humor is kept in check by the nurturing aspects of your personality. Whenever you're on the brink of going too far or closing a door (although you do like a good exit scene), you bite your tongue and back off. Humor is also an outlet; it keeps you from taking yourself too seriously and puts an optimistic spin on any difficult situation. The sun is going to rise tomorrow, and you intend to be the first one on the block to see it.

Love, Sex, and Marriage

Once you calm the domestic butterflies, you make a wonderful parent. Nesting comes naturally to you, and you want a home that's a cozy castle for all who dwell there, from Joey's hamster to the soul mate who said, "I do." No matter how far you fly or how many zillions of hours you work at what you do, you need more than just a place to store your stuff, and you do accumulate a lot of it. Love, laughter, and commitment are the main ingredients for a place to be a home.

Love and sex don't necessarily go together, but when they do, it's an addictive high that keeps you coming back for more. "I love you," doesn't jump out of your mouth easily to a prospective mate, and you delay talking about tomorrow or making any plans until you think the magic has staying power. Since you love unconditionally, it's essential to find a mate who shares your values, visions, and hopes for the future.

Money and Career

Nothing but the finer things in life will do for you, and you are diligent about getting the required resources for the domicile and lifestyle you want. You enjoy having plenty of money to spend on others as well as yourself, and enjoy a comfy home plus exotic vacations. You care about the people you work with and make sure they know it. No matter what your title, you don't hesitate to work long hours, alone or with a staff, to see a job gets done. As an executive, you take pride in being able to coax everyone to produce an outstanding product.

The true-blue loyal type, even when a better job beckons, it's a difficult decision to move on and leave the folks who count on you. Still, you need change and action; you do so abhor the humdrum. You do very well in any spot in human resources, standing on a stage, as an inventor, or in entertainment, politics, and teaching.

The ♈6 Potential

Empathetic and nurturing, you find a way to deliver the most difficult news or severe criticism with a light, soothing touch. You're a tough cookie with a heart of gold and firmly believe that truth is the basis for living a good life.

You seek harmony but will battle with all the tools in your considerable arsenal should anyone attack someone close to you. Your battle cry makes the staunchest opponent cringe. Revenge is hollow, but it takes a few times of getting it before you figure that out. Once you do, it becomes easier to keep to the high road. Be the leader who sets a good example and encourages everyone to reach their full potential. The gift you give the world is your faith in others. The gift the world gives you is unconditional love.

FAMOUS ARIES SIXES

Eddie Murphy	4/3/1961	Rosie O'Donnell	3/21/1962
Francis Ford Coppola	4/7/1939	Sandra Day O'Connor	3/26/1930
Wilbur Wright	4/16/1867	Leeza Gibbons	3/26/1957

♈ • 7
Aries Seven
"The Scientific Psychic"

♈+	7 +	♈-	7 -
Assertive	Analytical	Arrogant	Aloof
Creative	Technical	Impulsive	Secretive
Passionate	Articulate	Jealous	Repressed
Enterprising	Perfectionist		

Whether you're a teacher, actor, scientist, or writer, your true talents aren't obvious from a casual glance. You go after what you want, but only after an objective analysis of the situation, with pertinent data in hand. And that's a hand you won't play unless tactical strategy and politics fail to get you what you want. Sometimes you enjoy the game for its own sake, not caring to win, but when you tire of the match, you detach and walk away, much to the bewilderment of adversaries. Just because you know how to make miracles doesn't mean you always have a reason to do so.

Education provides the needed rudder to guide you in any direction you choose to sail. Your curiosity knows no limits and you're always ready to pick up your laptop and head off to distant shores. You, Aries Seven, are a mixture of a bold pioneer, reserved perfectionist, and pragmatic psychic. When learning how to drive, make love, earn money, or acquire any skill, you stick with it until you can do it right every time. Of course, with a quick grasp of complex concepts and a competitive spirit, you aren't afraid to try almost anything.

As a young ram, you butt heads over matters trivial, but the Seven's influence teaches you to pick battles with care and not for abstract principles alone. You become a master at hiding your feelings unless you decide it's a better maneuver to reveal all. This trait makes foes fall into the tender trap of thinking you're predictable and then *wham—sha-bam!* With succinct words and flawless logic, you set the record straight. Mouths drop open as you back up what you said with an action plan or a printed dossier of facts.

You're fascinated with history, law, politics, religion, medicine, plus things psychic and spiritual, too. More than just reading about such topics, you like getting hip-deep in the action. Pondering the mechanics of space travel, sifting sand at an archaeological dig, or attempting a Vulcan mind meld, you try anything intriguing, but may never mention it to anyone. You so like your secrets. As psychologically astute as you are, you are surprised (often pleasantly) when someone is able to surprise you.

Love, Sex, and Marriage

The chemistry starts with an unusual meeting. Maybe you met in a dream long ago, or you were startled at an acting class when he spoke your favorite line from *Hamlet* to make a point and was looking right at you as he spoke. The chill up and down your spine coupled with the cerebral connection bewitched you enough to make your move the moment class was over.

Sex can be an expression of love for you, but you also crave a touch of the erotic and experimental to be happy. Marry an intellectual equal, psychically connected, and with a physical appetite to match your own. If any of these three elements is missing, avoid the altar talk, and enjoy the relationship for the present only. When an Aries Seven finds the perfect fit, the intellectual warrior is transformed into a dedicated spouse and imaginative playmate.

Money and Career

You aren't keen on managing people unless they are as educated, dedicated, and talented as you are, plus share similar career goals—however close to the cutting edge (also known as the fringe) they are. In that unusual but not impossible situation, you make an excellent shirtsleeve manager. Always demanding respect, your drive for perfection, tireless hours on the job, and eagerness to train others makes you a demanding but rewarding boss.

A "generous tightwad" sums up your saving and spending patterns. You don't throw money around, but use it appropriately and as needed with an occasional splurge to go first class. Rich or poor, you always have enough to take care of yourself and usually have more cash tucked away than anyone in the neighborhood would guess.

The ♈7 Potential

It's as easy for you to be the man behind the scenes as it is to be in front of the camera. A private person, you require lots of solitude for balance. Conversely, you have a keen scientific mind and knowledge to share. You take your time growing up, but once you develop specialized skills, you gain confidence and do very well for yourself.

Later in life, you wax philosophical and pump out a book or two. Along the way, you sometimes blur the line between what's acceptable and what isn't. When that happens, you find Experience to be an effective teacher. Develop your mind to gain the wisdom you seek.

FAMOUS ARIES SEVENS

Leonard Nimoy	*3/26/1931*	*Emma Thompson*	*4/15/1959*
Eric Clapton	*3/30/1945*	*Elle MacPherson*	*3/29/1964*
James Woods	*4/18/1947*	*Picabo Street*	*4/3/1971*

♈ • 8
Aries Eight
"The Inspired Professional"

♈+	8+	♈-	8-
Assertive	*Capable*	*Impatient*	*Indecisive*
Generous	*Professional*	*Excessive*	*Workaholic*
Enthusiastic	*Open-minded*	*Headstrong*	*Money Problems*
Creative	*Sensuous*		

To you, the difference between right and wrong is a matter of perception and choice. There's also that mixed bag of tantalizing opposites you have slung over your shoulder wherever you go. Is it a gift, you wonder, to be able to see the rewards and consequences of any action you might take? Yet fiery Mars won't let you sit back and be an observer instead of leading the fray. Well, if this sounds like you, honey, you're in good company. Buddha, yes, THE Buddha, was an Aries Eight extraordinare, and doesn't that help put things in perspective?

Destined to spread your wings and range far from home, whenever facing a dilemma you must solve, you ponder carefully before making a selection. No vacillating wimp, you're ready to back up (and sometimes reconsider) any decision with legal action or sword, whatever is most appropriate to protect those who look to you for guidance. And many do, don't they? From Mom to your college roommate, folks recognize the impartial and fair advice you dish out on request. You never tell anyone what to do; but you do tell them what you would do in the same situation while pointing out why or why not that would work for them. Since this started at an early age, you're used to others expecting not only friendship, but protection and guidance, too.

Always tolerant, you refuse to let anyone box you into a corner. You know today's truth might not read the same tomorrow and insist to keep your options open. At some point, maybe as you observe the ridiculous wrangle between two women in the grocery store over the last ripe avocado, it dawns on you that not everyone sees the world the same way you do. Once that light bulb turns on, you want to illuminate everyone's way through the maze.

Love, Sex, and Marriage

You search the planet for a person who is a skilled and complementary reflection to call your other half. A partner who wants to be an equal, is able to stir your passions, contributes to the family budget, and doesn't mind keeping the home fires burning when you dash off is the one you need at your side. Of course, you want to be home as much as possible to enjoy the sensual pleasures you find in each other's arms. Enjoying sex is as important to you as the most glorious philosophical meeting of the minds. Adaptable to a lover's whims and fancies, even between the sheets, you're a fair player. Both of you must be serenely satisfied before the teasing and caressing are over.

A balanced combination, Aries Eight is an intellectual and sensual combination. You have an intense drive to experience, a hunger for physical pleasure, and the mental dexterity to create and play out fantasies. Your partner needs an equal imagination, the stamina to last, and must be able to relish the wonders you can offer.

Money and Career

A poet, banker, minister, lawyer, politician, or judge, you try to make a difference whatever you do, and want to see results for your efforts. You need to be in a position of authority where you can direct others to achieve measurable success. Success means accomplishments, and the one that makes you feel the most valued is to help others mold dreams into reality. No matter where you work, you are respected. Wield the power you have wisely.

Money is more cyclical for you than for most. Either you're rolling in it or struggling to make ends meet. Since the Aries influence demands you stay independent, you eventually find ways to minimize the ups and downs through careful money handling. Work is a joy to you, and money represents the recognition and reward for your efforts.

Career and marriage are often united in a common venture for you and your partner. You can be a formidable team, once your respective roles are clearly defined.

The ♈8 Potential

Combine your unique outlook with authoritative qualities and the ability to manage a diverse group of people to be an influence that produces far-reaching results. You work as hard as you play, but shouldn't take yourself too seriously. You alternate between being driven to succeed and kicking back to enjoy the wonder of a brilliant sunset over the bay.

Over a lifetime, you change career tracks a few times and in the process become a treasured resource and friend to many. Develop a balance between the spiritual and physical worlds. As soon as you can accept that desire alone won't change everything that's wrong in the world, the quicker you make progress toward doing exactly that!

FAMOUS ARIES EIGHTS

Johann Sebastian	*3/21/1685*	*Aretha Franklin*	*3/25/1942*
Bach		*Chaka Khan*	*3/23/1953*
Warren Beatty	*3/30/1937*	*Elizabeth*	*4/15/1933*
William Wordsworth	*4/7/1770*	*Montgomery*	

♈ • 9
Aries Nine
"The Enterprising Performer"

♈+	9+	♈-	9-
Dyamic	*Artistic*	*Impulsive*	*Possessive*
Creative	*Compassionate*	*Naive*	*Moody*
Active	*Charismatic*	*Headstrong*	*Inconsistent*
Leader	*Worldly*		

No one knows how to get attention better than you do. Moments out of the womb, eyes bright with anticipation, you gazed at your first audience—doctors, nurses, attendants, and oh, yes: Mom and Dad. Everyone was so pleased with the entrance you'd made, including you.

You aren't quite like the rest of your classmates in Ms. Green's kindergarten. Somehow you know without being told what makes people tick. You can make them laugh, cry, and let you have your own way. Yes, due to the blinding charm and naive trust you broadcast, you do get away with more than most kids. Folks have just got to respond to charisma like that.

Since you always take the road less traveled, remember to inform the bevy of believers following in your bootsteps before exiting the main highway with them in tow. The members of the entourage may change, but you do need the approval of adoring friends. To your credit, you are quick to step down off the pedestal if it looks like anyone might get hurt. You're a realist who carries a wide-angle lens to view the world.

Enthusiastic with energy to spare, you have an ample share of disappointments to make you quite the expert on recovery, bouncing back, and starting over. A practical visionary, you want to achieve notoriety, but have your hands full living the abundant life. You're a gutsy creature who continually cuts through uncharted waters with the hope that the new and distant shore won't evaporate before you reach it. Faith and determination have always helped you get there before, and you don't expect that cosmic law to change any time soon.

Love, Sex, and Marriage

True love presents a serious quandary. You want a loving family and simpatico spouse but recoil from the idea of staying in one spot long enough to make it happen. Because you do anything and everything to the fullest, you're a delight as a lover. There's no such thing as a routine roll in the hay with you. A lover quickly learns new rhythms to keep up and occasionally takes the lead if they intends to stay with you.

A smart partner won't nag about housework or being there every single minute. No, it takes more than cunning to keep you in the cottage—a child for example. A child is a wondrous gift, and you approach parenthood as you do everything else—curious, fearless, and determined to make a good job of it. You want to be there from the first steps until college graduation. Likewise, you are your partner's greatest cheerleader in anything he wants to accomplish. And of course, your partner is smart enough to pick a spotlight different from your own in which to shine, isn't he?

Money and Career

Others marvel at the high energy and fast pace you keep. No matter from what direction the ton of bricks hit you, you shake the dust off and get moving again. That talent and your ability to include *everyone* in a plan make you a dynamic boss with a loyal crew. As long as there is a reward in the offing, you will accept almost any challenge.

You manage to sustain a stable income, though figuring out how to do that is initially difficult, so you might experience a hard knock or two in the world of budgets before getting it right. Once you're in a position of authority, there are bonuses to be had and/or freelance cash to earn that make the effort worthwhile. Entertainment, law, forestry work, business, teaching, counseling, and the arts are all stimulating and profitable callings.

Family seldom takes a backseat to the time clock. As independent as you think you are, the people who hug you at the end of the day are the cornerstone of your life.

The ♈9 Potential

You're a free spirit with a multitude of people to help. Marriage seems unlikely, yet it is the ultimate experience that gives meaning to your life and color to everything else you do. A natural parent, you provide inspiration and direction for strangers with the same care you do for loved ones. You make every life experience 3–D and multitextured for all.

Overcome moodiness by seeing yourself as a citizen-at-large instead of succumbing to self-pity or longing for whatever is over the next hill. It isn't easy being in the flow and living in the moment, but it *is* the path to achieving the accomplishment you long for the most—true love and old-fashioned happiness.

FAMOUS ARIES NINES

Eliot Ness	*4/19/1903*	*Gloria Steinem*	*3/25/1934*
Harry Reasoner	*4/17/1923*	*Bette Davis*	*4/5/1908*
Paul Michael Glaser	*3/25/1943*	*Jennifer Grey*	*3/26/1960*

TAURUS

●

♉ • 1
Taurus One
"The Bold Builder"

♉ +	1 +	♉ -	1 -
Ambitous	*Decisive*	*Impatient*	*Inflexible*
Industrious	*Determined*	*Hot-tempered*	*Willful*
Determined	*Daring*	*Jealous*	*Myopic*
Steadfast	*A Leader*		

A Taurus One seizes life by the horns: no cowering for you, just bulldozing ahead! You firmly believe that everyone and everything has its place; yours, of course, is toward the top of the food chain. But in your honorable world, there are no small roles, only small actors. Every human being is a vital cog in the machinery of society. As Taurean One Karl Marx wrote, "From each according to his abilities, to each acording to his needs."

No one understands better how the system works. While you favor maintaining the status quo, you're fiercely dedicated to improving situations. For all your traditionalism, you're an iconoclast, with a cool rebellious streak. But it's cleverly concealed behind your proper exterior. You recognize that image is everything, and present yourself very carefully. You believe fervently in keeping up appearances and keeping up with those darned Joneses (if you aren't a Jones yourself), but you're not showing off, just staring down the competition. Yours is the football-coach-as-self-help-guru philosophy, practicing winning through intimidation. The car you drive makes a statement, your home is a showplace, and if you have any skeletons, you're not stupid enough to let them hang out in a closet, you bury them where they belong. Of course, *you* know it's all an act, but that doesn't mean that the people you're negotiating with have to, right?

Your Achilles' heel is your temper; it's imperative that you let off steam gradually, instead of periodically erupting like Vesuvius, burying anyone around you in red-hot verbal torrents. Aware of this tendency, you're probably a big fan of regular exercise as a way to burn off stress, not to mention calories from those fancy biz dinners. Those who love and respect you understand that the stomping and snorting are part and parcel of your ardent approach toward life. Most people don't, however; if someone unintentionally waves a red cape at you, try not to bully him or her into waving a white flag.

Love, Sex, and Marriage

You'll likely have frequent amorous scrapes, though you'll rarely bleed on the field of battle between the sexes. While Taureans usually like taking their time about romance, and Ones are supremely level-headed, you occasionally lose your head in matters of the heart. You can get yourself into some pretty sticky situations, in both love and work. Nonetheless, being fundamentally sincere, if you make the wrong choice, you'll stubbornly stick it out. Honor, tenacity, and responsibility are marvelous qualities, but remember that love doesn't always last forever.

Once you've settled down, you tend to view your mate as your possession. Since you wouldn't respect a partner without equally strong opinions, this leads to quite a few fireworks. Fortunately, they're usually carried over into the bedroom; after the Sturm and Drang is over, you switch immediately into kiss-and-make-up mode. Since you're the make-out champion, you score more points in the afterglow than in the heat of the moment.

Money and Career

You respect what power accomplishes, and work diligently toward a position of authority, which turns you on more than cold hard cash. A brilliant conservator of money, you'd do well as a CFO, lobbyist, image consultant, or fundraiser. You devise inventive and exciting ways to enrich the coffers, knowing exactly how to calculate risks and odds. Bank president to theatrical managing director, you excel at develping promotional strategies that improve your company's reputation.

You're just as careful with your own finances, and could doubtless retire at forty, if you don't float away on a golden parachute. You can be surprisingly penny-wise and pound-foolish; don't begrudge loved ones an advance on their allowances for some "nonessentials" when you just spent $75,000 on a Town Car for its prestige factor. (Actually, you'd convince the company to buy it for you.)

The ♉1 Potential

You're smart enough to know that bluster and bravado carry the day only so far. Your self-confidence is perhaps your greatest asset, but it can be your undoing if you become too inflexible and unwilling to listen to others. Few people have a better grasp of what it takes to get things done with both amazing grace and stamina. Lead by examle, and don't let your impatience get in the way. You genuinely want everyone to feel happy, secure, and productive, so remember to factor others' opinions and perspectives into your final decisions. Then you can help build a world that really will be the better place you tell everyone you want for your kids.

FAMOUS TAURUS ONES

Jack Nicholson	*4/22/1937*	*Dennis Rodman*	*5/15/1961*
George Clooney	*5/6/1961*	*Carol Burnett*	*4/26/1933*
Isabella I of Spain	*4/22/1451*	*Judy Collins*	*5/1/1939*

♉ • 2
Taurus Two
"The Kittenish Charmer"

♉ +	2 +	♉ -	2 -
Ardent	Accommodating	Slow-moving	Unassertive
Hospitable	Understanding	Complacent	Shy
Calm	Gentle	Overdeliberate	Sulky
Loyal	Modest		

To all outward appearances, you're adorable, dimply, and cuddly: Mr. Teddy Bear meets Ms. Barbie. You're so charming you could probably throw an "end of the world" party and make it a funfest filled with love and laughter! Despite your entertaining skills and fondness for your social club's bridge tournaments or theater outings with your best friends, part of you would much rather snuggle up to your sweetie with some microwave popcorn and *Casablanca* on the tube back home. Taurus Twos are remarkably sensitive and understanding; you crave stability and offer it in return. Hence, individualistic types might find you demanding and dependent.

Although you know just where to stroke ruffled egos, you can wield a deceptively steel hand in a velvet glove if someone crosses you deliberately, especially when your security or that of loved ones is threatened. You're the type to pick fleas off Fido's coat and release them in the woods, craftily preferring the art of compromise to out-and-out warfare. Stubborn, opinionated Taurus can lock horns with the meek, peace-loving Two. They can merge productively: While you need tranquillity, you're not afraid to confront your nearest and dearest if you feel they've misbehaved. This makes you a natural parent, combining doting and discipline in equal doses. You'll hold your children's hands all night through an attack of the measles, weaving magical tales of pink polka-dotted porpoises to calm them, then gently singing them to sleep in your undoubtedly soothing, melodious voice. You long to find a partner who will then croon a lullaby to you while cradling you in his or her arms.

Love, Sex, and Marriage

You're incredibly caring and devoted. You take love very
seriously indeed; though you may not always show it, you're
easily bruised. You prefer a lengthy courtship, allowing
friendship to form the foundation of true love. Total honesty
is imperative, though you cringe at the thought of causing
pain. You'd never cheat, for example, but you'd rather know
if your partner does; then at least your trust won't be
shattered.

The irony is that you're so nice that potential mates sometimes feel you're not challenging enough. You need someone secure with high self-esteem; otherwise he or she is
likely to break it off with "Honey, you're wonderful, everything I always wanted. So what's wrong with you that you
want me!?" Though you crave a 50/50 relationship, you
place your loved one on a pedestal, like a delicate china
figurine. Problem is, he or she is flesh and blood, with individual needs, agendas, and desires that can conflict with
your own. So before you play bull in the china shop, look
for warning signals that your partner resents being on display on the credenza.

Money and Career

Whatever you choose to do, it's with an eye to helping
others, improving their conditions, or beautifying their surroundings. It's not that you shy away from hard work, even
physical labor, but you need to see the fruits of your concrete contributions. Weeding, mowing, and pruning as a gar-
dener, sure, since your artistry would be apparent . . . but
manufacturing mulch, even for millions, never! Your tact,
taste, and refinement could lead to a diplomatic career, acting, painting, landscaping, interior design, fashion, even
flower arranging. Your own finances usually blossom, as
you have a green thumb in more ways than one. Your taste
is exquisite but eclectic, your living room cluttered, even
clashing, that eighteenth-century Chinese cloisonné horse
you just *had* to have contrasted with a stunningly simple
black halogen lamp.

The ♉2 Potential

   You're here to set an example simply by being your unruffled, loving, generous self. You're the eternal pacifying voice of reason, the worked-out strong shoulder, the gentle yet firm guiding hand. A steadfast friend in times of need, you shouldn't be afraid to ask for help yourself. You may not receive the recognition you richly merit for your unassuming dependability, but your absence would actually leave a painful void in many people's lives; whenever you feel unappreciated, remember how fortunate you are to be gifted with your Taurean resilience and fortitude. Nice guys may not always win the race, but they virtually never finish last.

FAMOUS TAURUS TWOS

Jay Leno	4/28/1950	Michelle Pfeiffer	4/29/1958
Pierce Brosnan	5/6/1953	Shirley Temple Black	4/23/1928
Sugar Ray Robinson	5/3/1920	Ann-Margret	4/28/1941

♉ • 3
Taurus Three
"The Teasing Traditionalist"

♉ +	3 +	♉ -	3 -
Sensuous	Imaginative	Sensual	Trivial
Artistic	Debonair	Lazy	Dishonest
Buoyant	Carefree	Gluttonous	Dissipative
Boisterous	Sociable		

Taurus Threes have a mischievous, even willful side that pops up at unexpected moments. You're the one who enlivened your cousin's wedding by doing a bump and grind with the bride's grandmother before stripping to the disco version of "Hava Nagilah." You probably identify with those great thirties screwball comedies and sometimes objectively view your life as a French farce with larger-than-life characters, ridiculous misunderstandings, and slamming doors. Of course, you're the author, director, and star player around whom the action revolves. Chances are you play or would relish the role of dotty Aunt Agatha or the family's dashing black sheep.

You have a wonderful sense of life's essential absurdity. You have verve, vim, dash, flash, and flair to spare. A whiz kid, you wowed your parents and teachers; so "talented, clever, and polite," they cooed. Of course, you had an ulterior motive: you wanted attention and flattery. As a result you're usually a teensy bit spoiled when you enter the "real world." You expect to bowl it over, but it won't roll over! Where are the adulation, acclaim, and advancement you thought were yours by divine right?

There's a valuable lesson here. You shouldn't just coast on your considerable charm and natural gifts. You know how to butter up, suck up, if you want that promotion handed to you on a silver platter; tell your superior's wife that horizontal stripes really *are* slimming. But with earnest effort—and yes, a dash of torturous toil—you can indulge your outrageous side without fear of constraint.

Love, Sex, and Marriage

You not only appreciate but hunger for beauty and elegance in every aspect of your life. While you seek these attributes in a mate, you also require mental compatibility and a similar outlook. Not to mention a willingness to put the paperwork down in favor of a good cuddle. You need a headquarters for your zaniness, so your ideal mate can throw confetti all over your New Year's Eve party guests . . . and start vacuuming the moment they leave. After a little whoopee, of course, then reminding you to drink five glasses of water and take one thousand milligrams of Vitamin C and three Advil before you go to bed.

For you sex is a frolic, a joyous romp in the hay, grass, river, wherever. You love to wallow in your surroundings, and probably entertain secret, deliciously silly fantasies of Victorian bordellos with plush red velour canopied beds and seraglios with jeweled embroidered pillows and satin sheets scented with jasmine.

Money and Career

Your madcap lifestyle requires money, and you do have an eerie knack for finding it on trees. Of course, your Taurean side carefully nurtured those trees from saplings, even as the Three influence impels you to sell kindling to finance the next shopping spree. Whatever you do, you'll be an entertainer. Even if you're just slinging hash, you flip the burgers behind your back to amuse the diners.

Acting, singing, writing, and directing satisfy your need for showmanship. Your work will always be distinguished by your charm and wit. You're no nine-to-fiver—you'd know just where to punch that time clock—but can thrive in an unstructured office environment where you're allowed to brainstorm and come up with ideas, half of which will be utterly dazzling, half absurdly unfeasible. Clever, creative, and innovative, you add flair to the most mundane situations. For all your Three influence, the Taurean side knows exactly when to stop partying and get to work, even if the grindstone is Himalayan and your nose is bent out of shape. Taurus helps channel that scattered Three energy; you need that adrenaline surge and sheer unadulterated panic, but you rarely need a jump start from someone else.

The ♉3 Potential

You're here to improve on reality, to water anything "garden variety" and watch it bloom. You know just how to add that accessory that makes an outfit come to striking life; that rare skill can be applied to anything you want, since your presence animates every situation. Your zest for living livens up every partnership; even a brief encounter with you will be memorable. You could easily go on cruise control, but set a new challenge for yourself every day, and you'll attain virtually any goal you set your mind to.

FAMOUS TAURUS THREES

Salvador Dali	5/11/1904	Stephen Baldwin	5/12/1966
Ella Fitzgerald	4/15/1918	Audrey Hepburn	5/4/1929
Frank Capra	5/18/1897	Bernadette Devlin	4/23/1947

♌ • 4
Taurus Four
"The Constant Contractor"

♉ +	4 +	♉ -	4 -
Stable	Hardworking	Rigid	Unimaginative
Patient	Traditional	Solid	Argumentative
Diligent	Persistent	Stubborn	Skeptical
Dependable	Constructive		

As a kid you were always laying tracks for toy trains, building the better dollhouse, assembling model planes, constructing futuristic skylines with Erector sets, even dissecting frogs. Whether a boy or a girl, you also had an affinity—and talent—for playing house and doctor. As an adult, you haven't changed one bit. You buy every how-to and do-it-yourself guide and probably emulate Bob Vila and Martha Stewart.

A Taurus Four is as solid as the proverbial rock, and brave enough never to hide behind it. Yet even if you disagree with someone, you always listen as long as they've done their homework; sincerity, sturdiness, accuracy, and dependability are qualities you value highly. The game you probably hated most as a kid was Telephone, since it infuriates you when someone doesn't get the facts straight. Establishing a strong, efficient network of communication is one of your priorities, both at work and at home. There's probably a cell phone growing out of your ear, since you recognize the importance of staying in touch.

Though a realistic and pragmatist, you believe in people's inherent goodness, that if given the choice, they'll do the right thing. After all, you usually do. Whenever proof is offered to the contrary, you're almost naively hurt, though you're expert at rationalizing others' behavior. There's no question you deserve that "Good Citizenship Award" on your mantel. But despite your seemingly sober side, you can be the practical joker par excellence. You're the one who short-sheeted your best buddy in camp, and engineered the hole-drilling in the wall of the girls' (or boys') locker room. That basic human warmth and touch of bawdiness underlying your conservatism have always been your keys to success.

Love, Sex, and Marriage

You exude earthy sensuality and enjoy your pick of one-nighters. But ultimately no fly-by-nights for you: you're in this for the long haul, and you want an equally capable, loyal partner. Still, you love sex, and yes, you'll respect them the morning after the first—well fifth—date. (You will even chivalrously give them their choice of French toast or eggs Benedict with their café au lait.)

Physical compatibility is important to you: but you're not only looking for the looker (you don't want *all* eyes turned to your beloved), just someone who spoons perfectly and enjoys a late-night tryst with the refrigerator (in which case you don't mind the crumbs of coffee cake in bed). Forget complicated discussions over where a relationship is going, you just want it to move forward at its own pace. As with everything else, your approach to courtship and marriage is "meat and potatoes." That includes sex: you like to get down to basics, and your basic training was probably quite thorough. Your endurance and libido are both legendary, and variety is in your spice rack; if your partner has something different and exotic in mind, he or she should just whisper it while nibbling on your ear.

Money and Career

Your enviable steadiness and patience make you a phenomenal researcher in any field. Constructing things and taking them apart to see how they work come naturally. This makes you a superb engineer, architect, scientist, or master craftsperson, able to build a house or a theory brick by brick. Your organizing and people skills are equally well developed; you're the ideal middle-level manager, entrusted with implementing orders and seeing them through to the finish. Although you have a few ideas of your own, you generally prefer perspiration to inspiration. Execution is your middle name. Though your checkbook isn't always balanced, an IRA sprouts the minute you find a secure job, and you're sure to keep a few shares of blue-chip stocks tucked away in the underwear drawer.

The ♉4 Potential

You're a pillar of society and the salt of the earth; but don't become so set in your ways you turn into a pillar of salt. Resist the temptation to become too complacent in the present; instead build consistently toward the future. You're not the type to go off on tangents; anything occupying your thoughts remains with you no matter what the situation. That single-minded intensity serves you—and the rest of us—well, but remember that a detailed breakdown of why trickle-down theory would jump-start Third World economies isn't exactly scintillating conversation at a cocktail party for Friends of the Ballet. You can find the joy and humor in everyday things, so relax and enjoy sharing the fruits you've so richly earned.

FAMOUS TAURUS FOURS

Bono	5/10/1960	Sigmund Freud	5/6/1856
Harvey Keitel	5/13/1939	Roberta Peters	5/4/1930
Rosie Perez	5/16/1963	Bonnie Tyler	5/8/1953

♉ • 5
Taurus Five
"The Mischievous Master Builder"

♉ +	5 +	♉ -	5 -
Elegant	Flexible	Greedy	Fickle
Self-reliant	Resourceful	Unfaithful	Reckless
Genial	Curious	Self-indulgent	Gullible
Decisive	Articulate		

Unlike many Taureans, you're bullish on change and never met an experience you didn't want to explore and savor. Never content with munching on the clover in your own backyard, you actively search out greener pastures in which to graze. Variety and versatility are vital to your well-being. You like going from Brie to bratwurst and black tie at a Metropolitan Opera gala to black jeans at a Mets ball game. Taurus Fives are a mesmerizing, mystifying combination of free spirit and military cadet, Clydesdale and bucking bronco. Even your looks and style are often slightly unconventional, and you ooze sex appeal without even trying.

You'll work deceptively hard when young, but it's really because you dream of early—and luxurious—retirement. But your'e not the type to play gentleman farmer. (Well, okay, you might buy and meticulously restore eighteenth-century stone farmhouses as a hobby.) No, you'd much rather buy a yacht and sail around the world. That doesn't mean you don't want a traditional home and roots, merely that you'll inevitably sow seeds in far-flung places. You'll accomplish virtually whatever you put your mind to, so you must get a series of goals for yourself to avoid boredom. You likely had five- and ten-year plans stashed away in your high school locker; when you unearth them at thirty you giggle at your choices, having improvised all the way.

You have an intuitive understanding of your role in life. From an early age, you could pinpoint your exact stimilarities to and differences from your peers. Your Taurus side knew just how to curry favor from those in authority, the Five could coax your contemporaries into thinking you were the next James Dean. You've learned how to play one against the other, in both your outer and inner lives. You're a walking example of having your cake and eating it, too, because your substantial charm enables you to do as you please even when your ideas clash with others'.

Love, Sex, and Marriage

You're difficult to pin down romantically. You know a relationship is in the cards but prefer to hold all the trumps. Not that you want a dummy sitting opposite you, quite the contrary, but you want to make sure that your mate for life can not only read your moods but can synchronize his or her own to yours. Obivously, establishing that connnection takes time, which is a most precious commodity in your life.

Still, your overpowering need for physical outlets means you'll always have someone in tow and probably under toe.

You believe in fidelity, but if dissatisifed at home might be propelled into a few extracurricular encounters. You'd rationalize that such discreet indiscretions actually help preserve a sagging relationship by burning off negative energy and satisfying curiosity. But anything on the side will usually be a one-shot-only deal, because you won't violate the sanctity of your marriage. You'll never endanger its stability—unless you feel your loves ones are building a higher fence around your grazing grounds.

Money and Career

Taurean Fives are usually endowed with breathtaking grace, fluidity, and dexterity, as well as incredible pure strength and stamina. You could probably pirouette while free-lifting a two-hundred-pound barbell. Any career that exploits that physicality to the limit is ideal: athlete, dancer, acrobat, trainer, or physical therapist. You'd also make a fine officer in any of the armed forces, with courage to spare and a mind designed to strategize. Your magnetism makes performing another option, while your disciplined yet inquiring mind could lead to writing or composing music. You'd also make a dynamic Freedom Figher or muckraking journalist exposing corruption.

You view money as a utilitarian means to a utopian end; you usually manage to make a bundle, and spend it on creature comforts, extravagant homes, and exotic travel. You also have a generous streak that many a friend takes advantage of . . . not that they're fooling you for an instant!

The ♉5 Potential

You have a tricky mission in life: to show people they can be revolutionary in their lives without flouting every convention. No matter how fidgety, even flighty, you may appear, you have a rock-steady core. But that balancing act rarely places you on an emotional seesaw. You have a powerful sense of your identity and won't be deflected from your goals, but would never stoop to devious means to attain them. You'll always be true to yourself, which explains your mass appeal. That combination of self-assurance and willingness to explore and experiment will probably sway quite a few people you encounter. Use the gift wisely.

FAMOUS TAURUS FIVES

Uma Thurman	4/29/1970	Andre Agassi	4/29/1970
Gary Cooper	5/7/1901	Dennis Hopper	5/17/1936
Irving Berlin	5/11/1888	Sören Kierkegaard	5/5/1813
Grace Jones	5/19/1952		

♉ • 6
Taurus Six
"The Sensuous Materialist"

♉ +	6 +	♉ -	6 -
Loyal	Sensitive	Possessive	Opinionated
Responsible	Conventional	Covetous	Narrow-
Magnanimous	Loving	Conventional	minded
Down-to-earth	Pampering		Obdurate

A Taurus Six is not just the salt of the earth, but the rich bountiful harvest itself. Chances are, even if you didn't grow up on a farm, you always loved the idea of milking cows and strewing chicken feed. Mother Nature and Mother Nurture rolled into one, you personify sturdiness. Your self-imposed mandate to provide for your family spurs you on to build, if not an empire, then at least a safe, secure haven replete with two-hundred-channel satellite dish and hot tub.

You're a man's man and a woman's woman, and take great pride in playing traditional roles. No matter what, there's something of the chauvinist about you. A fierce defender of your family and beliefs, you always look to elevate the status quo and tend to be staunchly conservative, not necessarily politically but in your demeanor. You're easygoing, as long as your cozy situation isn't disrupted, you believe firmly in living and letting live. Your credo is that everyone can lead the good life—and you're just the one to lead the way.

You're a caregiver at home and a caretaker at work, almost superhuman in the way you fulfill your obligations. Your promises really are as good as gold, and their market value doesn't fluctuate. You'll throw that family reunion, even if you know your nephew Bobby will crash several vases playing ball in the house. And you'll cut a board meeting short rather than miss Lisa's first piano recital. You're just as protective of your own parents, respecting them for the strong values they instilled; if your mate thinks a nursing home is the best alternative, you'd argue persuasively how much your own kids could benefit from Grandma's presence.

Obviously you're an incredibly indulgent spouse or parent, humoring every whim of your nearest and dearest—unless, of course, they must be taught a life lesson. Oh, you'll sternly deliver advice while uncannily resembling that portrait of your grandfather, but every scolding is followed by a warm hug and a "How much do you need?" as you whip out the bankroll.

Love, Sex, and Marriage

No surprise that a Taurus Six likes things settled: you prefer to stake out your own little piece of prime pasture where you can graze happily until the cows come home (which had better be sooner than later—you like to share time with your mate after work and rarely, if ever, stray into another bull's territory). When you marry, it's not just till death do you part, it's for eternity, and you'll weather all the little crises and testy moments with confidence.

Yours is the time-tested courtship approach: a loaf of bread (maybe that pane rustico studded with black olives from the gourmet deli), a jug of wine (Château Latour if you please), and thou (just the way you are). You adore the feel of silk sheets or silken hair, and could rub, caress, fondle, and massage for days. But to you love is a feast for all five senses: the whiff of perfume or almond shampoo, the faint salty taste of the neck, the drawn-out sighs, are as essential as mother's milk.

Money and Career

The glad-handing, back-slapping type, you're made for the world of business meetings at the golf course and innocent locker-room jokes. Genuinely friendly yet tough as nails as you hammer out a proposal, you leave everyone thinking, "What a great guy (or gal)." Your warm yet dutiful nature makes you a fine manager or executive, although your fastidious attention to detail makes it difficult for you to delegate authority. You're highly musical, indeed responsive to anything sensuous, and are drawn to all the artistic professions. Teaching is an option, since you love setting an example for everyone else. You'd also succeed at "home ec" jobs like chef, fashion or interior designer, and realtor.

You like beautiful objects, good hearty grub, and very comfortable surroundings; your home is your castle and you expect it to be furnished accordingly, though you'll tease your mate unmercifully about how much of your hard-earned money is going down the new gold-plated drain.

The ♉6 Potential

You're the hail-fellow-well-met of everyone's dreams. Universally popular, you set an example simply by being the nice, dependable human being you are, ambitious only for family and friends, wanting everyone to live in harmony. You can also share your appreciation of the finer things without pretension. Don't allow yourself to fall into ruts and routines. You need people around you who can push you to perform and reach your potential, otherwise you might sit a little too heavily in the lap of luxury.

FAMOUS TAURUS SIXES

Stevie Wonder	5/13/1950	Christine Baranski	5/2/1956
Robert Browning	5/17/1812	Duke Ellington	4/29/1899
Fred Astaire	5/10/1899	Al Pacino	4/25/1939
Halston	4/23/1932	Debra Winger	5/17/1955
William Randolph	4/29/1863	Joe Louis	5/13/1914
Hearst		Mike Wallace	5/9/1918
Randy Travis	5/4/1959		

♉ • 7
Taurus Seven
"The Conceptual Conjurer"

♉ +	7 +	♉ -	7 -
Determined	Inventive	Stubborn	Choosy
Alluring	Analytical	Haughty	Aloof
Imaginative	Selective	Stingy	Introverted
Commonsensical	Specialized		

A secret inverse snob, you'll attend opera premieres and enjoy the see-and-be scenes, yet have just as much fun line-dancing or slipping a Chippendales dancer a tip. Only a lucky few will be privileged to savor both sides. You delight in being an eternal contradiction, keeping people guessing whether you're a brain or a bombshell; isn't it amusing how difficult it is for folks to reconcile the two?

You project a mysterious allure, at once earthy yet ethereal. Your deameanor and humor are both deliciously dry and droll. That sly wit and apparent nonchalance belie your perfectionist precision and ferocious competitive drive. You cultivate a store of trivia, factoids, and fun anecdotes to regale with and sometimes distract them, deflecting them from discovering your true motives. You're no sneak or snitch, but you *would* make a terrific spy! Your Taurus side is so genuinely genial and hearty, permitting entrée wherever you go, while that Seven can calculate, absorb, analyze, and interpret like a Deep Blue chess computer.

You burn to create something incredibly specialized of lasting value to humanity, though you'd never admit—even to yourself—just how much you want that candy bar named after you. It might surprise people to learn that at the very least you chair a charity of your own creation. You pitch your ideas perfectly: they're invariably just distinctive and cutting-edge enough to be commercial, though never in an obvious way. If you created a "jiggle" sitcom, the lead character would be a stripper working her way toward a Ph.D. in astrophysics. Title? *Celestial Bodies*.

Love, Sex, and Marriage

Your affectionate nature compels you to be in a relationship, yet your craving for solitude, independent streak, and insistence on hving it your way can push potential lovers away. You intellectualize love far more than the average Taurean, but you're still more comfortable expressing your emotions through your considerable sensuousness and physicality. Thus you require a partner who can verbalize feelings for you both. Still, you're the least likely Taurean to marry; you might well choose to play the "other" in a thirty-year triangle or carry on a long-term, long-distance relationship.

'Twould be folly not to quote the great Taurus Seven expert on love, William Shakespeare. "Let me not to the marriage of true minds/Admit impediments. Love is not love/ Which alters where it alteration finds/Or bends with the remover to remove" (sonnet 116). In other words, once you've made that bed, you'll lie in it, having already determined that you can't bounce a coin off it, when your soul mate is tucking the sheets. If you find someone with a body and nerves of steel and a mind like a steel trap, you can easily enjoy a tranquil, devoted fifty or so years together.

Money and Career

Your intuition, insight, inspiration, are manna to any creative endeavor and you're naturally drawn to the arts. But with that instinctive touch for what will sell to the masses, you could easily be an inventor or product developer. You're a technical, scientific, and mathematical wizard, though you prefer doing something with tangible, quantifiable results that you can point to proudly. You can also take someone else's projects and put just enough spin on them to make them fly, or synthesize competing proposals into a harmonious whole: an architect of ideas. Lobby your company to create a "creative director" position for you so you can research for hours alone in your book-lined office.

You'll probably end up a millionaire, but you'll rarely brag about those extra zeroes in your various bank accounts. Your net worth comes out in the collection of Model T Fords or Fabergé eggs, all displayed to the most discriminating eyes—your own.

The ♉7 Potential

You're here to endow the commonplace, everyday, and humdrum with a dose of magic. At your greatest, you're an alchemist of the human soul, allowing people to see things as they truly are, then recognize the extra in the ordinary. Your success will likely transform you into a symbol of hope, inspiration, or merely status to many. Without even realizing it, you have a knack for juggling your worldly and private concerns. You're a authentic role model, analytic yet warm, likable yet reserved: a truly balanced human being.

FAMOUS TAURUS SEVENS

Queen Elizabeth II	4/21/1926	Jerry Seinfield	4/29/1954
Harry Truman	5/8/1884	Candice Bergen	5/9/1946
Katharine Hepburn	5/12/1907	Reggie Jackson	5/18/1946

♉ • 8
Taurus Eight
"The Empire-Building Executive"

♉ +	8 +	♉ -	8 -
Determined	Capable	Materialistic	Workaholic
Unstoppable	Professional	Calculating	Driven
Imposing	Authoritative	Avaricious	Power-hungry
Steadfast	Ambitious		

The minute your high-school voted you most likely to succeed, you probably scheduled a business meeting the day after graduation! Powered by a state-of-the-art eight-cylinder engine, you've meticulously charted your course in that inimitable Taurean Eight fashion. You don't need a slick car salesman touting your abilities: you're sure to be drowning in a cash-flow flood by the time you're through, with a nest egg that's hatched into quite a coop. Even an apparent knockout punch won't keep you down long, thanks to your bullheaded endurance depsite all obstacles. Fortunately, the warm golden touch of Taurus combines with the Eight's cool-headed appreciation of long-term opportunities, smoothing the bumpy financial ride many Eights take.

You're at ease strolling the corridors of power, but there's a softer side to your nature that few are privileged to see. Oh, they'll encounter the almost superhuman charm, grace, and insight, but they'd be shocked to see your inner sanctum, replete with—*gasp!*—a smiling, politically correct photo of you and your family on holiday. You refuse to parade the intimate details of your life for casual acquaintances, let alone the tabloids. Though you love deeply and truly, it isn't always easily expressed. Rather than flowery speeches or poems, you'll surprise your nearest and dearest with small but exquisite trinkets like a Balinese shadow puppet for your son, a Tahitian black pearl for your spouse—both bought on-site, of course.

Despite loving home, family, and country, you know you were meant to perform on the world stage. You project an air of authority and knowledge that crosses all borders and cultures. What's more, you respect other traditions as much as your own, which commands automatic trust and gains you entry to the upper echelons of power wherever you go.

Love, Sex, and Marriage

You're an equal traditionalist in matters of romance; you won't rush deciding on your life partner. It takes you a while to share both your heart and bank account, but when you're ready you'll back the Brinks truck up to your door; adding your honey's name to your checkbook will be first on your checklist. You're an amorous tactician, thinking out your plan of attack the same way you strategize for a board meeting. Once you make up your mind, you're virtually unstoppable in the seduction department; most people happily surrender to your advances. You realize that money can't buy love . . . but it sure can buy hothouse orchids, Cristal rosé, beluga caviar, and a butler on a moonlit terrace.

You're rarely jealous, but Taurus can be incredibly possessive. Though you're not the unfaithful type, you're quite aware of your extracurricular possibilities, and expect your partner to entertain a fantasy or two. You hope he or she will whisper it in your ear, rather than act on it with the cutie next door. Of course, after slaving away at the office, you forget that you're too exhausted to murmur sweet everythings in your loved one's ear. At least once your mate gets your attention, the lovemaking is likely to go on and on: Remember that horsepower!

Money and Career

King Midas must have been a Taurus Eight. You're a magnate in the making: a magnet for money, power, and prestige. Even if you never scale the Fortune 500 ladder, you'll achieve a position of prominence. You have so many fingers in pies, irons in the fire, and pots on the stove that you're an antitrust suit waiting to happen. You're particularly adept at global affairs. International law or banking, import/export businesses, tax shelter expert, portfolio manager, CEO or CFO of a conglomerate, or that wonderfully vague word "consultant" suit you.

Though most of your time is spent shuttling between conference room and executive dining room, your home will be lavish. After all, you'll need an extravagant space to entertain clients, with works by the hottest up-and-coming artists on display and tasteful yet pricey bibelots and first editions scattered unassumingly about. You'll gladly spend thousands on a baseball card or 1910 upside-down stamp to fill that annoying gap in your collection. Acquisitive by nature, with a discerning eye and palate, you look for the best bargain in the galley or on the wine list—even if it's a two-hundred-dollar bottle that you think ten times superior to the fifty-dollar selection.

The ♉8 Potential

Your persistence and diligence make you a potential role model for everyone you meet. Don't settle into comfortable routines and even cushier circumstances, otherwise the Eight economic rollercoaster might make you queasy. Don't emphasize the material and sensual worlds at the expense of the spiritual. Resist the temptation to become dictatorial in your business and personal dealings. Then you'll rake in the green and graze in greener pastures. Always remember you were meant to share your wealth, whether by funding a new hospital wing or giving of your undeniably valuable time to dispense practical advice to an entry-level exec in your empire.

FAMOUS TAURUS EIGHTS

Pope John Paul II	5/18/1920	Barbra Streisand	4/24/1942
Ulysses Grant	4/27/1822	Emilio Estevez	5/12/1962
Catherine the Great	5/1/1729	Daphne Du Maurier	5/13/1907

♉ • 9
Taurus Nine
"The Ingenious Genie"

♉ +	9 +	♉ -	9 -
Affectionate	Compelling	Indolent	Careless
Creative	Compassionate	Orthodox	Daydreaming
Purposeful	Spiritual	Smug	Self-interested
Unflappable	Generous		

You've always had a wisdom and kindness beyond your years. There you are, all of eight, tenderly cradling a pigeon with a broken wing in your hands. "Ugh," remonstrates your mother, "Put that thing down: it's dirty and disease-ridden!" "Well, yes, Mom," you gently but firmly remonstrate, "but it'll die if we don't nurse it back to health." Your atitude toward human beings is similar, believing that everyone can fly if they're given the chance . . . and that they have a right to comprehensive medical and dental insurance! Retaining that fondness for underdogs into maturity, you develop a robustly healthy dislike of anyone who plays top dog and plays it rough.

You're deeply spiritual, if not religious in an orthodox

sense. The Taurean in you wants absolute proof, of course, but you also daydream about reincarnation and extraterrestrial life. That doesn't mean you let doctrine or dogma Hale-Bopp you over the head, although you *are* surprised the first time meditation leads to an out-of-body experience. You accept anyone's form of worship without question, as long as it doesn't interfere with others'. On the other hand, you preach that any belief system can become a cult when its members claim they're the chosen ones.

It's hard to imagine you won't become involved in some kind of volunteer work; you especially like hands-on assignments where you can feel you're really making a difference to an individual. But you have such a talent for wheedling money out of tightwads that you'll eventually join the board of directors of a struggling theater company, "Save the sperm whale" foundation, and AIDS hospice. Needless to say, you'll also end up chairing the annual ball, as well as storming the decorating committee and besieging the caterer and florist with special requests.

Love, Sex, and Marriage

Love with you can be an unexpectedly stormy passage, and you wouldn't have it any other way. With your emotional sixth sense, it's often "love at first sight" and your stare burns through everyone else on that sardine-packed subway car until your quarry takes notice. But you can be confusing to your loved ones. On some level, it's as if you hold a part of yourself back from the public to give to your partner, yet reserve part of yourself for your public persona. Your loved ones soon learn that what they see isn't always what they get.

Sex with you is utterly delicious. A neck nibbler and toe tickler, you have a nose for erogenous areas as unerring as a veteran traffic cop's for parking violators in a tow away zone. Though your foreplay forehand is your best stroke, you're oddly backhanded about the aftermath afterglow. Your mate may never become accustomed to the way you turn off when you're ready to turn on the tube to watch a news report on your latest rally.

Money and Career

You genuinely enjoy networking, doing the chitchat thing with seeming aplomb. While you value good public opinion highly, you crave the respect of your peers and those in the power structure even more. You're an incredibly persuasive salesperson, especially if you believe in the product. You project a sensual appeal to the public, and are confident you can bring anyone around to your point of view. If inveigling and finagling don't work, you're not above playing martyr to get your way. With your passionate interest in improving humanity, you're drawn to jobs such as minister, missionary, journalist, and political or spiritual advisor.

Though you amass plenty of money, you do like to give it away. After donating $1,000 each to the battered wives' shelter and local symphony, pledging $500 to your alma mater, loaning three friends $250 apiece, which you know you won't see again, and several singles to the homeless people on your way to work, your weekly paycheck didn't stretch as much as you thought.

The ♉9 Potential

You were born to be special, meant to illuminate the way for others and help them appreciate their own unique gifts and abilities. Never shy away from your true self, fearful of what people might think. You're remarkably lucky in terms of the advantages that come your way. There are no guarantees in life; opportunities can vanish as suddenly as they occur. Take the bull by the horns and you might just hit the bull's eye.

FAMOUS TAURUS NINES

Henry Fonda	*5/16/1905*	*Cher*	*5/20/1946*
Linda Evangelista	*5/10/1965*	*Shirley MacLaine*	*4/24/1934*
Michael Palin	*5/5/1943*	*Orson Welles*	*5/6/1915*

GEMINI

●

Ⅱ • 1
GEMINI ONE
"The Liberal Leader"

Ⅱ +	1 +	Ⅱ -	1-
Gracious	*Courageous*	*Scattered*	*Cynical*
Articulate	*Direct*	*Nervous*	*Selfish*
Intellectual	*Independent*	*Noncommittal*	*Stubborn*
Versatile	*Innovative*		

After consulting several maps, you choose the most direct course between where you are and where you want to be. Obstacles disappear under your speculative scrutiny, and few can resist surrendering to your disarming patter once you take up a banner. No matter how casual a conversation might be, you keep your wits about you and refrain from revealing a single bit of information you deem best left unsaid. A discerning sort, you know how to deflect the most carefully worded questions away from private territory. Some call you a genius when you adroitly turn the tables to extract equally classified material. Deft and direct, you rarely meet your match in this kind of face-off.

While you appreciate approval, you don't consciously

seek it. Sure, you're congenial and like a full social calendar, but you won't die without it. In fact, it's the retreat from the spotlight that provides the chance to develop one of your never-ending streams of visionary ideas. You say you take life as it comes, which is true regarding difficult detours and unexpected setbacks. The future is a different story; you know what you want and leave nothing to luck when you go after it. Motivated and capable, you're used to getting what you want.

Freedom is a priceless possession you believe is everyone's right, and it troubles you when someone else's idea of freedom infringes on your own. You can be counted on to stand up for the right of all people to hold different beliefs, even when you don't agree with *what* they think. A perfect society makes allowances for the population to flourish as individuals.

Others depend on you, and you pride yourself on being there to get Mom to her doctor's appointment, cheer Tommy on to a home run at Little League, and still manage to overnight your fashion sketches to the design house on time. You don't assume that anyone will take care of you, but you do require reciprocal support from the home sector.

Love, Sex, and Marriage

You want an intellectual match to share secrets and make love under the full moon. And it won't hurt if he's a good cook, too. Clever enough not to get caught in a commitment, you aren't afraid to pursue any captivating candidate. No problem if the chase is all there is—sometimes it provides enough memories to see you through.

Still, life is sunnier when you aren't sleeping solo, and as independent as you are, you long for a companion you can count on. Besides, sex—be it soft and sensuous or blissfully bizarre—is better with someone you love. If you find all of these talents wrapped up in one package, you stop saying you won't ever get married and start shopping for shiny satin sheets. As much in control as you like to be, once the romance ritual begins with the first red-rose delivery, you gladly relinquish the reins and let the relationship roll.

Money and Career

An excellent memory and the ability to make small talk sprinkled with easy jokes and pertinent points are the secrets of your success. You like notoriety when it's due, but are sharp enough not to fall victim to false flattery. Working with a staff that's as versatile and cooperative as you are is the most important criterion when deciding to stay or push on. You could be with one company for your whole career, as long as you get to do a variety of jobs, including being a boss.

Long ago you decided that leisure time was more important than lining dresser drawers with money, but you never scoff at a genuine opportunity to make it. There's always a plane ticket to buy, and retiring early sounds mighty good to you. Then you can do what you really want—maybe open an antique store or learn how to cut gems and make jewelry.

The ♊1 Potential

You provide ideas with workable outlines to make them real. There's nothing you won't consider when options must be found. Though your views are noncomformist and somewhat cosmopolitan, they are given full consideration because others respect you. From behind a conventional facade, you provide hope and alternatives that show a deep understanding of the human condition.

With a touch of imagination, quick wit, and determination, you can take your place among a fine array of artists, musicians, and politicians if you want. But first learn how to weave a group into a team, share your unique sense of humor, and don't be so courteous and civilized that you're thought to be superficial. Be real and get real rewards.

FAMOUS GEMINI ONES

Wyonna Judd	5/30/1964	Noah Wyle	6/4/1971
Lisa Hartman	6/1/1956	James Arness	5/26/1923
Yasmine Bleeth	6/16/1968	Jonathan Pryce	6/1/1947

♊ • 2
Gemini Two
"The Ambidextrous Diplomat"

♊ +	2 +	♊ -	2 -
Articulate	Patient	Scattered	Moody
Gregarious	Thorough	Gossipy	Sensitive
Adaptable	Supportive	Nervous	Argumentative
Curious	Diplomatic		

The reason you never thought you were a typical Gemini is that you're a Two, too! With all the social graces of a lively, charming Gemini, you've got the Two's natural caution and reserve. Gregarious but selective, you're never so witty that you forget to be diplomatic. Your dual nature is twofold, twins doubled, which makes more than two sides of you. Getting to know you is a real challenge. A clever chameleon, you mold the outer you to fit the situation and protect the real you from casual scrutiny. There are secrets you intend to keep.

You believe change is good, and like to regularly zoom off in new directions, following one of your uncanny hunches. Your meticulous nature doesn't let you go too far, though, before you build a factual foundation to support the quest.

The truth is important, but not at someone else's expense— you can let it hide behind superficial conversation. In fact, you don't mind superficiality as much as being rude or vulgar. Oh, you're no namby-pamby and have got a four-letter vocabulary to fire off at the appropriate times, but prefer to avoid uncivilized behavior in public. Should anyone mistake your noblesse oblige for "anything goes," or try to walk all over you, you simply color them Out of the Picture.

A natural collector, you have a variety of interesting items in your home—from bonsai plants to the latest computer gadget. You also have a large selection of artwork, books, and music. As for people, you collect useful phone numbers but not people per se. You have a select circle of friends who share your interests and *never* let you down.

Love, Sex, and Marriage

The perfect partner knows which kinky buttons to push to keep the relationship lively. No amateur button pusher yourself, you like to get as good as you give! In addition to sharing the same sexual appetites and keeping up with that considerable intellect of yours, your heaven-made match is someone you don't have to change. You want a lover to live *with* and be alone with *together*. When another bright, curious, chatty creature crosses your path, you leap into marriage, stunning friends and family with the speed of the "I dos."

Marriage is happy as long as mutual appreciation and support prevail. When Relationship Road gets bumpy, you retreat to wait for the tempest to blow over. Withdraw too far and the repercussions are felt in the bedroom and could go all the way to divorce court, which you don't want since you consider it a miracle that you found anyone who loved you enough to marry you in the first place. For all your double duality, you believe in fidelity and never stray further from a mate than a casual conversation, and even that is kept in neutral waters.

Money and Career

If you're promoted to the position of manager, it doesn't take long, maybe just one whining employee, before you're ready to turn in those extra stripes. Confrontations, especially this kind, just aren't your thing. You want a responsible job, but only want to be in charge of yourself. Manage a project or be a consultant or technical guru to be happy. You also do well as a computer whiz, in medicine, teacher, diplomat, arbitrator, or writer.

Regarding money, you have a classic split personality: You want to have gobs of cash but abhor the idea of working long hours at a stressful job to get it. When you have it, you spend it, and when you don't, you know how to squeeze the juice out of every penny. Since you refuse to let work rule your life, eventually you learn to balance income and outgo. Luckily, you don't need that much money to be happy (just enough to buy those toys). Educated and resourceful, most Gemini Twos live better than they think they do but not as well as they would like to.

The ♊2 Potential

You take your obligations seriously, and when the going gets tough, you set your chin against the wind with determination and keep moving forward any way you can. After you've given 200 percent effort, if something isn't working out, you can dump it and walk away without a backward glance.

Relationships, particularly intimate ones, offer the greatest rewards and demands. You have no problem connecting with people, but taking it past sociably polite is beyond your comfort zone. When you trust your instincts and open yourself to honest interaction, you find out how many wonderful people there are out there. Being a master of discretion and having the ability to learn almost anything are the keys to your self-respect and success. Never underestimate yourself—you have what it takes!

FAMOUS GEMINI TWOS

Sally Ride	5/26/1951	Frank Lloyd Wright	6/8/1869
Sally Kellerman	6/02/1938	Joe Montana	6/11/1956
Leslie Uggams	5/25/1943	Bob Hope	5/29/1903

♊ • 3
Gemini Three
"The Versatile Romantic"

♊ +	3 +	♊ -	3 -
Vivacious	Artistic	Restless	Extravagant
Literate	Romantic	Indecisive	Easily
Generous	Sociable	Self-deceptive	Distracted
Versatile	Imaginative		Gossips

The word on the street is that you're a hopeless romantic, and Mirror, Mirror says you're an eternal optimist. You *do* wish the heavens would plop Mr./Ms. Soul Mate in your path before you're too old to care (can't imagine when that might be). Or that Universal Studios would call with praise for your screenplay. Disapointments? Yeah, you've had a few—well, a dump truck full. When you manage not to drown in personal-pity parties, you bounce back faster than the average romantic because underneath that stylish exterior is a survivor. Then the phone rings: the corner coffee store Barista (Italian) invites you out for dinner again or a friend calls with work at a fashion show and the clouds clear.

You're not satisfied having one iron in the fire at a time. Your hearth looks like a beach bonfire on the Fourth of July, it's so packed. Quantity in motion means that *something* will come to fruition. It's your job to stick the irons in, stir up the fire occasionally, and stand ready to grab the white-hot one and run with it. That doesn't stop you from envisioning Brad Pitt arriving on the doorstep, but it does give you concrete reasons to celebrate victories, large and small, when they come.

People love to join you for lunch or visit your home. Not only are you a gracious host, but you always have a provocative guest list. A few from the A list, the coffee-shop group, several of the crew at work, plus new friends and some you've known forever and ever. Matchmaker? No, you don't consider yourself a matchmaker for business *or* pleasure, but if something *should* happen between these lovely and charming people whom you judge to have sooo much in common, then, well, wouldn't that be lovely?

Through the confusion of constant activity, you have an eerie talent for "knowing" what's going to happen before it does. Of course, it's more reliable when it's about someone else rather than yourself. Those special visionary tidbits are shared with only a precious few friends.

Love, Sex, and Marriage

A nice home, accomplished spouse, bright kids, and a real estate career on the side are all you ask. You want it all, but would settle for two out of four at a time. Because you recognize potential when you see it, you give that insistent barista a second look, and don't hesitate to buy a fixer-upper for your first home. The children? You take parenting seriously and intend to enjoy your children as adults as well as bambinos.

Nothing captures your heart faster than an enlightened brain and enthusiastic sex. Gifts don't hurt either, and you aren't too fussy. "Take me to Tahiti," you offer, "and let's see what kind of magic music we make together." Hey, did you say that out loud? I didn't think so, but try it next time and maybe you can pick out another black-pearl pendant on the island for your collection.

Money and Career

Money is here today, gone tomorrow, here this morning, gone on Tuesday. On the days it's gone, you drive yourself crazy worrying about how to make ends meet, and then the bucks are back. Your money cycles can be a hairy roller-coaster ride, but you do manage to hold the family heirlooms intact, faithfully drop ar shekel or two in the rainy-day pot when the coins are pouring in, and never let the kids feel too deprived.

You like to be busy, you like to work and enjoy chatty conversations with co-workers. Your services don't go to the highest bidder, though, they go to the most interesting job offer in front of you at the time. Boredom is death to you and you honestly would rather return recyclables for porridge than bear the tedium of sour-faced associates and monotonous tasks. Always looking for a creative outlet, a Gemini Three often turns a hobby into a business.

The ♊3 Potential

Merry old soul that you are, you appreciate any good fortune and try to spread the wealth around. Generosity begets abundance, and you take every opportunity to prove this philosophy, be it with time, guidance, conversation, or presents. We are all in this together, like it or not; you know it, and know the world would be a better place if we all acted as if we knew it, too.

You have an eye for beauty and are a resilient spirit. Youthful at any age, try to finish what you start and not get side-tracked so long that treasured relationships unravel. Self-discipline turns every talent into an amazing asset. The world needs you to not take itself so seriously, but first you have to learn to do that for yourself.

FAMOUS GEMINI THREES

Brooke Shields	5/31/1965	John Wayne	5/26/1907
Annette Bening	5/29/1958	Billy Dee Williams	6/4/1937
Joan Rivers	6/8/1933	Liam Neeson	6/7/1952

♊ • 4
Gemini Four
"The Inquisitive Realist"

♊ +	4 +	♊ -	4 -
Clever	Persistent	Restless	Lazy
Curious	Responsible	Verbose	Contrary
Gregarious	Practical	Inconsistent	Undemonstrative
Explorer	Capable		

You're never short on words or moxie—even close chums don't know what to expect from you next! They think you lead a stable and sorta traditional life until they find out about the latest trek to Machu Picchu. You do like a Monday-through Friday routine. The day starts with a quick nod and smile to the building security officer at 7:00 A.M. every day as you dash to the cafeteria for breakfast and conversation or to finish reading a newspaper article. Even when you've got plans for the scrambled-eggs-and-toast hour, you put everything aside when a needy soul plops down and apologetically says, "Can I talk to you?" You know you're the reason the person came early.

No one expects you to tell him *what* to do. You've made it quite plain that you believe everyone is in charge of their own lives. They come to you because you have an open mind and an unprejudiced view of possibilities that you can help them see. Besides, you root for the underdog (having played the part yourself), and you actually listen to others and understand the worries that keep them up all night.

The clock is always ticking. When it's time to go, you detach from the conversation and rush headlong up the corridor to be at your desk before starting time. You hate to arrive after anyone, even the boss. On the job you juggle phone calls and memos and still accomplish more in one hour than most co-workers do in two. Not that you can't be sidetracked by a so-true-too-funny Dilbert cartoon, but when there's a schedule to be kept and a deadline looming large, you pause for only a nanosecond to chuckle. Who's in charge of your life anyway? You, and only you, and you intend to keep up.

When you're fired up for a quest, ideal, or objective, nothing stands in your way, except maybe a cold bucket of common sense. And then not always. You take the risk factor seriously, but like famous Gemini Four Harriet Beecher Stowe, abolitionist and antislavery author, if the cause is just, or compelling, you consider the risks, then do it anyway.

Love, Sex, and Marriage

When it comes to a real relationship, you've got strict standards and definite ideas. The list you handed Cupid plainly stated that you must share an enthusiasm for the same lifestyle, be it living in Trump Towers or in a cozy cottage at the beach. An amiable travel companion is a must. And while you're not a physical fitness freak, you stay healthy enough to be an active handful through your nineties, and expect your mate to do the same.

Sex is no game to you, no bargaining chit either, but when the moon is right and the right mental bond has been forged, you hold nothing back! All physical requirements met, the final request is for a practical dreamer who can provide the counterweight you need to keep from drifting in over your head or in the wrong direction without ever trying to take over the helm.

Money and Career

Creature comforts are almost as important as security, and you strive to keep your bank account even with the "I want, I want, I want" account. Since Geminis don't need much money to be happy (except to have what they want), and Fours want to accumulate cash, property, and good credit, you send your accountant conflicting signals every time you meet.

Always anxious to flex your intellectual muscles, you never doubt you can do any job that's handed to you. Higher-ups don't doubt it either, which is why you're often tapped to move up the ladder. But you usually have other plans to start your own company or clear the calendar to be with friends in Sante Fe. Besides, you always have more than one endeavor to bring in money at the same time. But why not? You love to work as much as play.

The ♊4 Potential

Even the things you do to relax keep you busy. There's not too much of a line between work and play because you do what you love to do every step of the way. You inspire friends to be more flexible, try new things, and not be afraid of stretching. The fact that they see you fall flat on your face now and then makes your advice credible; they believe you when you say something is possible but not easy to do.

You size up people quickly and seldom are proven wrong even after you get to know them. Friends are from diverse backgrounds, and they all find you to be an open-minded, reliable rock to bounce off decisions and worries. Do you have it all figured out? Of course you do—be the captain of your soul and stay on course. On the other hand, if it doesn't feel good you know enough to not do it, don't you?

FAMOUS GEMINI FOURS

Adrian Paul	*5/29/1959*	*Priscilla Presley*	*5/24/1946*
Paul McCartney	*6/18/1942*	*Harriet Beecher Stowe*	*6/14/1811*
Donald Trump	*6/14/1946*	*Helen Hunt*	*6/15/1963*

♊ • 5
Gemini Five
"The Clever Communicator"

♊ +	5 +	♊ -	5 -
Articulate	*Resourceful*	*Superficial*	*Restless*
Intellectual	*Versatile*	*Manipulative*	*Impulsive*
Generous	*Energetic*	*Impractical*	*Fickle*
Entertaining	*Inquisitve*		

Details are important, and if someone says you're too fussy, you know you're right on track. Oh, you can laugh at yourself surrounded by a dozen pairs of shoes as you try to match them to your earrings, but that doesn't stop you from finishing the task. If you lose sight of the forest because of the trees, you quickly shift the view to see all angles and land the best deal. You never underestimate the importance of connections. Skilled networker and smooth talker that you are, you can make friends with anyone, anywhere, and score interesting info in the process. And hey, you are interested in absolutely everything, aren't you?

Considerably restless since childhood, you're ready to go anywhere almost anytime. Unless there's a better reason to stick around; to, say, star in a Broadway show—bows, applause, and money to tuck in the bank. Then you hop on a plane to the white-sand beaches of Florida for a well-deserved vacation. And while you're down there, you might as well look up that fellow you met in Houston who owns a chain of health food stores. Keeping connections current is another detail that matters.

Intrigued by the mysterious and unusual, you love a good yarn and can spin a good one yourself. From the careless pieces of conversation you overhear at the water cooler that don't fit together to a bona fide criminal investigation on the evening news, you want to be in the know. As you roam from place to place, the curious snatches of this and that fuel the storyteller seed in you. You could (and may) write a book!

Your mix of genteel manners and ethusiasm opens doors. The

ability to deliver what you promise gets you your own passkey. Getting where you want to be is seldom a problem for a resourceful rambler like you. The only glitch is getting you to stay put for the long haul. You tend to exit before the big payoff is plopped down, especially if it's a long time in coming.

Love, Sex, and Marriage

Too refined to race after just any pretty little thing that turns your head, you want a proper introduction. No, you're not the stuffy sort, but you do want a biographical sketch of your intended before the first chatty phone call. Cautious about commitment, you want an intellectual and sexual fit. But should you find the perfect person to parent your children, that can be enough to make you pop the question.

If you don't marry young, you may have trouble fitting it into your life through the thirties and forties. Eventually you realize you were meant to have a soul mate at your side, and search for one with the same vivacious energy that has made other relationships bloom. You think you're a noncomformist when it comes to the saying the vows routine, but find out that you, too, adore the whole scene—house, kids, puppy, et al.

Money and Career

You'll be relieved to hear that you won't ever settle down to one tedious job to do day after day after day. Expect to have a minimum of three major career changes, with lots of minor ones along the way. With your varied interests, you succeed in any business that deals with the public—tourism, entertainment, and leisure activities in particular. Marketing, sales, journalism, publishing, acting, teaching, and psychology are all intriguing areas to you, too.

Money is the material to build the life you want. It gives you the freedom to stay out of the office and provides the bucks to buy planet tickets and call friends in Norway. You aren't particularly astute with your money, but more than able to make what you want and do what you want to do. Being disciplined enough to do it is the highest hurdle you have to jump.

The ♊5 Potential

You have an uncanny talent for knowing what the public wants before they do. You might not be the one to give it to them, but are generous with ideas and a master at putting people together who can benefit more from knowing each other than they do from knowing you. When you find two such people on opposite ends of the earth, you feel it's your destiny to bring them together; being a conscious link gives you great satisfaction, especially when they click.

Find an anchor early in life. It might be a family of your own, a fascinating business to run, or the purchase of an island hideaway. That anchor, whatever or whoever it is, serves a vital purpose. It makes you stop and count to ten before making an irreversible decision, or from being too hasty to cut and run on a whim. Practice the same wise counsel that you dish out and you will have the life you dream of having.

FAMOUS GEMINI FIVES

Sir Arthur Conan Doyle	5/22/1859	Courteney Cox	6/15/1964
Michael J. Fox	6/9/1961	Jessica Tandy	6/7/1909
Lionel Richie	6/20/1950	Isabella Rossellini	6/18/1952

♊ • 6
Gemini Six
"The Free-Spirited Humanitarian"

♊ +	6 +	♊ -	6 -
Articulate	Conventional	Manipulative	Self-sacrificing
Persuasive	Responsible	Arbitrary	Moody
Versatile	Loyal	Scattered	Possessive
Gregarious	Idealistic		

You don't take anything for granted. You've been behind the scenes enough to know what goes on there. Besides, you're comfortable in front of or behind any curtain and flexible enough to be effective in either position. So what if you favor the spotlight; when you're in it, it loves you back.

When plans depend on advice from experts, you don't hesitate to approach the brilliant and the best for assistance. In addition to acquiring information, you enhance your own teaching and learning skills in the process. Though you are curious about almost everything under the sun, people, successful or striving, top the list. It's easy to imagine yourself in someone else's shoes, and to suggest ways to improve their lot in life. You look out for others. You aren't always as careful about your own spot in the universal hierarchy though and have been known to make major sacrifices for the sake of love and family. Making the decision may have required countless hours of internal debate, but once the choice is made, you accept it and the responsibility that goes with it.

Teaching is as great a joy to you as learning, and you do it naturally from dawn to dusk, whether standing in front of a class of hyperactive youth or not. Family is high priority to you and provides a constant flow of support and self-knowledge. Becuse you require solitude as much as companionship, the way you teach comes by example, general conversation, and reaching out to others through artistic mediums—music, storytelling, acting, lectures, books. You are a profound influence and a prolific producer once you discover how to use your talents to uplift, enlighten, and entertain.

Consider the accomplishmetns of three famous Gemini Sixes who have gone before you and then imagine the possibilities. Edward, Duke of Windsor, sacrificed the Crown of England for the woman he loved; Patrick Henry with his inspiring oratory pulled revolutionarires together to help give birth to America; and Ian Fleming, the author who breathed life into the dashing James Bond and sent him on dozens of missions to save mankind.

Love, Sex, and Marriage

Playing the field is a discreet operation for you. At least it's your intention not to end up on the front page of the newspaper in an embarrasing situation. An exotic enchanter may catch your eye, but it's simple beauty, inside and out, that makes you think about making a commitment. The deal clincher is if this beauty knows how to laugh, is smart and capable, and kindhearted, too.

As vocal as you may be about staying footloose, you know marriage is a better situation for you than living the single life. A chat and a cuddle brighten the end of any weary day, and you look forward to the golden minutes you can spend with those you love. Children are a part of your dream home, but you may be too concerned about being a good parent to actually have them. This would be a shame because the world needs more parents just like you—after the storybook wedding, of course.

Money and Career

As an educator, probably college level, the life lessons you teach will be remembered long after class ends. Of course, that will be true for everyone around you no matter what you do for work. A professional spot that allows you the freedom to make your own schedule is best for you. Writer, physician, chef, or decorator, you like work that lets you interact with people on your own terms.

With money at your fingertips, you can be a philanthropist and benefactor, and that suits you. Without it readily available, you raise what you need and encourage everyone to be creative in making the needed improvements. Running your own show, you develop a loyal group of employees who return the favor of your faith in them by doing well enough to give you the flexibility and freedom you need to thrive.

The Ⅱ 6 Potential

Count to a hundred and listen to the advice others give you. Strive to sacrifice just enough to live up to your word, extend a helping hand, and still be able to tilt the deck back to a level position. Seek balance and moderation to improve the quality of your life and better maintain resources, including the skill to be a crackerjack mentor.

Learn to receive as well as give. Folks feel good about helping those who have helped them which you do so readily. Remember, you aren't the only one with this particular lesson. You do a fine job of opening minds and showing others how to succeed. When they turn left instead of right as you told them, love them anyway. Don't take it so personally when they try to fly on their own, and crash and burn instead. Be proud that they have the confidence to try because you showed them how, and believed in them when maybe no one else did.

FAMOUS GEMINI SIXS

Beverly Sills	*5/25/1929*	*Lou Gossett Jr.*	*5/27/1936*
Gladys Knight	*5/28/1944*	*Tom Berenger*	*5/31/1950*
Melissa Etheridge	*5/29/1961*	*Bjorn Borg*	*6/6/1956*

♊ • 7
Gemini Seven
"The Gregarious Scholar"

♊ +	7 +	♊ -	7 -
Curious	*Analytical*	*Inconsistent*	*Aloof*
Witty	*Perfectionist*	*Impatient*	*Secretive*
Versatile	*Articulate*	*Nervous*	*Cautious*
Detail-oriented	*Private*		

At age eight you slipped out of the house during the full moon to see if there really were any werewolves in the woods behind the barn. Next morning Mom was relieved and you were disappointed when she found you fast asleep under the old oak tree. Her worried scolding fell on deaf ears; both of you knew it wouldn't be the last time you went looking for proof of the strange and unusual. Classmates are fascinated with your exploits; that is, when you aren't too shy to share them.

Your world before adulthood is filled with wizard tales, Technicolor dreams, and a magic library card. By the time they hand you your diploma, you have about, oh, a hundred or so things you want to find, prove, and do. You've got the makings of a professional student, shrewd politician, movie mogul, or breakthrough scientist. Or the glamorous world of film and fame could snag you. The wide range of your interests and abilities creates an ever-expanding array of choices.

Knowledge is power, and you can keep a secret, almost for forever, to be divulged only after its power is gone. Strangers and friends trust you. Many think they know you better than they do, and that's okay, because you would rather have it that way. Courtesy prevents you from being publicly nosy, but you do like to "know," so develop sources to keep up-to-date with the juicy jewels making the rounds. You have a fascination with the unconventional and a flare for piecing together bits of unrelated info.

Your insatiable thirst for knowledge puts you in quirky places and circumstances that keep your batteries charged up. Once in a while the situation turns sticky, but with your mesmerizing patter, you emerge from the fracas a bit bruised, but breathing. The experience has to be worth the risk you took, at least in your eyes, and you do think things through before starting out. Who knew the paparazzi would be stalking a celebrity photo at the next table where you were staging a reunion with an old lover? Even you don't know everything.

Love, Sex, and Marriage

Leave it to you to kick off a romance with a clandestine candlelight picnic—a carefully planned impromptu feast with a sumptuous selection of gourmet food and a heady variety of wine. Alone at last, you prepare to dazzle your intended. Fanning the sparks to flame while prolonging the anticipation is one of your best skills. More than building a relationship, you know how to make delicious memories.

Friendship has to exist before marriage can be considered. And it isn't easy to find a person with the same sense of humor who understands the perfectionist in you. In the outside world, you want a mate with the grace of royalty and a movie star's glamour. In private, you delight in a quick switch to scientific collaborator or tantalizing tempter as the mood moves you.

Money and Career

Your voice sounds like money. No wonder—with your education and stellar network of chums, doors open to you at the hint of a knock. Though you understand power and are frequently pushed into an authoritative role, you're just as happy to earn a living doing lab reports or medical research. There are times when you don't want to be the one everyone else thinks can solve their problems, and other times you know you're the one who can.

If you donate to charitable causes, it's a well-kept secret. You do what you do quietly, and it's a respectable amount if you think it's needed. To make money, you take advantage of those connections, but once you think you have enough for a while, you loosen the harness to get back to painting watercolors. Selectively generous, but never careless with your money, you invest wisely with an eye to tomorrow, when you hope to be writing a Broadway musical.

The ♊7 Potential

Your perception penetrates the thickest smoke screen to cut right to the heart of a matter. Extensive observation has made you an expert about the actions and reactions of your fellow travelers on the planet. Good or bad, little surprises you, which is why you believe so firmly in teaching others the concept of logic and how to use it.

Leave room in your schedule to be spontaneous sometimes—it will do you good to spend a Tuesday afternoon at the Museum of Natural History gawking at dinosaurs with nephew Timmie. And don't ignore doubts and nagging nitpicky problems lest they turn into huge scandals or investments gone bad. Let other folks gamble; you stick with researched risks. And always use your imagination and intellect for the power of good.

FAMOUS GEMINI SEVENS

Marilyn Monroe	*6/1/1926*	*President John F. Kennedy*	*5/29/1917*
Dixie Carter	*5/25/1939*	*Ilia Kulik*	*5/23/1977*
Peggy Lee	*5/26/1920*	*Barry Manilow*	*6/17/1946*

♊ • 8
Gemini Eight
"The Entertaining Executive"

♊ +	8 +	♊ -	8 -
Versatile	*Professional*	*Impractical*	*Impersonal*
Curious	*Ambitious*	*Gossips*	*Materialistic*
Generous	*Authoritative*	*Indecisive*	*Workaholic*
Articulate	*Global View*		

In or out of big business, you approach everything with professional panache. Actor, judge, corporate tycoon, rancher, parent, lover—once you accept the label, you turn full attention to living up to 100 percent. That's after many hours of vacillating back and forth between the options before you finally shout, "Okay, I can *do* this!" Then the enthusiasm surfaces and no Web site is left unaccessed or resource untapped in the search to collect enough data to ensure a blue-ribbon performance.

So on Monday you agree to coordinate a benefit drive for a homeless shelter, then on Tuesday you score the only two tickets in the city to a Mariners baseball game for your son's birthday, plus pick up the new flat monitor for your PC. A justifiable expense since you work at home almost as much as you do inside those blue cubicle walls on the third floor downtown. Wednesday, who knows? An assignment in Chicago? A late night dinner date?

To be truthful, only, say, three hundred days a year are like this, but you love the variety and showing off your versatility. The other sixty-five days you relax as only you can—rafting the Colorado River or taking Mom to Paris. You don't want to miss anything, and while you fully intend to celebrate your ninetieth birthday you know you might not, and everyone knows that hearses don't have luggage racks.

Though you grew up quickly, your youthful sense of humor keeps you lively. VIPs and grocery clerks brighten up when you zap out a zinger as you walk by. Add a sensuous smile to the most innocent of phrases and you leave them hoping you come back soon. You daydream about wiggling out of the thick of things to set up housekeeping in a wilderness cabin. Then reality sets in: the computer, the VCR, the *telephone!* You're too technically dependent to leave it all behind for more than a retreat—a blessing for the rest of us; your cheerful smile would be missed.

Love, Sex, and Marriage

Marriage is the biggest commitment of all, and though you giggle and tease through the courtship stage, the enormity of the walk down the aisle is always at the back of your mind. The other bump that could trip you up in getting to the church is the Workaholic You that vies for equal time with the Amorous You, however sizzling the love spell might be. When pillow talk turns to deals and deadlines though, the right partner can take it in stride.

You would never marry for convention or convenience; in the love department you are sentimental and faithful. Sharing your life with someone is a scary concept, and unless you find the open-minded, forward-thinking sort with an old-fashioned view of vows and such, you may never take the plunge. That's only because you believe in forever, and only because you want to say "I do" only once.

Money and Career

Delegating everything you can fulfills two purposes: you shine as a capable executive and in the process help those under your command stretch and grow. An intuitive judge of character, you know just how much to push the group you proudly call your staff, which is never so much as to discourage them from ever reaching the finish line. You learn as much from those who call you boss as you do from the CEO.

Thinking about money gives you a headache. You know when an idea is hot and admire those who can turn nickels into gold bars. Not enough to sacrifice Lauren's ballet recital, or a trip to England, but enough to at least turn five cents to a hundred to score the bonuses you do and not lose any sleep wondering how you could have turned it into more. Appreciation is a must, and you will take a lower salary for the chance to use your creative intellect and collect kudos for doing so.

The ♊8 Potential

You might not always be able to make every lemon life hands you into lemonade, but it's to your credit that you try not only to turn it into lemonade but take it one step further and turn the lemonade into profit. And we're not talking only about hard cash here, but a benefit like a cloud's silver lining. If there is one, you can find it and will use it.

Endeavor to move one mountain at a time and not over-schedule the day. Trust others to honestly mean it when they say, "I love you." And refrain from spouting off a glib retort that can't be retrieved. People do believe what you say. You have enough personal power to go where you want and mix with an assortment of characters. The message you bring to the party is "You're okay and I'm okay, so let's dance!"

FAMOUS GEMINI EIGHTS

Stevie Nicks	5/23/1933	Sir Laurence Olivier	5/22/1907
Lea Thompson	5/31/1961	Joe Namath	5/31/1943
Naomi Campbell	5/22/1970	Igor Stravinsky	6/19/1882

♊ • 9
Gemini Nine
"The Effusive Explorer"

♊ +	9 +	♊ -	9 -
Gregarious	*Creative*	*Restless*	*Demanding*
Open-minded	*Compassionate*	*Superficial*	*Careless*
Versatile	*Impartial*	*Indecisive*	*Self-absorbed*
Curious	*Entertaining*		

"And so," you tell the reservationist at the friendly skies place, "That's *N* as in knickers and *E* as in Aesop." Yuk, yuk. No, you don't *try* to be a smart-ass, but you do like to stand out in the crowd, to be remembered with a smile. Gemini Nines are performers, right? You're *on* almost everywhere you go, which is anywhere you please, whether up behind theater footlights or not.

It isn't so much that you crave attention (well, maybe a little), but you believe anything worth doing is worth doing well, and deserves to be noticed. Oh yeah, and then there's the do-whatever-feels-good part. Sure, it's a dangerous set of rules to live by. Sure, sometimes you get your wrist slapped, but you're adroit at recovery and clever at staging a comeback. Or maybe this time you just move on. It depends on how many promises you've made to people you respect to stick around.

You and the effervescent character Auntie Mame have much in common. Life is a banquet—so much to sample, so much to enjoy, so much to learn, and an enormous golden heart with compassion to spare. From artsy friends to Buddhist priests, you have a penetrating question for everyone you meet. But should they need a place to sleep or spiritual solace, you quickly switch roles and become the teacher instead of the fun-loving student.

A staunch ally in the face of injustice, you stand by strangers when they need to be guided over rough spots. You could do nothing less for friends and family. When confronted, you don't mince words, and because you continually add to your collection of facts, opponents find you better armed than they expected. You can't make everything right for everyone in the world, but many folks bless you for giving it your best shot.

Love, Sex, and Marriage

One thing you aren't is the love-'em-and-leave-'em type. Oh, you might talk that way when chatting with a cute young thing at the corner club, but you wouldn't have even struck up a conversation if you didn't think more than a meaningful two hours together was possible. You're a sucker for big blue eyes that promise depth and complexity, and you don't stop looking for the pair that fulfills that potential.

You are a very attractive person. With the vibes you send out, you don't have to be drop-dead gorgeous to get phone numbers shoved at you constantly. Once the novelty wears off, you sit yourself down for a little talk. Yup, sex is important, yup, brains count, yup, must be easy on the eyes, but most important is unconditional love, innate understanding of the human condition, and to always be willing to set an extra place at the table for the parade of people you bring home.

Money and Career

Minister, counselor, surgeon, novelist, or performer, you don't usually find an office setting to be a happy environment for you. And you shy away from being a manager. You've got your hands full getting your work done and keeping your life together. You don't want to be contractorily responsible for anyone else. But you do take responsibility for any and everyone as the spirit moves you. You do best as a professional on your own, or in charge of a function, rather than in charge of a group of people.

There are wide swings in your bank account. You make enough to get by, and frequently can earn bonuses or freelance cash on the side. Money doesn't have much meaning for you; it's a tool to finance adventures, buy books and gadgets, feed the family, and help the needy. Your money goals are to have enough to cover these expenses, but your ability to make it is so much greater than that.

The ♊9 Potential

A quick hug, a casual comment that touches the heart, and a word of hope are the gifts you readily give. And you give them gladly because you know that this life isn't a free ride. Disappointments can be devastating, but in the process of working through your own pain, you emerge stronger and more capable for the next time.

Cherish your privacy and don't expect your soul mate or children to share you every day with everyone. Set aside time to be alone for meditation as well as time for family. You tend to lose yourself in the buzz of activities and assignments and let your aura lose its healthy glow by taking on too much. Slow down, kick back, and listen to music. As it soothes your jangled nerves, let's hope the next critter to pop up in need of affection is MacGregor, the kid's faithful Scottie dog.

FAMOUS GEMINI NINES

Tara Lipinski	6/10/1982	Richard Hatch	5/21/1945
Rosalind Russell	6/4/1907	Cole Porter	6/9/1893
Pam Grier	5/26/1949	Morgan Freeman	6/1/1937

CANCER

•

♋ • 1
Cancer One
"The Diffident Dynamo"

♋ +	1 +	♋ -	1-
Persistent	Original	Moody	Willful
Understanding	Individualistic	Sullen	Know-it-all
Plucky	Gutsy	Passive-	Blustering
Intrepid	Self-reliant	aggressive	

A Cancer One could never be the king crab in someone else's salad! One way or another you'll claw your way to the top, though you'd never use your pincers, except in self-defense. Chances are you'll be counted among the million-aire ranks, but may not achieve success until later in life. You must wrestle with your personal demons and need the stabilizing influence of a home or family. Then you'll gladly work all night or travel half the year on business, because your goal is never to make money for its own sake, but rather to feather the nest (and it's a tragic scene worthy of the Greeks when the birdies fly the coot, uh, coop).

Yours is a tough shell for anyone to crack. That driving logical One influence can't entirely tame those cardinal Cancer moods. You can be disarmingly open and sensitive one moment, withdrawn and stormy the next. Your ego clashes with your fundamental sweetness and need for approbation, just as you yourself oscillate between justifiable pride in your accomplishments and deep-rooted insecurity. Even those closest to you find it difficult to reconcile these abrupt mood swings. Of course, they're perfectly understandable from your perspective; you can't help but pick up vibes and respond instinctively. The surest way to inflame you is to call you irrational; pushing that particular hot button could set off nuclear detonation!

Cancer Ones of both sexes often suffer from outmoded societal concepts of appropriate behavior. The men need an outlet for their caring and sensitivity. The women require an outlet for their assertiveness. Male or female, you can weep copiously over a tear-jerking movie or a puppy caught in the tree yet coolly order cutbacks in the company's best interests, projecting a rare combination of empathy and efficiency.

Love, Sex, and Marriage

The ultimate provider, you take enormous pride in caring for your loved ones and anticipating their needs. You have a tendency to feel you know what's best for them; very often you're right, but they may not always see it that way. You're a most satisfying "dater." The minute you get home you'll note in your calendar the day you promised to call, while the roses will arrive punctually each week. Your Cancerian side prefers tried-and-true methods of courtship but the unconventional One influence encourages you to make a fool of yourself with a spontaneous serenade of his or her fifteenth-floor terrace if it helps you land your catch.

You'd be the first to admit you're not always easy to live with, though. Sensitive to real or imagined criticism, you sometimes feel misunderstood, primarily because you don't make your feelings known and expect others to intuit them magically. This can lead to unnecessary temper tantrums; once the squall blows over, you become your sunny self, and wonder why on earth everyone else is suddenly so gloomy! The ardent glow in your eyes always says, "I'm sorry" and "I love you."

Money and Career

Your exceptional understanding is a natural for the arts, especially writing and acting, which allows you to express the powerful emotions you often keep under wraps. You'd function just as effectively behind the scenes, as a director, producer, curator, or conductor, where you'd be in control. You have an unerring instinct for both mass appeal and an opponent's jugular, and delight in bold, unexpected moves like a grand master in chess. This suits you for the world of suits, where you can forecast others' moves and act accordingly.

You know the value of a buck and don't mind paying for quality; in fact, part of you is tempted to leave the price tag on just in case your impeccable taste isn't readily apparent. You know what you want in love, business, and shopping. You have a knack for picking the perfect gift, for your boss, best friend, mate, or kid; naturally they find it almost impossible to buy anything for you. But you genuinely prefer giving to receiving, and anyway can winklingly hint about those golf-club covers you covet.

The ♋1 Potential

Once you've learned to control your Cancerian moods as well as you do your business negotiations, the sky's the limit. Although you could easily perform every task you set for yourself, delegate responsibility and recognize that others need both their space and a chance in the sun. You can make the most caring leader. Be willing to express your feelings more often. Believe it or not, people have much to learn from your rainbow of emotions; you have the admirable ability to integrate your masculine and feminine sides, just as our shrinks have been advising us to do since Freud!

FAMOUS CANCER ONES

Tom Hanks	*7/9/1956*	*Tom Cruise*	*7/3/1962*
Ernest Hemingway	*7/21/1899*	*Josephine Bonaparte*	*6/23/1763*
Della Reese	*7/6/1932*	*Kristi Yamaguchi*	*7/12/1971*

✆ • 2
Cancer Two
"The Conscientious Counselor"

✆ +	2 +	✆ -	2 -
Sustaining	*Supportive*	*Brooding*	*Dependent*
Emotional	*Considerate*	*Insecure*	*Self-conscious*
Intuitive	*Cooperative*	*Over-*	*Timid*
Gentle	*Tactful*	*impressionable*	

Wonderfully sensitive and insightful, a Cancer Two can read others like a book, and read between the lines, too! With your genuine empathy, your heart goes out even to the most heartless criminal. Your faith in humankind is such that, despite any evidence to the contrary, you could make even Jim Jones come off like Joan of Arc when you've concluded your spirited defense. You certainly know your own limits, your feelings having been forged in hot steel. You firmly believe that everything, no matter how painful, is a learning experience, though you sometimes wonder if we ever receive our diplomas! You could easily join the John Gray/Marianne Williamson lecture circuit to discuss the maturation process and coming to terms with the emotional legacy of all our relationships.

It's ironic for a home-loving Cancer and ultra-shy Two, but it's imperative that you assert your independence and invividuality at an early age. You may have had an idyllic upbringing, yet you never forget a slight; the harsh word, carelessly said in a moment of anger, is emblazoned on your memory. You sometimes feel as though your life were one long cinematic flashback; present events often evoke incidents from the past. Very often we repeat patterns learned from our parents. Though you're occasionally timid, your confidence will soar when you break free of that early conditioning. You're such a psychic sponge and emotional chameleon, intuiting what others need, that your hardest lesson is divorcing yourself form situations and putting yourself first.

You have an unquenchable thirst for knowledge, not necessarily from books but from people. You hunger to make sense of this mess we've made and understand why we behave as we do; you turn that same laser penetration on your own actions. Your unfailing optimism and refusal to quit cause you to endure near-impossible situations, but you're determined to unravel the enigma called humanity, then publish your discovery to the universe.

Love, Sex, and Marriage

You're sometimes in danger of *not* showing your potent emotions, as if you fear overwhelming both yourself and your partner. Many would never suspect how fragile your feelings and how easily frayed your nerves can be. This can lead to passive-aggressiveness and manipulation, because you loathe confrontation. Your pride and reserve won't allow you to call someone after the first date, yet you wonder why he or she doesn't call you. But after a week's suspense, your curiosity and longing win out and you leave a message, a plaintive, slightly incriminating note in your voice. The call isn't returned immediately, so you call again, aggrieved. Turns out they were in Kalamazoo on business for the week and you end up apologizing profusely.

The moral: Don't let your overactive imagination run away with you, and never sell yourself short. You'll find someone just as caring and thoughtful as you who will reciprocate your deep feelings. You have a tendency to cling to relationships that have outlived their usefulness or even those you find unsatisfactory, for fear the next one might prove worse. You take others' guff, even when your common sense tells you you're being victimized. Avoid using relationships as a cocoon to protect you from life's harshness. Don't let people walk all over you; at least hold out for someone who realizes you're a Persian carpet, not a doormat!

Money and Career

You're passionately concerned with justice and reform; you feel you were meant to be an agent for lasting social change through your arbitrating skills. Your natural empathy enables you to reach people on a gut emotional level. You might be a consumer advocate, writer, public defender, or psychologist. You're impatient with bureaucracy and red tape, yet you have the patience to work to change the system from within. Your kind, tolerant nature and enthusiasm to get the job done make you a superb motivator; though you fear leadership, feeling unworthy, you often end up in positions of authority, especially behind the scenes, which you prefer since it keeps you out of the spotlight. You can be a tightwad, since you equate financial and emotional security. But you'll loosen up and loosen the money belt as you mature and gain confidence.

The ⚋2 Potential

Learn not to take every little detail personally, not to be everyone's savior or play the martyr for a cause. It's not your responsibility to save the planet, though you understand its problems better than most. You have the power and perceptiveness to enlighten the world; don't waste your precious energy on people who can't appreciate you. True, you're here to nurture others, but you must focus on your needs, letting the people you care about work through their own problems without your profound insight.

FAMOUS CANCER TWOS

Kevin Bacon	7/8/1958	John Glenn	7/18/1921
Gustav Mahler	7/7/1860	David Brinkley	7/10/1920
Kris Kristofferson	6/22/1936	Sidney Lumet	6/25/1924
Rose Kennedy	7/22/1890	Marc Chagall	7/7/1887
Edmund Hillary	7/20/1919		
Amy Vanderbilt	7/20/1908		

♋ • 3
Cancer Three
"The Intuitive Optimist"

♋ +	3 +	♋ -	3 -
Kind	*Visionary*	*Touchy*	*Self-interested*
Well-intentioned	*Imaginative*	*Defensive*	*Chaotic*
Instinctive	*Talented*	*Nervous*	*Gossipy*
Perceptive	*Romantic*		

A Cancer Three sees the humor in little everyday things, turning Fido the Pomeranian chasing Fluffy the Persian into a real-life Looney Tunes cartoon. Deliciously witty, you effortlessly volley one-liners on the internet with the adroitness of Andre Agassi at the net. You view your life as a gothic romance novel, albeit the contemporary versions where the heroine is a capable CEO of a multinational conglomerate too busy for love until an Italian count who owns a vineyard empire and half of Venice changes the flat tire on her Maserati. You adore all those tempting foreign phrases, seeking a melange of *l'amore, la dolce vita,* and *la vie bohème* (though you'd limit starving in a garret for your art to a six-month trial period).

Part of you senses you weren't meant for this world. You feel like a walking anachronism: where are the good old days? you might grouse, wishing you were off shooting grouse and partridge at an elegant hunting party. Well, make that a photographic safari, since you couldn't bear to hurt another living creature. (You eat lobster, sure, you just won't pop it into the pot.) You long to live in another time, perhaps of the harpsichord and minuet, or the Charleston and bathtub gin. With such escapist fantasies, any era but the present seems more glamorous.

You're just as sensitive and affectionate as other Cancers, albeit with a greater tendency to skim the surface of waters, rather than explore the depths. You howl at the moon while skinny-dipping: where do you think we got the word *lunatic* from anyway? You're quite chatty, occasionally catty, even bark when you're "in a zone," but never intentionally hurt someone's feelings. If you do, he or she will receive a handwritten note of apology in your most flowery calligraphy and a flamboyant floral topiary.

Love, Sex, and Marriage

Romance? Yes, please. Keep those scented candles, bubble baths, champagne picnics, and long-stemmed roses coming. You send thank-you notes after a night at the opera, call punctually, hold doors open (yes, you gals, too): as attentive and ardent a suitor as anyone could wish. Of course, just when the full moon backlights your sweetie perfectly, you propose . . . a midnight taco run. But guess what's stuffed into the ground meat? So your intended breaks a filling, then choked on the ring. You perform the Heimlich with a neck nuzzle and muffled giggle.

You'll want oodles of kanoodling, which will lead to oodles of kids. What a grand parent and grandparent you are; an overgrown kid yourself in many ways, you know just when to giggle and just when to give them a poker face that sends them into fits of screaming laughter. And you spoil them rotten, although sometimes your guilt impels you to lecture them on saving their allowance. "Practice what you preach" is the inevitable saucy retort.

Money and Career

Whatever you do, you establish an utterly unique style. Your gentle humor, sympathetic nature, and sheer enjoyment of life prime you for many careers. You mine daily life and domesticity for chuckles, whether dallying at the water cooler discussing your co-worker's steamy soap-opera travails, or writing about them. Your Cancerian sharp eye for detail and the Three's sharp ear for dialogue make you a wondrous screenwriter, comedian, actor, and advice or gossip columnist. But you'd excel in any of the arts thanks to your trailblazing originality. You're extremely mediagenic, radiating just the right mix of pizzazz and accessibility, with killer timing on your punch lines.

Unlike other Cancers, it's sometimes more important for you to play the dashing wolf, rather than keep the wolf from

your door. Three extravagance overwhelms your Cancerian
thrift; both endow you with such exquisite, expensive taste
you'd need an Ivy League–sized endowment to purchase
everything that catches your eye. You're prudent and shop
around for bargains first, then spend spend spend anyway
when you feel you deserve it. Your mate had better do the
coupon cutting; it strikes you as a tad cheap.

The ♋3 Potential

You're a luscious loon; even the rare Cancer Three curmudgeon will be lovable. Everyone thinks you're just a little
bit crazy, but you're here to point out the absurd little details; the world would be a far duller place without Cancer
Threes. Besides, your cockeyed perspective keeps you
youthful and alive when others are counting the days toward
retirement. In fact, you're so indefatigable and bursting the
damn with a flood of creative ideas that you won't stop
working; even on your deathbed you'll be dictating the latest
installment of your memoirs, getting irascible when the ste-
nographer can't keep up with your inexhaustible flow of
anecdotes.

FAMOUS CANCER THREES

Bill Cosby	7/12/1937	Neil Simon	7/4/1927
Abigail Van Buren	7/4/1918	Ann Landers	7/4/1918
Joe Torre	7/18/1940	Louie Armstrong	7/4/1900

♋ • 4
Cancer Four
"The Gentle General"

♋ +	4 +	♋ -	4 -
Conservative	Persistent	Miserly	Resentful
Solid	Loyal	Unforgiving	Disorganized
Comforting	Thorough	Pushy	Overcommitted
Contented	Enterprising		

You're the true salt of the earth, though you sometimes think the entire planet is on a sodium-free diet. You toil so unceasingly for people, and it seems as if they take your efforts for granted. Everyone views you as the dependable Rock of Gibraltar; inwardly you do feel the waves lapping and eroding your strength. You grumble to yourself how lost they'd be without you to hold everything together. Wouldn't it be fun to leave a note on the fridge saying you've run off with that drop-dead new neighbor, or an E-mail for the boss saying you've absconded with the payroll to Rio? Sure, the aggrieved Cancerian may daydream, but the conscientious Four will always be there to put bread on the table and butter it, too.

To feel happy and secure, you need the rent paid in advance, the larder fully stocked, and the college fund set up the moment of conception. No Mother Hubbard, you, though in a pinch you can darn the socks, grout the bathroom floor, and placate the plumber for another week. Indeed, working with your hands relaxes you after a stress-filled day. Your idea of a good evening is a yoga class, puttering around, spackling, gardening, alphabetizing the CDs, and painting wonderfully detailed miniatures.

Four translates the Cancer dreams into reality; though you enjoy playing traditional roles, part of you wants to strut your stuff on a larger stage or run away to join the circus. Chances are you won't, but your rebellious streak manifests itself in the choice of an unconventional mate or a tattoo emblazoned on a body part only your honey can see. You're not nearly as meek as you appear; you'll slug it out in the trenches for a cause or a loved one.

Love, Sex, and Marriage

Settling down helps focus you, since you have other mouths to feed. Though you project the serenity of a Renaissance Madonna, you have some pretty turbulent emotions; you're touchy-feely and can get touchy if your spouse isn't into a little huggin'. Physically and emotionally expressive, you have an endearing directness; you make eye contact and often touch someone's arm to make your point. You trick your babycakes into a hammer hold and liplock; giving a total stranger artificial respiration is probably a secret fantasy.

When you're comfortable, you exhibit an (expletive-deleted) earthy humor and a racy side that people wouldn't expect from your demure first impression. You're wild and woolly beneath that dyed-in-the-wool exterior, and others soon discover that you're no starched stuffed shirt. But only your mate knows how wanton you can be in your own bedroom, with lots of role-playing, role reversals, and reversals of position!

Money and Career

People rave about your inimitable sense of structure; you're a groundbreaking architect, landscaper, or urban planner. A skilled office manager, you employ a deft combination of receptiveness and firmness with your employees. You know just how to marshal the forces to get the job done in time. Helping others to "get it right" and "make it work" is your mantra. Your natural fluidity and grace also suggest dancing or athletics; the old-fashioned part of you might want to take up a sport like fencing, though tennis appeals more to your capitalist nature and your love of elegant movement.

You're quite practical about finances.You invest wisely for maximum return, doing your homework before listening to E.F.Hutton's minions. You can haggle like a bazaar vendor. You like the high life but at a low cost, and somehow manage to snatch a penthouse at a bargain-basement price. Nobody better mess with you at a Neiman-Marcus sale!

The ☉4 Potential

You have a lusty, straightforward approach toward life that wins friends and influences people. Even if you rocket to the top you remain "just one of the guys," visiting your old haunts, dishing the dirt with your high school buddies. You're enormously reliable; as they say in the film industry, you "get it right in the first take." True, people come to expect this of you and you can feel underappreciated. But remember you're the glue that holds so many things together, and you'd never let your nearest and dearest fall apart.

FAMOUS CANCER FOURS

Chris O'Donnell	6/26/1970	Pamela Anderson	7/1/1967
P.T. Barnum	7/5/1810	Henry VIII	6/28/1491
Barbara Stanwyck	7/16/1907	Leslie Caron	7/1/1931

69 • 5

Cancer Five
"The Hopping Homebody"

69 +	5 +	69 -	5 -
Self-aware	Adventurous	Snappish	Dissatisfied
Alert	Quick-witted	Hypocritical	Temperamental
Curious	Outgoing	Self-indulgent	Reckless
Emotional	Free-spirited		

You may cultivate a Goody Two-shoes appearance, but there are some bloodred spiked stilettos lurking in your closet. From high heels to hiking boots, your moods are far-ranging and fluid. Cancer Fives love hearth and home, but you also have an exploratory side. Think of the hermit crab, forever casting off its shell in search of a newer, better one. You're one crab who loves scuttling out from your little hole in the sand, especially if it seems like your carefully hatched plans are about to be scuttled.

The combination of restlessness and reliability in your nature is much like the tides; even your moods are predictable. Unlike many Cancers, you resist being tied down, requiring both the freedom to pursue avenues of self-expression and a home base from which to operate. That home will be both a showplace and a workplace, with an eclectic collection of souvenirs from your extensive travels, from Balinese fertility idols to Banbara war masks, and the library of research materials you gathered before the trip.

You'll never stop absorbing as much information as you can, avid for both book knowledge and life experience that you can share with others. And you always return from your latest exotic holiday with baubles and bubbly tidbits of information for your entire crowd. Exhibit A: the shrunken head from Papua New Guinea. Exhibit B: a detailed discourse on the headhunter table etiquette and how they only eat those victims they deem brave in battle, believing they'll then possess their spirits.

Love, Sex, and Marriage

You're not one to settle for mere bed and "bored" when you marry. You seek a fellow traveler, geographically and spiritually. You like writing your observations down in a journal when you go exploring on either level but would just as soon turn someone on the arm, whispering, wide-eyed and excited as a kid, "Look at that!" You love sharing experiences, but are just as content exchanging anecdotes at the end of the day. You have an insatiable need to communicate every thought and feeling as it occurs; your partner must be equally animate, articulate, and emotionally forthcoming.

The curious Five influence softens your Cancerian shell; rarely reserved, you want to talk things out if there's a problem and welcome constructive criticism. You've probably read every book on intimacy there is, but you respect your mate's privacy and don't take offense if conversation is tabled for another night. You'll find ways to reinvigorate a stagnant relationship. Maybe an impromptu trip to watch leatherback turtles nest on a secluded Caribbean isle. Or take sex with your partner outside the bedroom (well, maybe just the kitchen while whipping up a soufflé). And if worst comes to worst, wouldn't it be a gas telling your friends what couples therapy is really like?

Money and Career

You're expert at creating ideas as a Five, while your Cancerian sympathy ensures that even the dreariest droid under your care will feel he or she has made an invalauble contribution to the team. This makes you a powerful motivator; you're often put in charge of a department and allowed to run it as you please since you always get results. This also enables you to triumph as a producer or director, while your intuitiveness and liveliness form a natural performer.

Whatever you do, you prefer to be in front of the house, schmoozing with the clients. Obviously you find anything that expands your scope of knowledge and brings you in touch with other cultures enormously inviting. Ethnobotany, hotel management, restaurateur or caterer, cultural anthropology, public relations, advertising, teaching, and travel and tourism are just a few excellent job opportunities; besides, that way your trips would be free, expensed, or at least tax-deductible!

The ☉5 Potential

You possess a winning, winsome appeal and accessibility, adept at both superficial chitchat and deep thought. Relating well to people is imperative to your well-being; you're unhappy in situations where you can't find some common ground or connection. "People person" is such a cliché, but that's what you are; you take the time and effort to get to know people, making them feel special by remembering the little things, like a child's birthday or a book they casually mentioned interest in, and they appreciate it.

FAMOUS CANCER FIVES

Liv Tyler	*7/1/1977*	*Carly Simon*	*6/25/1945*
Helen Keller	*6/27/1880*	*Hermann Hesse*	*7/2/1877*
Jerry Herman	*7/10/1932*	*Donald Sutherland*	*7/17/1934*

♋ • 6
Cancer Six
"The Happy Homemaker"

♋ +	6 +	♋ -	6 -
Tender	*Domestic*	*Overprotective*	*Domineering*
Sentimental	*Loving*	*Cranky*	*Smothering*
Giving	*Dutiful*	*Stifling*	*Self-sacrificing*
Solicitous	*Reliable*		

To you the entire world is a stray waiting to be taken in. Even Cancer Six men are homemakers, humming happily as they empty the cat litter or cook the cassoulet. Everyone comes to you for homespun advice, which you dispense readily, along with homemade chicken soup. (A Cancer Six probably first said chicken soup was a cure-all.) You also offer unsolicited advice and take it personally when the mailman doesn't heed it. Mother Nurture, that's you; waving your pincers at anyone who gets in your way when you have loved ones to feed, caress, and protect.

You need a family on whom to lavish your considerable love; even if you're gay, you'll likely adopt. No matter what your gender, fussing like a mother hen is mother's milk to you. Clinging and clucking are your ways of controlling people; you can be as virtuosic as the stereotypical Jewish mother at subtly inducing guilt. But that guilt runs both ways and runs deep. If you snap at someone, however justified, you'll agonize over it long after your "victim" has forgotten. You boast a photograhic memory for special occasions and dote on throwing surprise parties.

You have to be involved at all costs, feeling shut out when your loved ones have their own lives. Whatever road you take together, you're the backseat driver. But that craving for constant reassurance can drive away even the people who love you most. Kind words make you crabs happy as the proverbial clam, while offhand criticism makes you clam up. Love and respect yourself; only when we proudly assert our inividuality we can truly merge with another. Then your mate will experience your love not as limiting but liberating, and you'll make the best partner of all: firm yet giving and always extremely devoted.

Love, Sex, and Marriage

You mate for life, being "a truly, madly, deeply" type whose love never wavers. Ironically fearful of rejection, you often don't make a move, your intended never intuits your interest, and your emotions become so overwhelming that you have to repress them. Generally your angelic air attracts more aggressive types who'll never admit how much they want to be wanted. Should you misjudge your first partner, a fairly frequent occurrence because you're so trusting and so desirous of a stable home, your second marriage will work because you're wiser, having learned not to confuse sympathy for love. You can drive the poor darlings crazy with your insistence on accounting for every moment spent out of your sight. You're not jealous, you just long to share every intimate detail.

Your love can be overwhelming; you should have kids and a full menagerie of pets to share in the bounty. The kids may squirm when they get older; don't you know that kissing isn't cool in front of the other dudes and dudettes? You'd deny them a driver's license if you could, but you deny them little else. Try not to spoil the little monsters or go to the opposite extreme and ground them for every candy bar they buy with the milk money. Yes, it's okay to make them floss.

Money and Career

You genuinely enjoy cooking, cleaning, gardening, anything to do with the home; it helps you relieve stress. You'd thrive in any job that involves caring, helping, or providing for others. Chef, realtor, healer, doctor, nurse, masseur, physical therapist, dietician, teacher, and social worker certainly lead the list. Contact is vital; you could work from home if you have that brood to brood about, but otherwise you like interaction, the more hands-on the better.

Your closets probably overflow with boxes of love letters, term papers, beaten-up sneakers, and a series of your magnificent obsessions, from Broadway original-cast albums to dainty dolphins. Your home will be comfy, lived in, its look, if not traditional, then retro. Classic, kitschy fifties design appeals to you, like Formica counters, soda-shop barstools, chairs that morph with the shape of whoever sits there, and wonderfully abstract vases (especially in soft seashell colors).

The ☺6 Potential

You have remarkable strength of purpose and belief in others, if not always yourself. The ultimate homebody, you offer the milk and cookies of human kindness to the world. But you must remember that not everyone can live up to your expectations. Even at your most Cancerian clinging vinish, you grow on people, becoming inextricably bound up in their problems. You need to distance yourself from others, recognizing that only they can deal with their issues and you can't force them to grow up. Allow others to mother you in return; this creates an equal relationship and helps your partner feel more important.

FAMOUS CANCER SIXES

Sylvester Stallone	7/6/1946	Meryl Streep	6/22/1949
Linda Ronstadt	7/15/1946	George Steinbrenner	7/4/1930
Elisabeth Kübler-Ross	7/8/1926	Bill Blass	6/22/1922
Oscar Hammerstein II	7/12/1895	Nathaniel Hawthorne	7/4/1804
Buckminster Fuller	7/12/1895	Abner Doubleday	6/26/1819
Duke of Windsor	6/23/1894	Nelson A. Rockefeller	7/8/1908

♋ • 7
Cancer Seven
"The Adorable Academic"

♋ +	7 +	♋ -	7 -
Insightful	*Psychic*	*Withdrawn*	*Caustic*
Feeling	*Observant*	*Resistant*	*Secretive*
Protective	*Poised*	*Shy*	*Dogmatic*
Thoughtful	*Scholarly*		

A haunting dichotomy is at work in the Cancer Seven. Cancers desperately long to be understood fully; Sevens require their privacy and let only a select few inside. Since Cancers are not emotionally forthcoming by nature and can play the crabby hermit themselves, you often have difficulty expressing your deep wells of feeling. Even if you come from an enormous, loud, boisterous family, you somehow come across as an only child. You're forever searching for that elusive soul mate, not cellmate.

You require long periods of uninterrupted introspection to reflect and recharge your batteries. You find solace in your solitude; when you want to disappear you can make like Jimmy Hoffa. Friends might tease you with a Genius at Work sign, but you stare at them with maddeningly inscrutable calm. You need these emotional retreats, and those who love you come to accept that they're as natural and unstoppable as gravity.

Though you like the anonymity of the crowd, you might be slightly claustrophobic: no subway rush hour for you, thanks. You carry yourself with an innate dignity and impenetrable yet charming reserve that always command attention, even at a crowded July Fourth barbecue. You appear utterly innocent and unassuming until people get to know you. Then they shiver with the accuracy of your acumen. That sharp intuition trained on others can make them uncomfortable: the emotional equivalent of X-ray vision.

You understand better than most the concept of the defense mechanism. You recognize we're all locked up in brooding castles, replete with machicolated battlements and moats filled with snapping crocodiles. And for what? To hide the one thing that we arguably all have in common: our shameful vulnerability and longing. It takes a great effort for you to lower the drawbridge, but you hope for the best, understanding that it opens you up to a great deal of pain, but also much love.

Love, Sex, and Marriage

Traditional monogamy is your shining ideal, yet if your mate doesn't seem attuned, you can drift into an affair, hungry for that true connection. As comfortable as you are in your seclusion, you're deeply lonely unless you make the effort to reach out to others. You possess an abstract sweetness, absentmindedly petting your honey's head as you read the editorial section. You're a gentle, solicitous mate, as long as you're permitted your private moments and no one asks you to reveal your psychic journeys. Your sex drive is powerful but erratic; when you want it, you need it, and you lose yourself completely in the act. But then you always float off ethereally when the mood strikes. You can become so immersed in your projects that you temporarily forget your family, or disappear even at home, lost in thought. Make yourself as available as possible to your mate, children, and friends.

Money and Career

Your greatest success comes through accessing the inner child in us all. Acting, singing, directing, producing, and writing are among your potent outlets. You prefer to be left to your own devices in the corporate world, and might well contract to work part-time at home. Indeed, you're not comfortable until you've purchased your own home; you need that retreat, remember. Associates sometimes underestimate you because of your apparent complaisance, but underneath you're really a tiger; you dream, after all, and dream big. As a result, you can stir up more intrigue behind the scenes than Letterman and Leno clawing over *The Tonight Show*. You can be manipulative to achieve your ends and have a sense of occasion and rise to one every time. Try not to become too obsessed with the combo of intellectual attainment and worldly success.

The ♋7 Potential

You're an unusual, touching mix of innocent child and sophisticated adult. Your otherworldliness is confusing but mighty attractive. It confuses you as well, since you have a down-to-earth, even ribald side. Try not to overanalyze your flowing mood shifts and don't give in to them if they threaten to hurt you or those you love. There's nothing wrong with drifting off into another plane, and no one has the right to intrude, but remember that others can feel left out or left behind. Your bottomless emotions and penetrating intellect can glow like a beacon that illuminates our understanding of childhood past and future maturity.

FAMOUS CANCER SEVENS

Princess Diana	7/1/1961	Patrick Stewart	7/13/1940
Beatrix Potter	7/6/1866	Dan Aykroyd	7/1/1952
Arthur Ashe	7/10/1943	Olivia De Havilland	7/1/1916

♋ • 8
Cancer Eight
"The Determined Delegator"

♋ +	8+	♋ -	8 -
Nurturing	Just	Possessive	Materialistic
Tenacious	Ambitious	Diffident	Impersonal
Creative	Professional	Hypersensitive	Workaholic
Sympathetic	Global View		

Mastery of the self is your greatest challenge: You're so sensitive and objective that you might terrify and terrorize yourself until you learn to harness your energy! You have a mission, a vision, and a keen sense of your power, ambition, and charisma; yet because your passions are so strong, you often fear you'll use that magnetism for selfish gain, whether emotionally or materially.

Okay, you're intimately acquainted with your power-hungry, manipulative, controlling side. Combining Cancerian insight with the Eight's grasp of the big picture endows you with extrordinary entrepreneurial skills. You'll probably work long hours, even neglecting to call to say you'll be late for dinner. But you'll probably atone by showing up with petits four from the nearest five-star French restaurant. Cancer softens the occasionally no-nonsense Eight facade, while Eight gives Cancer greater resiliency and a more balanced emotional perspective.

You cut an imposing figure: people just know you make a devoted friend and an implacable enemy. You should allow others to see the *real* you more often—the soft touch, the sucker for a sob story. You often fear others will take advantage of that gentler side, or take it for granted. But it can get lonely in that huge boardroom with the "big picture" windows. You're a perceptive judge of character: use it to draw the right people into your life.

Love, Sex, and Marriage

Love with a Cancer Eight is a high-voltage high-wire act. Cancers are so sensitive they're the human tuning forks of the zodiac; combined with the Eight's magnetic allure, you might come on stronger than you realize. *You* know you're not as forbidding as you look, though you bark orders like a marine captain and tyrannize waiters when the filet isn't cooked to your exact specification. Between the shy Cancer and businesslike Eight, it could take prospective lovers a while to know where they really stand. Trusting is a difficult proposition for you control freaks. Nonetheless, there are times when you throw caution to the winds and pursue the object of your attention with hurricane force. As much as your Cancerian side loves courtship (and an engagement of Victorian-era length), the Eight itches to sign the marital contract and get back to work.

Initially cool, you heat up fast once the spreadsheets give way to the bedsheets. You sometimes dominate your lovers, but part of you wouldn't mind turning the tables. In fact, you need an equally strong partner. Just keep the control games in the office. Well, okay, a little amorous wrestling— "you pin me and I'll cook dinner, honey"—*can* spice up your sex life.

Money and Career

You combine Cancerian sensitivity to others with the Eight's savvy. Both excel at marketing and promotions; together they're irresistible with a pitch. Trust your hunches: you have an uncanny ability to predict trends, taking short- and long-term objectives into (bank) account.

Your masterful air and genuine empathy allow you to become a successful politician. That passionate concern about justice and the ability to see issues from all sides make you a fine lawyer, even judge. You'd function best as a CEO, preferably of a vast multinational conglomerate, or in some self-employed activity. Creative thinking is critical to your well-being. Although you'll slave for hours ensuring every last detail is right, avoid positions that entail mere grunt work.

Don't be stingy with credit due or a credit line, otherwise your success could rebound on you. Fortunately your cautious, conservative Cancer side should ensure you have some tidy sum squirreled away in a Swiss bank account.

The ♋8 Potential

If anything, you have a fear of SUCCESS. You can focus others' lives for them. Why not train your almost superhuman intuition on yourself—and lighten up? You *can* leave work at the office, and trust that your motives for getting ahead are actually purer than you think. You want money not for its own sake, but for the power it affords, the ability to live without restraints. Broad-minded, with penetrating insight into the world's internal workings, your overdeveloped responsibility to humanity often makes you feel you must be judge, jury, and executioner rolled into one. Couldn't it be that you simply want to provide for the people you love and contribute something of lasting value to humanity?

FAMOUS CANCER EIGHTS

Nancy Reagan	*7/06/1921*	*George Washington Carver*	*7/12/1861*
Mary Baker Eddy	*7/16/1821*	*Bob Dole*	*7/22/1923*
Estée Lauder	*7/1/1908*	*Anthony Edwards*	*7/16/1962*

♋ • 9

Cancer Nine
"The Pragmatic Performer"

♋ +	9 +	♋ -	9 -
Receptive	*Philanthropic*	*Self-pitying*	*Self-absorbed*
Artistic	*Spiritual*	*Reticent*	*Changeable*
Compassionate	*Magnetic*	*Self-destructive*	*Morose*
Sincere	*Compassionate*		

You have what in the twenties used to be called "It": good old-fashioned sex appeal combined with a seeming accessibility, an approachable fantasy figure. Your own imagination knows no bounds; you have a special genius for seeing the world a little askew. You can almost read others' minds and have a direct wavelength to their hearts. You know how to appeal to people's emotions, whether one on one or on the global stage. And are you ever funny: Whether through wry, dry wit or manic motor-mouth mobility, you keep your audience in stitches—even if only one person forms your audience—which is part of your ineffable magnetism.

Despite the Nine penchant for performing, your Cancerian side needs a retreat from the harsh glare of the spotlight to reenergize. The paradox is that you crave the trappings but not the trap of celebrity. You require a tremendous amount of recognition for your efforts. But you want to lead a "normal" life. Finicky and claustrophobic, sometimes you can't bear the crush of those adoring fans. To relax, every so often you take the phone off the hook and become obsessed with tidying and tying up loose ends. Time to clean out those closets and donate half your wardrobe to a homeless shelter, weed the garden and plant a row of dogwoods, catch up on your business correspondence (especially all those kind but firm rejections of your time).

You tend to be an extremist; either you're a wild child or you're the tranquil communing-with-nature sort. Either way, there's always a stable or untamed component to your personality that emerges unexpectedly. Often the Cancer Nine "crazies" make superlative parents, while the Cancer Nine good citizens take off to howl at the full moon while mooning a caravan of RVs.

Love, Sex, and Marriage

You're both an artist and artisan of love. You court someone with all the little attentions, the filigree work, the appliqué, the ormolu: the little embellishments that make dating you stand out. Marriage is a safe haven from the crazy world. For all your generosity and compassion, you sometimes require constant attention. If you're wise—and you are—you'll choose a partner who steadfastly refuses to treat you like a child and give in to every whim. And no temper tantrum, bawling fit, or your best offensive weapon, your inhuman charm, should be tolerated! You're a delectable sensualist in bed, verbally and physically teasing, murmuring sweet everythings and making your lover giggle in surprise and anticipation of your next move. If you have kids, you'll be a devoted parent, ensuring that you reserve "quality time" for them and imbuing them with your own gift for laughter.

Money and Career

You're a seeming paradox: an idealist and an opportunist. You'd rather wait tables and dig ditches than adopt a career that doesn't make you happy. Whatever you do, you need to feel you're an integral part of the creative process. You like starting from the ground floor of a new enterprise, becoming inextricably bound with its growth. And given any role in the decision making, you'll ensure the venture succeeds. On the creative side, a Cancer Nine's work might be coolly rational, yet invariably has a visceral emotional appeal, packing an emotional and financial wallop, tugging at both the heartstrings and the purse strings. Your work is never boring; you'll sing, act, and dance your guts out.

A performer with this aspect is more likely to do something he or she feels is gainful and enriching if the gigs aren't there. Like fellow Cancer Nine, Harrison Ford, you'd much rather be a carpenter than do underwear commercials; it's more soul-satisfying and at least you know you're building something of use. You probably write half your own dialogue, not because you're into power plays but because you go straight to the heart of a role and inhabit the character. You're the type to research a down-at-heels drunk on a bender on Skid Row or gain fifty pounds if the role demands it. This knockout combo of old-fashioned star power and character-actor versatility keeps you in great demand.

The ♋9 Potential

You're an amazing, baffling, charismatic personality; people are genuinely starstruck by your powerhouse presence. But you don't buy in to the star trip, rarely putting on airs. Sure, you have an ego, but you're just an entertainer. Whatever your role in life, that's your refreshingly plain attitude: make people laugh and help them get in touch with their inner selves. The only caution is not to use and abuse that dynamic presence for your own selfish purposes; you really do hold sway over others. Use that power benevolently.

FAMOUS CANCER NINES

Robin Williams	7/21/1952	Courtney Love	7/9/1964
John Cusack	6/26/1966	Barbara Cartland	7/9/1901
John D. Rockefeller	7/8/1839	Lena Horne	6/30/1917

LEO

•

♌ • 1
Leo One
"The Misunderstood Monarch"

♌ +	1 +	♌ -	1 -
Generous	*Innovative*	*Conceited*	*Dictatorial*
Passionate	*Independent*	*Arrogant*	*Boastful*
Noble	*Bold*	*Status-seeking*	*Impulsive*
Dynamic	*Original*		

You have enough pride for a pride of lions, but for a true King and Queen of Beasts, there's nothing beastly about your behavior. Granted, you *do* regard the world as your private playpen to stride through at will; you can't help but ignore those maddening No Trespassing signs. Nothing daunts you; you welcome all challenges and comers. If you can't conquer the world, you'd happily invent one, since you're also the world's great dramatist. You, of course, act all the parts.

You're not shy about trumpeting your abilities, yet you'll blow others' horns, too; you delight in encouraging others to live up to their potential (privately giving yourself credit). A natural take charge leader, your favorite roles are teacher and mentor. As far as you're concerned, there's little you can learn from others that you couldn't teach yourself. And if something arouses your curiosity, you study it intently until you've mastered the subject.

Even in kindergarten, you were calling meetings during recess. You'd have killed to be hall monitor in grammar school, the ultimate authority figure, but were savvy enough to realize it would make you unpopular; you were probably already concerned with making the right contacts to get ahead. Nor did you relish the role of school bully; sure, you could deck the brawniest kid in your class, but much preferred being respected for your sharpness and intellect. Your commanding presence stopped many a school-yard fight, and the skinny, short, four-eyed future techno wizards adored you.

Love, Sex, and Marriage

Your idea of seduction might be to dress in an impeccable gray Armani suit, pull up in a black stretch limo of just the right length, brandish a baker's dozen roses—twelve red representing passion surrounding one white signifying the purity of your love—then belt back a stiff one and invite your sweetie back to your apartment to admire your Dürer etchings and endurance. Yup, that goes for women, too: Leo One just plain makes you ballsy.

You tend to be equally magisterial in the bedroom, but surprisingly needful of reassurance. It's as if you don't quite buy in to the dashing image you cultivate. Those feelings of inadequacy actually make you a better lover, since you're more acutely aware as a Leo One of how your partner perceives your performance.

Extraordinarily magnanimous, you shower the one you call your own with extravagant gifts, and not just on the usual special occasions. Even an innocent holiday like Flag Day brings out your creative, amorous streak. You wouldn't mind being on the receiving end, but unswerving loyalty is far more important. You expect total fidelity—no, downright feudal fealty—in return for your largesse. No question you can be domineering, withholding favors if someone has displeased you. Although you love children and would make an exciting parent, you may opt not to raise a family; you're such a kid yourself that you might view your own as competition.

Money and Career

If monarch isn't a career option, you'll almost always gravitate toward a central position of authority (where you must curb your theatrical temper and know-it-all impatience). At least you cheerfully admit you require the lion's share of attention. You hate being controlled or dictated to. Forced to play second banana, you might just connive to make your boss slip on a peel. But no one questions your leadership abilities; you're the type who could rally the troops when they're outnumbered twenty to one. You're out to hit a homer in every at bat, but sometimes it's more effective to move the runners up base by base.

Obviously you require a position of creative or executive power. Anything that influences public opinion, especially TV, film, advertising, and the print media, is a natural. You might run a top fashion house or devise your own lines of perfumes and cosmetics. The more academically inclined could become a college professor or museum curator. Regardless of your job, you'll always demand recognition for your work: a big, brassy name plate on the door suits you fine.

The ♌1 Potential

Your nobility, ardor, and generosity can light the way for everyone in your considerable domain. Alwys be your sunny self and refuse to give in to negativity. Guard against arrogance arnd egotism; even the greatest monarch requires advisers, so remember to listen to your subjects' views now and then. Make sure you surround yourself with people who will stand up to you, in both your personal and professional lives. They can always cut you down to size when you need it; humility ain't exactly your best Sunday suit, but you *do* wear everything else impeccably! Even showing your flashier side invariably warms people's hearts. Face it: You're larger than life and wouldn't have it any other way!

FAMOUS LEO ONES

Magic Johnson	*8/14/1959*	*Henry Ford*	*7/30/1863*
Emily Brontë	*7/30/1818*	*Aldous Huxley*	*7/26/1894*
Mae West	*8/17/1893*	*Halle Berry*	*8/14/1968*

♌ • 2
Leo Two
"The Valiant Valedictorian"

♌ +	2 +	♌ -	2 -
Eager	*Extroverted*	*Temperamental*	*Sly*
Creative	*Friendly*	*Self-centered*	*Argumentative*
Cheerful	*Diplomatic*	*Childish*	*Hesitant*
Warmhearted	*Companionable*		

Leo Twos are the consummate survival artists. You have an extraordinary ability to bounce back from adversity, not only making lemonade from lemons, but selling it for a healthy profit. Leo provides Two with resiliency and bucks up its self-esteem. You quickly learn success results from two credos: "You wash my back and I'll wash yours" and "You watch my back and I'll watch yours." You're the finesse-meister and surgically precise spin doctor, your determination and craftiness cloaked in disarming affability. No one would ever guess how coolly you can wrap opponents around your little finger, or wrap yourself around them like a boa constrictor until they holler uncle. Waffle iron describes you perfectly. Your first instinct is toward compromise and you can sail like a kite whichever way the wind blows. But once you've made up your mind, you're unmoved and unmovable, nearly always getting your way.

As a kid you were the teacher's pet, yet weren't any the less popular for it. You curried favor with your peers by your eagerness to do their homework, sly comments about the teacher behind her back, and willinness to trade that dead tadpole for your Ken Griffey Jr. card (one of several, natch). As for any fellow pupils you didn't win over, if they only knew how much time and care you took selecting just the right apple, red, shiny, with not a wormhole in sight, they might have appreciated you more.

Pity the poor fool who stumbles into an argument with you. You're eloquent, cutting, dramatic, and impressive when crossed—besides, you don't let your adversary get a word in edgewise. You remember every slight, real or imagined, but will be the first to proffer a helping hand, so they can get back on their feet. Your roar is mostly for show anyway. You're like Aesop's fable of the lion felled by a thorn in his paw; any hostility or insensitivity and you're like a stray kitten.

If you do have a chip on your shoulder, it's that you feel constantly compelled to prove yourself. You're more at ease with people whom you secretly think your inferiors due to an unnecessarily negative self-image; when someone with an impressive intellect shows up, you automatically feel you must argue to make your point. If cajolery and charm don't work, you'll get "in their face," going (wo)mano a mano. The point is, Two craves approval, yet Leo demands respect.

Love, Sex, and Marriage

Of course, every star must have an entourage, even if it's only an audience of one, which is often what people in your life must become. A Leo Two's loved ones must tenderly stroke the bruised ego, restore the sunny optimism, overlook the (usually) innocent flirtations with "fans," answer the letters, and autograph your photo to boot, and while they're at it, balance the checkbook without nagging.

You overwhelm your mates with your largesse. You're like an emotional banquet, with a vast array of tempting dishes, and you want your loved ones to gorge themselves silly. You're incredibly demonstrative, leaning toward mushy PDAs, and can be easily hurt by a reserved partner who isn't as affectionate on demand. You do require constant reassurance and proof of devotion.

Money and Career

Twos are behind-the-scenes negotiators, while Leos grab the stage. You'll be a commanding presence whatever line of work you choose; when you retire you could earn a substantial living just acting as a figurehead, meeting, greeting, and looking regal. The ultimate actor-politician, you're incredibly telegenic and always speak in sound bites. What a trial lawyer you'd make, combining all your considerable skills; you'd make the *L.A. Law* and *The Firm* crowds look amateurish by comparison. And fittingly, your performing panache and directorial command are unmatched. You always know exactly how to sell yourself—or any product—to the public, which drives up the bidding. Even as a tycoon or an athlete, you'll consider running for public office. You hunger for responsibility even more than approval, yet can't be called power-hungry, since you genuinely believe your own script and think you can make a difference in people's lives.

The ♌2 Potential

Once you've decided on a course of action, you have an unswerving conviction that you know best. Very often you do; your good intentions are unquestioned. But while under pressure, you should watch out for a tendency to be alternately evasive and take charge. Twos run from the spotlight, but your leonine side is mopey and grumpy without a stage. You have an uncanny knack for finding co-stars who understand you; you function best in supportive partnerships and teams, helping everyone to shine.

FAMOUS LEO TWOS

President Bill Clinton	*8/19/1946*	*Woody Harrelson*	*7/23/1961*
Angela Bassett	*8/16/1958*	*Jacqueline Kennedy*	*7/28/1929*
Madonna	*8/16/1958*	*Onassis*	
		Malcolm Forbes	*8/19/1919*

♌ • 3
Leo Three
"The Charisma King"

♌ +	3 +	♌ -	3 -
Dashing	*Generous*	*Flirtatious*	*Vain*
Stylish	*Fun-loving*	*Inconstant*	*Garrulous*
Entertaining	*Spirited*	*Faddish*	*Cynical*
Vital	*Congenial*		

The quintessential smooth talker and operator, you probably handed out embossed business cards during Freshman Week. You knew from an early age that you wanted to go first-class or not at all. Leo Threes are typically so irresistible they could sell a Yugo off the used car lot, but *naturellement* they wouldn't be caught dead near anything but a Jag, Rolls, or Mercedes!

You were born to entertain. The consummate host, you'll remember everyone's favorite drink and cook an elaborate dinner. Then you let the dishes mount up until some guest tactfully offers to help clean up . . . but before accepting you'll struggle between your inherent hospitality and distaste. Hiring a caterer, if you have the money, would allow you to mingle, but it lacks your trademark personal touch. Besides, you couldn't resist the best. Why go for the pressed Sevruga when the beluga is only twenty dollars more per ounce? After all, you're only inviting your thirty absolutely closest friends.

If it's not your party, you love stirring things up. With your tremendous theatrical flair, you can't resist the shock effect of a scarlet gown at the White Ball. At the very least, you delight in dressing up; even when you dress down, it's showy in some way— the jeans ripped just so, the mascara running in one perfect tear.

You almost chauvinistically believe in the courtly concept of the shining white knight and fair damsel. You want to be King Arthur and his Round Table rolled into one; true love is your Holy Grail. You dream of unicorns, rainbows, and pots of gold (which you'll need to keep yourself in the style to which you'd die to become accustomed). Of course, even Camelot was a messy sty, with serfs toiling in abject poverty and unsanitary conditions and inequity between classes, but it still pains you to discover harsh reality. Your fantasy world remains untainted by the small-minded or shallow. You're a soft touch for scam artists whether in love or business because you desperately want to believe in your shining ideal; this wraps you in a radiant mantle of old-fashioned glamour and purity.

Love, Sex, and Marriage

You're spendthrift emotionally, too, with operatically extravagant feelings. Your life is a series of crushes. The only drawback is that if you're constantly in love, you can't very well be constant. You seek an all-consuming grand passion: Romeo and Juliet, except, of course, for that tragic part. You're monogamous in principle, but sometimes have difficulty living up to the contractual obligations. It isn't that you *want* to cheat, just that you require continual attention from a bevy of admirers. And it would be so rude if you turned down a well-timed advance.

Dating? It's more like storming the citadel. You'll besiege your amour, even staking out the apartment if you fear competition. Obviously you have an active romantic imagination; reality rarely lives up to the fantasy. Sometimes you fall for the superficial appearance; needless to say, the part of you that requires intellectual stimulation and playfulness is inevitably disappointed. You need someone who can help ground your dreams, translate your noble ambitions and high-minded ideals into substance.

Sexually, you adore all the little toys of seductions. Naughty black lingerie arnd edible underwear tickle your fancy and sense of the absurd even as they heighten sexual tension and pleasure.

Money and Career

If only flirt, *bon vivant,* and *Beau Brummell* were job descriptions! An inventive idea person, you loathe routine and get bogged down in the nitty-gritty. Of course, you'll rise above petty pencil-pushing politics. You make a perfect PR person or fund-raiser (though once you've cajoled the money, you shouldn't be trusted with its disbursement, thanks to your grandiose schemes and dreams). You traffic in illusion; therefore, film is your natural medium. Hey, it pays better than the circus. Beauty, fashion, jewelry design, and the art world are other media for self-expression. You'll require lots of earning power, since you indulge yourself in the same lovely nonentities that surround you at work.

The ♌3 Potential

With your innate style, buoyancy, and sheer joy in living, you have only to be yourself. People may try to tear you down, but you remain your devil-may-care self. The world needs dreamers and conjurers like you. You weren't meant to lead a conventional life, though you may sometimes tire of playing poster child for *la vie bohème*. Avoid mere sensationalism: you know, the *Playboy/Playgirl* centerfold when you're sixty. On second thought, if you got it, baby, flaunt it. And whatever "it" is, you're sure to possess plenty in reserve.

FAMOUS LEO THREES

Melanie Griffith	*8/9/1957*	*Wesley Snipes*	*7/31/1963*
Alfred Hitchcock	*8/13/1899*	*Peter Jennings*	*7/29/1938*
Ethel Barrymore	*8/15/1879*	*Connie Chung*	*8/20/1946*

♌ • 4
Leo Four
"The Hail-Fellow Hercules"

♌ +	4 +	♌ -	4 -
Loyal	*Accomplished*	*Pompous*	*Exacting*
Lusty	*Strong-willed*	*Show-offish*	*Contrary*
Jovial	*Committed*	*Pushy*	*Dogmatic*
Enterprising	*Strong Values*		

You're that rare aristocrat who doesn't mind mucking out the stables after your morning canter. No matter what the circumstances of your birth or upbringing, you consider yourself a "common (wo)man." Leo Fours measure people's worth by the size of their hearts rather than their bank accounts. You're earthy and direct, yet even amid telling an off-color (well, blue) joke, you still come across as a blue blood.

You genuinely believe that people can rise by sheer grit and honest toil, dedicating yourself to examining every situation in minute detail. You're capable and confident, with seemingly superhuman energy; even your second wind blows in with hurricane force. Despite your drive to get ahead, you can also have a indolent streak. Material success comes easily to you and once your creature comforts are satisfied, you make a perfectly blissful sofa spud.

When life disappoints you, you play your own heavy-mettle band, ranting and railing about how undependable folks are these days. Doesn't anyone have a sense of responsibility, care about a job well done? Your anger is genuine, but part of you enjoys putting on a good show. You're equally adept at the chillingly effective silent treatment. Even as a little cub, you knew just what it would take to motivate yourself and others. In truth, you're almost scarily efficient in your planning; you can also mow down adversaries through sheer perseverance. Think of your fellow Leo Four Arnold Schwarzenegger as the Terminator (in his kinder, gentler Part II incarnation, of course!).

Love, Sex, and Marriage

Your love life is important to you; you like to have it settled so you can worry about loftier matters. You're dedicated to working at your relationships, bringing optimism, determination, and emotionalism to any partnership. Since you loathe failure of any kind, divorce is the very last resort, though not for appearance sake. You simply don't like to admit you might be wrong, and your integrity demands that you find some way through the crisis, even if it means shouldering the lion's share of the blame yourself.

Your view of romance is a satisfying blend of idealism and pragmatism. You understand that everyone has walls, including yourself. But your attitude is, you're not storming

the fortress demanding to know someone else's most intimate thoughts, you're just knocking on the gate asking if
Jane or John can come out to play. When the wrestling
match begins, remember that very few are as, uh, inexhaustible as you.

Money and Career

A tireless worker, you won't stop until you're shining that
brass plaque on your desk, then earn that gold watch at
(enforced) retirement; with your innate discrimination, you'll
know if the title or timepiece is only fourteen-karat. You're
a born manager of men and money. Your only flaw as an
authority figure is that you forget how unique you really
are. It's nothing to you to wake up at 5:00 A.M. for a brisk
ten-mile run, followed by an energetic calisthenics program.
Your zeal to maximize production and increase efficiency is
admirable, but your employees are already jumping at your
command, so you needn't institute a daily routine of jumping
jacks. Naturally any Leo will want to seize center stage;
whatever your job, there's a bit if the performer in you,
especially when higher-ups are watching. A job combining
beauty and practicality, such as horticulture, also appeals.

Your probing mind makes you an excellent stock analyst,
pollster, or research scientist, while your strong constitution
is well suited to athletics. Don't be surprised if your career
takes a ninety-degree turn and you end up doing something
entirely different; you have an aptitude for being in the right
place at the right time for sniffing out new opportunities.
You'll finagle a three-year contract first, of course. As for
expenses, you're no cheapskate, but you're hardly extravagant. Your purchases must perform a necessary function,
whether a stationary bike or a car that gets forty miles to
the gallon. But first you pay off the mortgage and invest in
several IRAs.

The ♌4 Potential

One word: unlimited. The combo of Leo enthusiasm and
Four persistence is unbeatable. You're cast in a heroic mold:
an old-fashioned doer and go-getter, a Horatio Alger story

come to life. By exerting an earnest effort in every area of your life, you set an example for those around you. You're a quiet hero, but the blush is for effect: you know that you deserve all the accolades you receive. Just don't argue for argument's sake; listen to others' viewpoints. And recognize that most humans are by definition merely mortal and, yes, even flawed. Except you, of course.

FAMOUS LEO FOURS

David Duchovny	8/7/1960	Patrick Ewing	8/5/1962
Esther Williams	8/8/1923	Max Factor Jr.	8/18/1904
Shelley Winters	8/18/1922	Vida Blue	7/28/1949
Robyn Smith Astaire	8/14/1944	Geoffrey Holder	8/1/1930
Percy Bysshe Shelley	8/4/1792		

♌ • 5
Leo Five
"The Zany Zealot"

♌ +	5 +	♌ -	5 -
Magnetic	Free-spirited	Impetuous	Self-indulgent
Courageous	Peppy	Hotheaded	Hasty
Exuberant	Communicative	Ostentatious	Undisciplined
Expansive	Resourceful		

You have a voracious appetite for any and all experiences; Mick Jagger, another rolling-stone Leo Five, penned your anthem, "I Can't Get No Satisfaction." But you try and you try. You're seduced by anything new, the more flamboyant the better, since you love shocking people out of their complacency. You even invent anecdotes to get a rise out of your stuffy neighbor, like the time you attended that Halloween party with three drag queens in tow. (The tranvestite part's accurate, but you chatted them up at a chichi he/she book party for a new makeup guide.) You don't give a damn about what others think; they can whisper behind your back, so long as they get the facts straight.

You may embellish occasionally for effect, but your life isn't fiction. You really *were* the first person in town to heli-ski in Antarctica. Your imagination and curiosity know no bounds; there's always something of the caged beast about you. The principle of independent thought and action impels you to do things your way, even if you know it's not the right way.

For all your bluster and bravado, you're unstinting with your time and money, especially if it means fun for all involved! You make friends wherever you go, and allow plenty of people to impose on your good nature. And you certainly don't put on airs. Sure, you enjoy a fancy-schmancy affair, but you'd end up at the Hell's Angel bar shooting a few games of pool afterward. Even if you became one of the fat cats, there'll always be a streak of alley cat, tomming about, everyone enjoying your tomfoolery entertaining.

Love, Sex, and Marriage

Insatiable and incorrigible, you'll sow plenty of wild oats (the tastiest kind!) in your youth. Your love life makes *Melrose Place* seem tamer than a dialogue between Saint Francis of Assisi and his birds. Actually, you need taming, though needless to say, you don't respond well to a whip and cage. Your lover(s) had better not be shy. We're talking major PDAs here; the sloppier the kiss in that five-star restaurant, the better. And in private, fuhgeddaboudit! You want love-making with wild abandon. You require constant stimulation and inventiveness, if not variety, in your lovemaking. The words you most fear having to say are "The passion just isn't there anymore."

So why are so many people willing to play a supporting role? Because life with a happy Leo Five is Rachmaninoff and roses, Handel and candlelight, a constant whirl of elegant parties followed by playfully amorous chases in the boudoir. Not to mention the fact that you simply couldn't attend the audience with the Dalai Lama without them.

Money and Career

You aim straight for the public eye. Whatever you do, it has to be on a grand scale. No way could you slave day after day on the same project in the same office. How dreary! Discussing the latest *X-Files* at the water cooler or on the Net isn't enough for you. You need to be bizarre and imaginative yourself. Free-lancing is your number-one solution. Since you require an audience, something that places you on the World Wide Web is primo, since you can satisfy your curiosity about other people and places. Performing? But of course! Just so the manager understands that you *have* to trash the hotel suite and entertain hookers; you don't *want* to, but you have your nutso reputation to live up—or down—to. Besides, as lewd and lascivious as you can admittedly get, you were only trying to straighten the gal's priorities out, not her finances. But you'd never let *A Current Affair* hear that side of the story. You have that reputation to protect, you rascal. And that silly green stuff? As long as you can shout, "Drinks on me!" every so often, what do you care?

The ♌5 Potential

You're a hell-raiser, no doubt about it, but you're here to loosen people up: to hell with convention and conformity! You live your life the way you please, which encourages others to break out of the doldrums and entertain a fantasy or two. Part of that wild streak is just for the tabloids, of course, but you genuinely believe that the party animal in all of us needs to break free of the zoo of dull daily life. Few people learn of your good works, because of that bad boy/girl rep you assiduously cultivate, but then for a Leo, shucks, you're actually pretty darned modest.

FAMOUS LEO FIVES

Gillian Anderson	8/9/1968	Sean Penn	8/17/1960
Jacqueline Susann	8/20/1921	Steve Martin	8/14/1945
Alex Haley	8/11/1921	Jill St. John	8/19/1940

♌ • 6
Leo Six
"The Humane Humorist"

♌ +	6 +	♌ -	6 -
Loving	*Home-loving*	*Vengeful*	*Jealous*
Faithful	*Protective*	*Domineering*	*Overprotective*
Magnanimous	*Responsible*	*Overbearing*	*Self-righteous*
Giving	*Loyal*		

Like all lions, even Leo Sixes will preen and primp in any mirror they pass, but the reflection isn't complete without a loved one and brood of kids: you display your pride with pride. You radiate a competent warmth, burning with the kind of steady blaze that both lights and heats whatever room you're in. You're an incredibly dynamic character, a walking book on seduction techniques without even trying. You have no idea how *tempting* you are as either an alliance or a dalliance; you could easily fall prey to misunderstood mates in need of affection. But you have morals, not to mention more nobility than a pride of lions and Burke's peerage put together.

You love without bounds; you're a fantastic catch because you have a healthy but not inflated ego. And you're oh so nice, kittenish, never catty. But that doesn't mean you're a pushover. Far from it! You always back up your convictions with more than your intimidating roar. Especially where love, family, and friends are concerned, your claws can be deadly. Ever seen a lioness defending her cubs? The interloper is not a pretty sight when she's finished.

But you're really just a big pussycat at heart. You love to see people happy. You're hysterical, making snide observations out of the corner of your mouth that leave your friends doubled over in riotous laughter. You're rarely downright cruel, but you do delight in puncturing posturing and pretension. Your imitations are absolutely devastating. Otherwise, your humor is usually so subtle that the targets of your derision may not even realize they're being mocked. If they do, you're immediately apologetic and solicitous, flashing that big, toothy grin. It probably hurts you more than them, because you'll remember it blushingly the next time you meet.

Love, Sex, and Marriage

If someone sets your heart racing and our blood pounding, you might race into commitment without thinking it out first; you're so eager, so dashing, so willing. Then you discover your partner didn't attend Princeton, and indeed, dropped out of high school. Even then you admire his or her smarts and street savvy. But you often fall for people who aren't your equals, because you want to hug, teach, and protect.

You voice surprisingly strong opinions at home and may run it more rigidly that your spouse would imagine, from those carefree dating days. You're a fine parent, scrupulously instructing your cubs in the laws of the jungle. As much as you'd like them to remain in the den forever, you know they have their own battles to fight and you want to prepare them for the inevitable conflicts. You're indulgent, yet if the kids break the rules, you don't hesitate to put down your paw.

Like all Leos, you want to come to someone's emotional rescue. You're drawn to people who need a strong shoulder and steadying hand. That element of compulsive generosity is present in all your relationships. Your healthy ego demands that you have an equal, independent partner with a career you can be proud of. You don't want someone beneath you or underfoot, but on some level they must be utterly dependent on you.

MONEY AND CAREER

You're a natural mimic and impressionist. The sheer range of your comic skills is probably unequaled: you can do slapstick, drawing-room banter, and imitations with equal aplomb. Naturally you gravitate toward acting, yet your inquiring mind and fascination with every detail of the creative process mean you'll probably segue into writing, producing, and/or directing as well. Then, just because you like to feed, entertain, and schmooze after hours, you open a restaurant or bar that immediately becomes the hottest watering hole in town or you might open a health club where people can sweat out those toxins and improve their looks. All these traits serve you well in business. You charm people at tedious cocktail parties, oversee every detail of a project and keep things—and co-workers—humming, and stroke the potential client perfectly over a dinner so drawn-out you'd like to strangle this jerk who's keeping you from rolling around with the kids.

The ♌6 Potential

You're cast in the heroic mold. You're here to protect and provide. Your tools are a strong shoulder, balanced perspective, trenchant mind, noble bearing, and a refusal to take things too seriously even when all looks bleak. These traits virtually ensure that you'll enjoy more than the "fifteen mintues of fame" promised by fellow Leo Six Andy Warhol. And if not, that's okay, too, as long as you have the respect of your comrades.

FAMOUS LEO SIXES

Robert De Niro	*8/17/1943*	*Christian Slater*	*8/18/1969*
Dorothy Parker	*8/22/1893*	*Kathie Lee Gifford*	*8/16/1953*
Linda Ellerbee	*8/15/1945*	*Ray Bradbury*	*8/22/1920*

♌ • 7
Leo Seven
"The Freethinking Trailblazer"

♌ +	7 +	♌ −	7 −
Aristocratic	*Reforming*	*Standoffish*	*Aloof*
Alluring	*Erudite*	*Arrogant*	*Repressed*
Gallant	*Dignified*	*Demanding*	*Inconsiderate*
High-minded	*Articulate*		

Leo Sevens flaunt an impressive but rather tangled mane indeed. You can be a series of apparent contradictions, even to yourself. You're just as enamored of mirrors as any other Leo, but you're haunted by what lies behind the dazzling reflection. You have a touch of leonine hauteur yet a becoming modesty that masks your genuine achievements. You never trumpet your accomplishments even if you feel you've mastered the subject. As a kid you hid your smarts behind a dumb jock(ette) facade, snuck off after lacrosse practice, sequestered yourself in the tree house you built yourself from recycled aluminum cans and discarded two-by-fours, and devoured everything from Waugh to Wittgenstein.

Despite a ravening curiosity about human nature, your initial research can be faulty. Sevens can have a blind spot about themselves. The Leo pride often exacerbates the Seven assumption of immediate knowledge. You soon learn that your first impressions aren't always as right as you'd like to think. You're surprisingly withdrawn for a Leo, but gradually become more extroverted as you mature. You'll never feel you've learned enough, of course. You recognized one of the eternal paradoxes of human existence from a shockingly young age: that the more you know, the more you know there is to know. At eleven, watching a shooting star, you contemplated the origin of the universe, and probably even called it a conundrum. If gaseous particles combined to form clouds, as posited by the Big Bang theory, how were they created in the first place? And even if they rose from a vacuum, isn't a vacuum something? After all, we have a word for it. Which, of course, left you to ponder the concept of blind faith. . . .

Love, Sex, and Marriage

Leo makes you ardent, and Seven choosy. Part of you can't make up your mind what you're really looking for in the ideal partner. It's like buying the right car. You know you want something sleek and sporty that bespeaks both status and class, so you'll go for the Jaguar, then realize the Ferrari's more your speed. Your tremendous need for freedom clashes with an equally potent need for love and terror of being alone. You come on very strong, then back off just as suddenly. A smart prospect won't appear too available, as that can make you lose interest. Your passion and longing get you into positions you must disentangle yourself from, making promises you'd rather not keep. Take it slowly, even when you get that "fated to be mated" feel. You'd counsel your friends there's no such thing as discovering your soul mate after one bottle of wine. Trust your psychic ability— except when it comes to your own feelings. You scare yourself off by thinking soul mate and intimacy too quickly.

Learn compromise, and remember that after the romantic glow comes the doubting period: is this really the person I want to spend my life with? This period is just as unrealistic as initial infatuation. It, too, will fade, as you allow greater intimacy into your life.

Money and Career

Just as with romance, your career places you in a quandary. There are so many avenues you'd like to follow. If you could, you'd become a professional student. Your gravity about learning suits you for the groves of academe; besides, you'd look fetching in a cap and gown. Once you've decided upon a course of action, you'll pursue it single-mindedly. Since you're big on understanding others' motives (though your own can remain a mystery), you make a sensational therapist or social worker, in whom compassion and reason blend nicely. You have enormous appeal as an actor, sporting either a sexy swagger or a gift for verbal and physical comedy. Attuned to universal harmonies, you can be a composer or musician of tremendous depth. Computer development or selling new technologies are also possibilities. Any job must give you the opportunity to learn something new every day or you'll become easily bored.

The ♌7 Potential

You've always been hard on yourself and never take the easy way out. When you think about it, that's pretty darned praiseworthy! You're a deserving role model, eternally anxious to learn from experience and books alike, then use your discoveries to benefit others in some way. Don't let your pride and analytical bent deter you from attacking life more aggressively. You are a true scholar; since you're usually mighty attractive and personable, your example might just lower the dropout rate!

FAMOUS LEO SEVENS

Antonio Banderas	8/10/1960	Lucille Ball	8/6/1910
Matthew Perry	8/19/1969	Bella Abzug	7/24/1920
Bill Bradley	7/28/1943	Myrna Loy	8/2/1905

♌ • 8
Leo Eight
"The Entertaining Entrepreneur"

♌ +	8 +	♌ -	8 -
Self-confident	Authoritative	Self-involved	Overpowering
Commanding	Insightful	Intolerant	Bossy
Competitive	Capable	Intractable	Workaholic
Direct	Sensuous		

A Leo Eight could coax anyone out of his or her portfolio and into something more comfortable. You have a majestic presence that automatically finds people kneeling at your feet awaiting your next command. You're extroverted and cocksure, with a daunting intellect. Even the resonant deejay timbre of your voice is imposing. Friends, family, business associates, even total strangers probably leave breathy messages on your answering machine sighing that you belong on the radio. And you'll always sound like you know what you're talking about even when you don't.

You have a severe, abstract sense of justice, and can be easily offended. You believe in live and let live, yet hold yourself to a rather rigid code of behavior; your own transgressions don't escape your scrutiny. You forgive readily but forget the forgetting part. You're the first to admit you have flaws and problems, but you resent anyone who dares expose them; of course, you often attract equally powerful, stubborn people into your life.

You're a scrapper with very definite ideas, and anyone who wants to capture your attention must appear to let you run the show. You're a lion in a cage, baring your incisors at any tamer daring to brandish his or whip. Youi thrive on competition and sexy, saber-rattling office power plays. You can be as deadly as a Borgia skulking behind the arras, dagger barely sheathed, if someone crosses you. When it comes to getting even, patience can be counted among your virtues, but if others demonstrate loyalty, you'll see them through any crisis, even as you long to call your pal a prize idiot for not seeing what was coming.

Love, Sex, and Marriage

With you, Cupid's arrow has the deadly accuracy of a stealth bomb, and you pursue the object of your attentions with SWAT-team efficiency. But it's difficult for you to think in romantic terms unless everything else in your life is running smoothly. You brood over an unsettled job situation, or if your sublet is running out in eight months and you haven't found a replacement. Your life is a running soap opera, and love is no exception.

Sometimes your pride and busy schedule get in the way of a promising romance. You're admirably straightforward: you enjoy spending time together, great. All you ask is that they be as punctilious as you. If they say they'll call, they should call. If they say let's have dinner next week, just name the day. Is that such a big deal? It is so unreasonable? Honest soul that you are, you *always* call when you say you will, no matter how hectic things are. When others don't follow through on their word, of course you're upset. But you're even angrier on an abstract level: it's simple courtesy. Don't they understand that you have a busy schedule, time's money, and with your appointment book filling up, you're just showing interest by penciling them in? It's not as if you're asking to move in after the third date!

Money and Career

You could never be a drudge and drone, buzzing around another's hive: you're quick to spot the flaws in authority figures and consequently find them hard to respect. If you're an actor, you'll become your own producer; if an athlete, you'll want to coach, or better yet, become the team's general manager. You're an astute judge of talent, stealing future stars in trades. Whatever your business, you're a hard-as-nails negotiator with a disarmingly soft touch. Your natural milieu is the penthouse boardroom. You end up being promoted so regularly that even the CEO fears your progress; but the company can't afford to lose you, and you emerge as the anointed successor. You may just start your own business at home in your spare time, perhaps public relations, proposal writing, market research, or demographic surveys. It'll take off, and so will you from your regular day job. Law interests you most among the traditional professions, since you love to argue and win any debate, followed by accounting; but the former contains too many loopholes, while the latter involves counting someone else's money. Well, maybe Supreme Court judge; you cut a dramatic figure in black. Just curb your urge to splurge, as your bank account will likely go through dizzying loop-the-loops.

The ♌8 Potential

You have enough drive to win the Indy 500 in a beaten-up Edsel. You may appear stern and authoritarian, yet underneath you're quite tame. You just like the perks of power and control, which is fine, but don't become so forbidding you lose all sense of human contact. Your life story and message to others is "How to Succeed in Business by Really Trying." Frankly, it comes easily to you, but you wouldn't respect anyone, least of all yourself, who didn't at least try to overachieve. Use your keen perspective of trends to lead others in the new millennium.

FAMOUS LEO EIGHTS

Martha Stewart	8/3/1941	George Bernard Shaw	7/26/1856
Annie Oakley	8/13/1859	Neil Armstrong	8/5/1930
Stanley Kubrick	7/26/1928	Sandra Bullock	7/26/1964

♌ • 9
Leo Nine
"The Vivacious Ventriloquist"

♌ +	9 +	♌ -	9 -
Charismatic	*Charitable*	*Bombastic*	*Chameleonesque*
Chivalrous	*Outgoing*	*Egotistical*	*Careless*
Dramatic	*Magnetic*	*Extravagant*	*Possessive*
Enthusiastic	*Daring*		

Leo Nines have a genius for putting words in other people's mouths. If you were a kid right now, you'd scheme how to coax the parents into letting you stay up to watch NBC's "Must See TV" block. "Gee, Pop, I really want to be a doctor, and *ER* is so REAL," you plead with saucer eyes. Is the answer ever in doubt? You're a real card, in fact an ace. You love to entertain, feeling it's an almost divine mission. In a sense, your concept of spirituality is that lifting people's spirits is the most uplifting thing you can do.

You'll be in the public eye, and ensure that the audience has 20/20 vision. Nine softens Leo's vanity; you still toss your mane, but it's silken, and temper your roar to a purr. You're magnanimous and caring in the extreme. You have a roaring ego, yet you're not so much selfish as self-important. You're that rare visionary who isn't blinded by the grandeur of his or her ideas, ignoring the real people. You realize that when it comes to human relations Copernicus was wrong: the earth doesn't revolve around the Leo Nine sun. Still, your showmanship compels you to do everything in a big way, and you're not afraid to flop. You're so comfortable basking in the glow of the spotlight that you see spots if anyone tries to train it elsewhere. You're the star attraction and all the world *is* a stage, after all!

Boy, do you have the gift of gab and a gift for, uh, embellishment. Everything that happens to you is larger-than-life. Namby-pamby words like nice, pleasant, and okay simply don't exist in your vocabulary. It's a superlative or nothing. That's not a mountain you made out of the molehill, it's Everest, K2, and Annapurna heaped atop one another. The whole world is colored by your dynamism. Objectivity may not be your strong suit, but your sincerity, mettle, and passion carry the day. You have almost childlike faith in your ability, if not downright superiority to get the job done, by swaying opinion if necessary.

Love, Sex, and Marriage

Despite the hordes clamoring for your precious attention and time, you know how to keep a relationship purring. But your mate had better understand that when you're "on," he or she mustn't upstage you. You're generous with your time toward everyone; whoever coined the phrase "I'll be there in spirit" was likely a Leo Nine. When you're angry or feel betrayed you don't pussyfoot about, yet beneath that stirring roar you always remain a pussycat at heart.

You can be a tad skittish at first; you need the stimulation, the thrill of the chase. If your quarry proves elusive, he or she might just win your heart. But if a potential amour threatens your independence, you toss your mane and majestically leave the room. Once you've mated you're faithful, though you have not so much a wandering eye as a farsighted, all-encompassing, omniscient one. You're aware of your quite devastating effect on others and don't lack for opportunities to stray. You're usually incredibly good-looking, with a striking mane and clear bright eyes. Despite your eternal youthfulness, you're surprisingly concerned about aging. Every sag, bump, and wrinkle heightens your appeal because they add character, but remind you how transitory mere physical beauty is. If you ever cheat, it's a one-time deal to confirm your attractiveness. Needless to say, you dote on being served, and being the center of attention. As long as your mate is willing to cater to your every whim (however kinky), you're happy.

Money and Career

Obviously Leos Nines are consummate performers. You like people feeding you lines and feeding your ego. If you can't be in the spotlight, you adore manipulating the action behind the scenes—after all, the director is the hub of the entire production. Whatever you do, it's bound to command attention in your field because it will be original, intellectually stimulating, and heartfelt. You're accustomed to getting your way and don't function well in subservient roles, which is why the corporate life isn't really for you. You can tap into your spiritual side and gain more universal understanding of humanity and its place in the grand scheme of things. Pity philosophy doesn't pay well or even fill the lecture halls. Needless to say, you'll lavish gifts on loved ones and, if you can, donate to numerous charities and endow scholarships to the amount of a Third World nation's GNP.

The ♌9 Potential

You embody seductiveness, on the physical, intellectual, and spiritual levels. It's a heady, heavy responsibility. You can't afford to believe your phenomenal press, admittedly unlikely, since you're surprisingly humble about your considerable talents. You understand that they're at the service of others for their education and edification. You feel you're part of a campaign to save the planet from itself; indeed, you're an enthusiastic environmentalist who wants to leave a legacy of clean air and clear heads to future generations.

FAMOUS LEO NINES

Robert Redford	*8/18/1936*	*Carl Jung*	*7/26/1875*
Dustin Hoffman	*8/8/1937*	*Whitney Houston*	*8/9/1963*
Julia Child	*8/15/1912*	*Jada Pinkett*	*8/18/1971*

VIRGO

●

♍ • 1
Virgo One
"The Gymnastic Genius"

♍+	1+	♍-	1-
Organized	*Inventive*	*Petty*	*Cynical*
Industrious	*Straightforward*	*Fastidious*	*Contrary*
Bright	*Focused*	*Hypercritical*	*Inflexible*
Health-conscious	*Self-willed*		

Virgo One is the health-nut, good-for-you-granola type. Physically, within three months of bearing triplets you could walk down a runway, while mentally you never say die: you're back in the saddle, whether thrown by your horse or thrown for a loop by your business partner. Male or female, you embody the phrase "bombshell with a brain."

Of course, your obsession with fitness could put you on a treadmill. By concentrating on the outer shell, you send a message to others—and subtly, to yourself—that the real you underneath isn't worth displaying. Will you feel better and live longer thanks to your sundry regimens? Absolutely! Just don't allow the low body fat/high muscle percentage to become a suit of armor that denies people entrance.

Anyway, your emotional tough shell is really just an act, protecting your unexpected, endearing vulnerability. You firmly believe that people should help themselves first. But when push comes to shove (and it often does), you'll dive into that polluted river without hesitation to save a drowning man or give that homeless Vietnam vet at the ATM everything in your pockets save your last bus token. You're an incorrigible softie and are terrified others will take advantage if they find out.

Whatever your background, you exude flair, style, and grace, to the manor born even if that silver spoon was really tin and tarnished to boot. You possess the drive and determination to make yourself the best you can possibly be. Many Virgo Ones have the uncanny ability to reinvent themselves in new surroundings. You're the original ugly duckling that turned into a swan, not just through genetics but application.

Love, Sex, and Marriage

Any potential mate must meet your exacting standards: the perfect combo of body and brains. You work at your relationship as you work out at the gym; as a couple, you and your significant other must be toned, fit, and appropriate for display, and not just physically. You must not only look right but seem right, functioning as a perfect unit. You want someone as exacting, logical, intelligent, innovative, and curious as you. If there's any trouble in paradise, you'd rarely admit it, even to your best friend.

You may appear reserved in public, but behind closed and double-locked doors you're a hellion, with a robust sexual appetite. You can surprise your partners with how verbal you are during the act, prodding them on, never hesitating to encourage them when you like what they're doing. You need someone whose lustiness matches your own, both in bed and in life. They should be as avid for knowledge as you, their stores of information complementing and enhancing your own, ready to chime in with the answer if you don't know it.

Money and Career

You're a force of nature in the workplace, resourceful and resilient. You know exactly what you want to accomplish before you confide your plans; you're also flexible and sufficiently quick on your feet to adapt to the prevailing winds. You take warranted pride in the ideas you generate, and prefer to supervise projects you've initiated directly. Fitness guru, trainer, athlete, and dancer are among your career opportunities in the physical sphere. Your searching intellect is ideal for publishing, whether editorial or sales; you could also create beauty or exercise books and videos, then hawk them on an infomercial. In fact, advertising isn't a bad idea either. You'd certainly make a splendid spokesperson for any product, including yourself. You are driven to be the best at whatever you do.

You also want to enjoy the best life has to offer. Your work and home environments reflect you: trim, neat, organized, and quietly elegant. You favor clean lines, open space, and lots of light, otherwise you feel cramped and hemmed in. Clutter, whether on your desk or in a closet, offends you, just as it does in your relationships. When it comes to personal expenditures, you buy all the latest home gym gadgets and sign up for grueling spa or adventure vacations.

The ♍1 Potential

You have a fine blend of vigorous body and rigorous mind. You enjoy being a role model, fulfilling your high ideal of service. You're a thorough perfectionist; although people inevitably look up to you, you *are* allowed to show a chink in the armor. Never doubt that others will appreciate the real you. In fact, realizing that nobody is perfect—not even you!—will spur them on to greater achievement. Always remember to show your human face and you can enable yourself as well as others to reach any goal.

FAMOUS VIRGO ONES

Sophia Loren	9/20/1934	Sean Connery	8/25/1930
Raquel Welch	9/5/1940	David Copperfield	9/16/1956
Jimmy Connors	9/2/1952	Queen Elizabeth I	9/7/1533

♍ • 2
Virgo Two
"The Constructive Consultant"

♍+	2+	♍-	2-
Decorous	Sincere	Insecure	Shy
Thoughtful	Conscientious	Finicky	Argumentative
Concerned	Gracious	Negative	Self-conscious
Service- oriented	Helpful		

Ever since you learned to write, you've kept a journal, precisely recording your thoughts, impressions, observations, feelings, and longings. Even when you're seventy-five, you know exactly where those old diaries are, and can recall a special entry in an instant. When you finally allow your grandkids a peek, they're amazed by the rich fantasy life you confided to your secret friend. Because you don't share your innermost thoughts readily, many people may dismiss your world as drab and monochrome. But you know it isn't. You're aware that nothing is black and white, but rather colored in a pleasing palette of grays, from pearl to charcoal, the classic cloud with a silver lining backlit by the sun and a rainbow just beginning to form.

You rarely had the chance to realize those dreams of being the first person to walk on Mars or winning the golf Grand Slam because you recognized your obligations in the real world. Your homework done on time, you made yourself available to tutor other students. Not quite popular enough to be elected class president, you were probably grateful; you knew the job was a figurehead and you'd have more responsibility and meaningful work as class secretary or treasurer. That pattern persists into a quiet, orderly adulthood. The neighborhood usually comes to you with their problems, asking you to mediate a marital crisis, reason Kenny out of the attic, and figure out why the lawn mower went bust.

Yet for all that, you feel like an underachiever, rarely giving yourself the credit you deserve. The people you let into your life are aware of your sterling qualities; you're so self-effacing you underestimate your abilities, fretting and second-guessing yourself constantly, reliving every moment of the day in vivid Technicolor because you're so hard on yourself.

Love, Sex, and Marriage

Your independence is really a front; you're wary of being hurt, fearful of being trapped in an unsatisfactory relationship. You have a delicate, fragile temperament, although you don't show it. Your image of yourself is utterly false: you imagine you're abrupt, halting, coarse, and vulgar (everything abhor in others). You're overly sensitive in romantic matters, a loveaholic: one hug too many, a million not enough. You crave a happy relationship, but recoil from the heartache and disorder finding one often entails. You tell yourself you'd much rather muck about in your garden than get all hot and bothered. Yet you can't exist without a partner, so you persevere.

A highly strung, exquisitely vibrating Stradivarius, you need someone low-maintenance to counterbalance your low self-esteem. Though you're not precisely prudish or inhibited, your fantasies sometimes embarrass you. A loving partner with just the right teasing touch can unlock a wonderful sentimental and imaginative streak in the bedroom by encouraging you to whisper your deepest desires. When you can check off more qualities on the good side of your plus/minus list of a prospective mate's attributes, you take the plunge gratefully. It's important for you to keep up appearances; even if your relationship shows more cracks than the San Andreas fault, you'll cheerfully plaster them up.

Money and Career

Your mission is to be the support network, the quiet glue that holds everything and everyone together. You make a winning arbitrator of any dispute. Alternative medicine is another strong lure; you could be a healing homeopath, chiropractor, or reflexologist. No stranger to insecurity yourself, you can help people overcome their fears through inspirational music and art. You can coach others, whether on a sports team or the lecture circuit, coaxing them to perform to their peak capabilities. An astute statistician, you could analyze demographic trends. And you're a whiz when it comes to trimming the fat from a payroll or schedule.

The ♍2 Potential

Don't play it safe and never settle for less than you know deep down inside you can attain. Relax and realize you deserve to reap the benefits of your 110 percent effort. Remember self-esteem is crucial; the key to loving and being loved is accepting ourselves, warts and all. Trust others to appreciate your astonishing gift for empathy and compromise. You're meant to scale the highest mountain you can, then encourage others to realize their own potential.

FAMOUS VIRGO TWOS

Ben Bradlee	8/26/1921	J.P. Morgan	9/7/1867
Jose Feliciano	9/10/1945	Tim Burton	8/25/1958
Joan Jett	9/22/1960	Nancy Travis	9/21/1961

♍ • 3
Virgo Three
"The Juggling Wizard"

♍+	3+	♍-	3-
Practical	Optimistic	Critical	Boastful
Meticulous	Sociable	Persnickety	Extravagant
Logical	Artistic	Judgmental	Unstable
Idealistic	Self-expressive		

Here's a workaholic perfectionist joined at the hip to a party animal with artistic aspirations! Virgo is disciplined and thinks in linear terms. Three bubbles over with so many ideas you might appear scatterbrained. But that imaginative mind set and teasing Three personality help Virgo laugh at itself and loosen up a bit. Virgo helps ground those flights of fancy, giving form and focus to your creative side. Your combination of precision and inspiration makes you about as maddeningly perfect as you've always dreamed of being. In other words, you're a Mr. Spock who loves to flirt.

Your typical day? Take a deep breath and . . . stay at the office until 1:00 A.M. Thursday, shop at the twenty-four-hour supermarket, chop the crudités, grab a few hours sleep, buy wine during Friday lunch hour, dash home at five, dust, take a quick bubble bath, then welcome guests to your weekly salon where seers mingle with CEOs, and sculptors with scalpers—unobtrusively emptying the ashtrays whenever you get the chance.

You retain an appealing eternal youthfulness. Underneath that angelic exterior lurks a sly devil: the type who cracked rude Freudian jokes in the back of psych class, then smiled demurely when teach whirled around. But just because you seem friendly and outgoing doesn't mean you're indiscriminate. Your natural curiosity and mental agility require a varied social circle; you derive sneaky pleasure from throwing an oddball lot together just to see what happens. Your closest associates needn't be intellectual snobs or even particularly eloquent, but each must offer something unique and stimulating.

That fussiness and pursuit of excellence apply equally to you. Virgo Threes are rather vain; it's important for you to dress neatly but stylishly, and remain in fighting trim. Everything in your life, from your neatly ordered desk to your carefully chosen comrades, is a reflection of you and your inevitably impeccable taste.

Love, Sex, and Marriage

While not exactly cuddly, you *are* surprisingly playful—not so much physically as verbally. Good dialogue turns you on: a Tracy/Hepburn battle of the sexes. Though Virgos are ironically sensitive to criticism, that jolly Three influence allows you to roll with the punches and puns. You're a delightfully sophisticated, intellectual flirt.

Many Virgos marry late in general; add that capricious Three influence and you could wind up a special guest on

The Dating Game's fiftieth anniversary (okay, singles night on *Book Chat*). When you finally run into someone who meets your exacting standards, you can make a fool of yourself, sending dried fruit baskets daily, or pithy love poems in all-too-free verse. The sight of you swooning is amusing enough to attract your prey, who, of course, replies that he or she is allergic to sun-dried apricots. The grand romance beings. . . .

You're essentially faithful when you have an easygoing, intelligent mate. That doesn't rule out the occasional fantasy, but it remains in the head. If anything, you're likely to take a very specific image (postition thirty-four in the Kama Sutra, adding a dollop of whipped cream), substituting your partner for that attractive stranger on the 7:02 train.

Money and Career

That fleet-thinking Three and meticulous Virgo produce a brilliant networker and creative problem solver, probably not above flirting to get that John Hancock. You also make extraordinary editors, genuinely wanting to improve your writers' work while respecting their voices. Your best moneymaking opportunities come through friends, who often recommend you for projects; your air of efficiency and winning charm make you sparkle in interviews and contribute people-managing skills.

Money is a dichotomy. Virgos are rather frugal; Threes are rather spendthrift. You'll literally argue both sides of a purchase: practical versus pretty. The Dapper Dan(ielle) is drawn to that exquisite dress or tie. It's more expensive than it should be and you really don't need it. BUT it'll improve your mood and make a good impression at that party or interview. Rather than give in to temptation every time, you'll splurge once or even launch into a shopping spree, then go on an austerity program, economizing beyond all reason.

The ♍3 Potential

A facile mind, reserved charm, Joe or Jane College appearance, dry–as–Dom Perignon wit. You're meant to network—

not in the crass commerical sense, but rather in bringing people of different cultures and interests together. You resist being categorized, so resist your temptation to compart*mentali*ze people. Accept, even embrace, others for who they are, warts and all; curb the urge to give everyone an instant makeover. Whatever your profession, you're the publisher and editor in chief of life's magazine, providing seductive layout, copy, and ads to prevent others from becoming too stale or staid.

FAMOUS VIRGO THREES

Michael Keaton	9/5/1951	*Johann von Goethe*	*8/28/1749*
Ted Williams	8/30/1918	*Cameron Diaz*	*8/30/1972*
Zoe Caldwell	9/14/1933	*Mrs. (Debbie) Fields*	*9/18/1956*

♍ • 4
Virgo Four
"The Tactical Technician"

♍+	4+	♍-	4-
Pragmatic	*Methodical*	*Self-effacing*	*Unimaginative*
Discriminating	*Organized*	*Hypochondriacal*	*Undemonstrative*
Painstaking	*Practical*	*Mechanical*	*Overcommitted*
Modest	*Principled*		

You're the Fix-It and Go To guy or gal, the actual and spiritual equivalent of the technical support to everyone in your orbit. You relish the role of bookkeeper, repairperson, and troubleshooter. Virgo Fours have always flourished in situations that most people would consider monotonous: playing scales endlessly to the predictable rhythm of a metronome, tossing five hundred straight foul shots in basketball practice, bellying up to the barre until you get the *en pointe.* As far as you're concerned, practice really does make perfect.

You're keenly aware that time is a precious commodity. Whether taking the SATs in high school or racing to meet the deadline for a new ad compaign, you hear every last tick and tock with excruciating clarity. No wonder small talk makes you nervous: isn't there something more constructive we could be doing? you muse. But you're a wonderful, reasonable listener. You calmly assess the situation and often find an escape hatch your friend never saw. Cautious and conservative by nature, you have a cleverly disguised risk-taking side, which may come out in that unusual solution to a problem or a hair-raising motorcycle ride at 3:00 A.M.

Your precise, dutiful nature often makes you feel like the little Dutch boy with his finger in the dyke staving off certain catastrophe. Spending so much time solving everyone else's problems, you sometimes worry that your own pet projects are dammed up or doomed to failure. Hence, for all your ain't I a good egg attitude, you turn down the occasional demand on your time and refuse to put all your eggs in one basket. Like the Energizer Bunny, you just keep going, never noticing your own disappointments, even as you help others manage theirs.

Love, Sex, and Marriage

You appear so conventional that you could turn off partners who don't realize the potential for untidy emotions lurking beneath your meticulous, ordered surface. Though you rarely mention it, you'd like your partner to acknowledge the sundry little things you do: paying the bills on time, arranging the car pool for school (and doing more than your share of the driving when the other parents beg off), coaching Little League, scrubbing the bathroom; the list goes on and on.

You understand that planting the seeds of love isn't enough: you must tend them carefully before they bloom. But you're not as good at interpreting the little signals of restlessness and boredom; a little spontaneity will keep your love life humming and your partner continually challenged. On the plus side, you have a regular, steady libido, with a healthy attitude toward sex as good old-fashioned exercise. You go at it with gymnastic fluidity and the stamina of a hockey player.

Money and Career

You're skilled at manual labor, dexterous with brushstroke and keystroke, with admirable hand-eye coordination. This makes you an excellent computer technician or software developer, handy person, dressmaker, contractor, draftsperson, artisan—anything utilizing tools. Though creativity isn't your strongest suit, your artistic pursuits are characterized by fine detail work. You're also a reliable overseer of others. You do something over and over again until you get it right, and expect the same of your employees and co-workers. You're usually content to remain at middle-level management. While those above and below may slip on the corporate ladder, you're almost never fired since you produce and persist in your unassuming way.

The original perfectionist, there's always some unfinished business to attend to. This attitude endears you to your superiors, if not your family. Then again, your loved ones know they'll never want for anything; your diligence insures there will always be money in the bank and food—nothing too fatty, of course—in the fridge.

The ♍4 Potential

In a world where most people are never content with what they have, you remind people to be grateful for the simple things and never take anything for granted. You can help them see that progress is often attained gradually, in small increments. Your discipline and powers of discrimination can genuinely help others improve themselves. Relax the tendency to criticize others, not to mention yourself, and you'll get the point across with your fundamental intelligence and sincerity. Then you truly can make the world a better place—and even receive some recognition in the bargain.

FAMOUS VIRGO FOURS

Keanu Reeves	*9/2/1964*	*Regis Philbin*	*8/25/1933*
Itzhak Perlman	*8/31/1945*	*Edgar Rice Burroughs*	*9/1/1875*
Joseph Kennedy	*9/6/1888*	*Grandma Moses*	*9/7/1860*
Arnold Palmer	*9/10/1929*	*Sid Caesar*	*9/8/1922*

Alan Jay Lerner   *8/31/1918*   *Frankie Avalon*   *9/18/1939*
Anne Bancroft   *9/17/1931*   *James Fenimore*   *9/15/1789*
                                       Cooper

♍ • 5
Virgo Five
"The Champion Cheerleader"

♍+	5+	♍-	5-
Perceptive	*Versatile*	*High-strung*	*Impatient*
Eloquent	*Active*	*Compulsive*	*Sharp-tongued*
Cultivated	*Quick-witted*	*Mercurial*	*Reckless*
Erudite	*Energetic*		

Virgo Fives are the all-American boys and girls next door who ran away for the day to the big city in search of adventure at the ripe old age of twelve. Sure, you might have employed a little deception to earn the bus fare. That aw-shucks, gosh-and-golly demeanor opened plenty of doors when you were collecting money for UNICEF; were you to blame if your benefactors didn't notice the box was just a sawed-off milk carton with a photo cut and pasted from an ad for Save the Children? Of course, back home safely, your highly ethical nature asserts itself (you could define super-ego even then!), and to atone you contribute your next month's allowance to those needy children. Anyway, you were a kid with a deserving cause: you had an unquench-able thirst for experience! You didn't have to go far to find it, and still don't. You don't look for trouble, mind you, but trouble has an odd habit of seeking you out, just to chal-lenge you and spur you to greater heights.

It's not that you have a criminal mind; far from it. But when you're good, you're very, very good, and when you're bad, you get away with murder. It's that sweet appearance; even when you get caught you're so irresistible with a com-back that people relent, collapsing in laughter. Face it, you're as cute and funny as a chimp with hiccups. Your parents learned fast that grounding you had no effect; you climbed nimbly out the window and shimmied down the drainpipe to freedom.

The searching nature of the Five combines with your exacting Virgo side to create a formidable, searchlight intellect. You illuminate the dark corners of human behavior, including your own. You can help others understand what motivates or inhibits them. Five makes you a freewheeling, spirited free spirit, while Virgo protects you from running completely wild and contributes remarkable self-control. You come across as fiercely independent, trenchantly witty, and shrewdly intelligent; but you're the kind of tough cookie who crumbles at the sight of the less fortunate.

Love, Sex, and Marriage

Because you're both hot-blooded and detached, you date several people simultaneously or engage in multiple affairs. You adopt the classic rationale that since it means nothing to you, you needn't even mention your occasional indiscretions. Though most Virgos are neatniks, many can go to the opposite extreme, becoming the sloppiest pigs imaginable. This sometimes applies to sex, as well. Hence, with some Virgo Fives it's always feast or famine, filling the gap between them by first wallowing in transports of joy, then ecstasies of guilt. You're not a sex maniac, you just have a healthy appetite for touch that requires release. When you marry, you generally settle down, as long as you have a honey who can keep up on every level. Your mate will probably be as much of a handful as you are; you might find yourself playing the domestic role and liking it!

Though not a natural parent, you'll be a real friend to your kids, genuinely enjoying their company (once they've begun to string words together). Eternally curious yourself, you'll buy them a computer rather than Easy-Bake ovens and Air Nikes.

Money and Career

Five endows you with quicksilver wit and networking aplomb while Virgo provides steadiness and dedication.

You're a comic commando, whether onstage or at the office. You're a supreme motivator, joking people out of bad moods, sparking their enthusiasm. If you had the patience, you'd be a fine manager. But you're no stuffed shirt: you don't want to appear like the first herky-jerky generation of robots filing out of the office dutifully. Still, you're a surprisingly hard worker when the job intrigues you. Advertising, magazine editing, and telecommunications could keep you in one place. Your vibrant, singular humor, always based on detailed observation of human behavior, makes you a scintillating comedy writer. Sitcoms and stand-up are really your métier. You also love being on the road and on the move, so regional salesperson, travel agent, athletic coach, and performer are other appealing options.

The ♍5 Potential

A fireball of energy and enthusiasm, you have that *je ne sais quoi* appeal that leaves them shaking their heads in wonder every time. You can stimulate others to bring out their nonconformist streak as well as their tiptop performance. You exist to promote individuality in everyone. The world's a far more interesting place, isn't it, when people let their hair down? But don't be disappointed or pushy if people don't respond. After all, a stick-in-the-mud can serve as another kind of guidepost entirely.

FAMOUS VIRGO FIVES

Lily Tomlin	*9/1/1939*	*Lauren Bacall*	*9/16/1924*
Gloria Estefan	*9/1/1957*	*Tommy Lasorda*	*9/22/1927*
Alfred Knopf	*9/12/1913*	*Jeremy Irons*	*9/19/1948*

♍ • 6
Virgo Six
"The Habitual Helpmate"

♍+	6+	♍-	6-
Dutiful	*Truthful*	*Nitpicking*	*Hypersensitive*
Trustworthy	*Obliging*	*Meddling*	*Outspoken*
Honest	*Kind*	*Crabby*	*Complaining*
Respectable	*Responsible*		

There's no other word for it: Virgo Six is a nag. But you're the most ideal, lovable, perfect nag imaginable. You typify that Virgo and Six ideal of service to others; in this case, multiply service by obsession and what do you get? Fetish. It's only because you hate to see wasted opportunities and potential and, like the army, urge loved ones to "be all you can be." Of course, sometimes your criticism of others is an outward manifestation of your own deep insecurities: are you worthy of your great mission (even if it's just taking out the trash)?

You can't help being a worrywart. Pity your poor kid when he or she breaks curfew by an hour; the earnest, heartfelt lecture about phoning home so you won't call the cops can wait until breakfast. A health fanatic, you're sweetly hypochondriacal by extension, to friends and family. "I know it's just a freckle, Jane, but I wish you'd let my dermatologist take a look." "A back spasm? You shouldn't take chances, Jeff, my chiropractor performs miracles. And while I still reserve judgment on alternative medicine, I happen to have the numbers of a Rolfer, a homeopath, and a Chinese herbalist." Your friends have long since learned resistance is futile.

Yours is the Julie McCoy, *Love Boat* cruise director approach to life. Is everybody happy? Is everybody active? The spawn of Batman's Boy Wonder and the chirpiest cheerleader in high school, you see yourself as an old-fashioned Western hero(ine), coolly riding off into the sunset after you vanquished the bad guys in a blazing shootout. Even though there may not be many evil Dodge Cities to clean up, nobody's faster on the draw to help those in need.

Love, Sex, and Marriage

No one is more well intentioned than a Virgo Six in love. This can be a double-edged sword, since you have an over-inflated sense of responsibility. The lovely thing is that words like *obligation* and *duty* don't frighten you as they do many others. Feeling wanted is all well and good, but you need to be needed. In fact, someone else's neediness, preferably concealed behind a deceptively independent facade, is an aphrodisiac.

You often select partners who are stormy, flamboyant, and, well, unreliable. They expect you to articulate their repressed feelings for them. You exhaust so much energy fussing over others that you have no time to analyze your own motives and determine whether this might really be the one or just another toad.

You go into situations expecting to be hurt, which doesn't exactly create an atmosphere conducive to a thriving, developing relationship. Strive to find your equal, someone as intelligent, affectionate, and imaginative as you. Consider role-playing, in and out of bed, to work through problems, even expose a few of those slightly kinky thoughts of mild bondage. Then you're less likely to find yourself psychologically enslaved.

Money and Career

Your idealism compels you to make a difference in the world. Part of you is perfectly content taking care of your own, leading an unobtrusive life. Yet you also realize instinctively that you can't give all that love to just a few people; the world can gorge on the substantial leftovers. The market for super-hero(ine)s being somewhat limited, you become a crusader sans cape. Forming or heading charities (soup kitchen or homeless shelter perhaps), education, and medicine are possibilities. If you enjoy working with your hands, horticulture and catering will please you. The arts also beckon. Any Virgo Six performer will express the yearning underneath the exterior, allowing the audience emotional, even cathartic, release. Writers will likely be concerned with social justice, the psychology of misfits, and the future's unlimited potential. As for moola, it's only good for improving your home and contributing to your pet causes. Your donations of money as well as time will be considerable.

The ♍6 Potential

The epitome of good taste and proper grooming, the dispenser of wise counsel: you're a perfectionist in an all-too-imperfect world. But as a result you hold yourself—and the people you love—to impossibly high standards. The moral? It's a fine line between duty and responsibility and obligations and burdens. Hey, nobody ever asked you to plan this party called Life, then load the dishwasher and empty the ashtrays. You *can* ask for help, you know. (Just stop harping, for goodness sake, your mother can shampoo her own carpets.)

FAMOUS VIRGO SIXES

Michael Jackson	*8/29/1958*	*Greta Garbo*	*9/18/1905*
Stephen King	*9/21/1947*	*H.G. Wells*	*9/21/1866*
Agatha Christie	*9/15/1890*	*Twiggy*	*9/19/1949*

♍ • 7
Virgo Seven
"The Academic Aesthete"

♍+	7+	♍-	7-
Refined	*Knowledgeable*	*Pedantic*	*Detached*
Patrician	*Truth-seeking*	*Overanalytical*	*Secretive*
Orderly	*Dignified*	*Supercilious*	*Suspicious*
Self-controlled	*Scholarly*		

You live in an exquisite ivory tower, an impregnable fortress of the mind that you've painstakingly constructed since childhood. Your aloofness is your allure; people want to pierce that seemingly inscrutable, impenetrable facade. You're incredibly desirable and coolly, devastatingly sexy, which fools people into assuming that banked fires must exist within. You *do* have tremendous intensity and pent-up energy, but hide it even from yourself.

You project an air of total self-sufficiency, with your Dewey decimal library and your latest high-tech gadgetry. You're intimately acquainted with mirror-gazing; you're not vain (although you can't resist a bit of fluffing and primping), you're merely staring into and beyond yourself, hoping to uncover the most hidden aspects of your personality. This does amount to a certain kind of self-absorbed snobbishness, though you're so democratic you probably have an argument on the tip of your tongue as you read this.

You wield a sly, self-deprecating wit. When it pleases you, you can be quite charming, even lovable, and there's something so noble about the way you condescend to descend from that tower to mingle. People are hooked before they realize it; they never suspect that you might be angling for tenure. Yet you're hardly an ivory chess piece; underneath, a poetic knight in shining armor struggles to break free. The problem is, you rarely reveal that side, confiding your intimate innermost thoughts to your diary. Perhaps the solution is to leave it out as obtrusively as you dare and let your loved one read it. (You, of course, are above such tawdry temptation, but recognize most others aren't.)

Love, Sex, and Marriage

It can't be said that you make the ideal mate or parent, and these traditional roles probably don't interest you much. Your idea of stroking is a deft keyboard; you prefer interfacing over face-to-face encounters. To you a beautifully bound hardcover feels as sensuous as soft, perfumed skin. You'd probably be perfectly happy conducting various affairs over the Internet: it's so much neater that way.

Your affairs are controlled and orderly, just the way you like it. You tend to hold your lovers at arm's length in a vise; in your odd, detached way you'll never really let anyone leave your life. You *do* love and want it in return, but on your own terms. Sometimes you'll deliberately pick a messy partner; your surface reality is, aha, someone to take apart and fix, but the deeper truth is, you envy that animateness. Let yourself relax and enjoy it. People leave you only if you refuse to communicate and listen rather than lecture. When you finally make the effort to reach out, it's with the awkwardness of learning gleaned from books, not real life. Still you try: your birthday gift to yourself might well be *The Joy of Sex,* but it's like following a recipe. Throw the tomes and disks away and intuit your partner's needs, as well as your own, more.

Money and Career

You're perfectly suited to a free-lance career or a job allowing you to work primarily out of your home. Wherever you work, you carve out your own little study/workplace anyway, a retreat from the hustle and bustle. The phone, fax, and computer suffice for interpersonal dealings. You love puzzling out problems and delight in minute analysis of human behavior. You have a deft hand for mystery writing, as well as troubleshooting. You're a computer whiz, so you could easily hack designing or safeguarding new systems and programs. Psychiatrist, essayist, medical reseacher, philosopher, editor, mathematician, inventor, dean, judge, film director, and television commentator are other apt choices. You can also become a musician of rare depth; melody automatically soothes you, and you enjoy the abstract task of making the notes connect and flow. About the only professions you avoid are those requiring manual labor; you much prefer mental gymnastics.

The ♍7 Potential

Remember that for all their acuity and analytic prowess, Virgo Sevens can have a blind spot about their own actions and a surprising unwillingness to change their spots. Exercise total detachment and try to see yourself as others do. Meditate occasionally to relax your overactive mind. You project incredible containment, concentration, and serenity,

which you can share with the world, but the key is expressing your feelings more often. You don't have to leave that
tower, just invite people in for a soiree or two.

FAMOUS VIRGO SEVENS

Hugh Grant	*9/9/1960*	*Leonard Bernstein*	*8/25/1918*
Peter Sellers	*9/8/1925*	*Harry Connick Jr.*	*9/11/1967*
Margaret Sanger	*9/14/1883*	*Tuesday Weld*	*8/27/1943*

♍ • 8
Virgo Eight
"The Organized Operator"

♍+	8+	♍-	8-
Disciplined	*Poised*	*Obsessive*	*Intense*
Clear-thinking	*No-nonsense*	*Overrational*	*Overstriving*
Self-reliant	*Efficient*	*Fastidious*	*Indecisive*
Shrewd	*Global view*		

Leave the rat race to the rats: a Virgo Eight places the ro-
dents in a maze to observe their behavior. You're not the
type to dig the trenches: that risks digging a hole for yourself. Your security depends on your maneuverability. Not for
you the front lines of battle: you're much happier and more
effective strategizing back at military headquarters.

No one is better at being calculating without being calculating. You know instinctually how to balance everything
from budgets to commitments. People look up to you automatically, without asking why. You radiate authority, profi-
ciency, confidence, and that underrated trait, competence.
You're not a big talker, yet you carry a big say in community
affairs and business negotiations.

This doesn't make you an automaton. You always find
time to listen to others' troubles, dispensing good cheer and
even better advice. Unless, of course, you think they're dog-
ging it. Then you read the riot act about how you can't
afford to slack off in a dog-eat-dog world. You play the rah-

rah coach, but ultimately you know it's all up to them. Carried to the extreme, you'll let someone start drowning in order to teach him to swim. "Sink or swim" sounds like a harsh philosophy, but you believe in natural selection and survival of the fittest. It's never enough to stay afloat: you've got to dive in and touch the finish line first, then celebrate. Beneath that stern facade, you genuinely see the beauty, or at least purpose, in everything and everyone. No animal is too ugly (in fact, the homelier it is, the more your heart swells), no murderer too vicious (don't people understand what an abusive childhood can do?). You shower attention and quiet affection everywhere. Your word is your bond, and not the junk variety.

Love, Sex, and Marriage

Though devoted and constant, you're a handful. Love almost always takes a backseat to work; moreover, you're not the type to tolerate backseat driving in your life. Still, you learned pretty early what the backseat of the family Ford was for. You can go long periods between love affairs, a camel in the romantic desert not by choice, but because you don't allow yourself a free moment. Even friends and family can feel merely incidental in your life. In that case, use your superhuman efficiency and organizational ability if you have to, and jot down reminders to call people in your Day-Timer.

You want a partner but won't enter into a relationship just for the sake of being in one. You don't have the time or inclination to date around or, worse, go through a messy divorce. You like that part of your life settled so you can get on with business; indeed you might insist on a prenuptial agreement. Which doesn't make you a cold fish: quite the contrary, if you find the right one, you'll fight like a salmon swimming upstream to spawn. But you *are* picky. When someone appeals to you, you switch gears immediately, pitching woo as well as you pitch a deal. Your sex life is intense yet private. No one would suspect how inviting your lap can be once you've put down the laptop.

Money and Career

Your business acumen is extraordinary. Your ideal situation would be as an integral cog, an indispensable team player, in a top executive position. You don't necessarily want all the responsibility, although people will probably beg you to assume it. You're happiest running your own department, preferably in an unstructured company that permits you maximum latitude in decision making. Of course, you'll step up and in if someone is running his or her own section into the ground. No one has a better sense of how all the parts fit in an organization. With your long-range vision you'll work diligently to move up the ladder. You're not a gambler. All your risks are calculated to within five decimal points; it's a safe bet that even if you did lose your shirt on one deal, you have plenty more in the wardrobe.

Your intellect is readily applied to the arts as well. Even as a performer, you'll have clear ideas of how everything should be run, and have sure instincts for producing or acting as an agent. Your most successful creative pursuits often revolve around the topic of power and its abuses or fanaticism of some sort.

The ♍8 Potential

Your immediate grasp of the whole picture and cool grace under pressure quietly dazzle. You'll never sacrifice your beliefs, or for that matter, anyone else's, to fit in. You project an aura of being upscale yet down-home in all your personal and professional dealings, which earns you respect and admiration. In many ways, you're a reluctant hero(ine), yet your shoulders can carry the weight of the world. You often find yourself in situations were you're either held up as a role model or come under attack for your policies. You never waver from your course, teaching others a valuable lesson in dignity and conviction.

FAMOUS VIRGO EIGHTS

Joan Lunden	*9/19/1951*	*Richard Gere*	*8/31/1949*
Ingrid Bergman	*8/29/1915*	*Tommy Lee Jones*	*9/15/1946*
Oliver Stone	*9/15/1946*	*Claudette Colbert*	*9/13/1905*

♍ • ⑨
Virgo Nine
"The Versatile Visionary"

♍+	9+	♍-	9-
Cultured	Imaginative	Nervous	Critical
Respectful	Spiritual	Reticent	Unsympathetic
Dedicated	Entertaining	Fussy	Bitter
Thorough	Careless		

Possessed of impeccable timing, you've always chosen your moments carefully for maximum impact. There you were, six months old, your parents despairingly wringing their hands over the crib; little John/Jane hasn't said a word, not one single gaga! Thirty-odd years later, Mom and Dad are still relating the moment you suddenly unleashed a perfectly formed sentence. It was probably something along the lines of "Get everyone else in here: you ain't heard nothin' yet!"

You have a bit of the magician about you, with an eternal rabbit in your hat. You're a clever sleight-of-hand artist intellectually, able to fool people into thinking you're doing or saying the exact opposite of what you intend. You love entertaining people and enjoy the good life. You'd happily open a restaurant, where you could hold court, dispensing good advice and great grub to all and sundry.

You're the kind of person often described as striking or dashing; you're not always classically attractive, yet you command attention. You make an unforgettable impression; it's your dignified bearing, almost dandified style, warm bonhomie, not to mention your far-ranging *Jeopardy*-type smarts, and the devilish gleam in your eye. Yet underneath you may hide a secret sorrow, since the world and your life rarely meet your expectations. That, of course, only makes you even more mysteriously appealing to others. You really yearn to make the world a better place, but often despair of how to do it. You may not realize it, but Virgo Nine is a healer. Oh, not with snake shows and laying on of hands and mumbo jumbo, but rather the restorative power of art, or a fine meal, something that reinvigorates the soul.

Love, Sex, and Marriage

You can invent a million excuses not to marry (human beings are not inherently monogamous, love can't last, look at the divorce rate), then another million why you shouldn't have children (the world's already dangerously overcrowded and we haven't learned how to harvest the seas hydroponically for extra sustenance, so why would you want to bring another life into this messy, messed-up world?). But it's mostly show; besides, you're quite fastidious in your choice of mate. You can be struck quite hard by the love bug, but the disease can only progress to a chronic stage when a firm friendship has been established; in fact, you're quite good at remaining pals with your exes.

You have a deep need for companionship and want someone around, but only when it suits you. Just when they're feeling lovey-dovey, you realize there's so much research to be done! Your combustible combo of intimacy and indifference drives you to passionate pursuit, but once you've captured your prey, your mind if not your heart strays. Love's all well and good, but what about work? Ironically, you often meet your mate through business. The ideal situation is that you work together on various short-term projects, then leave each other to sundry devices.

Money and Career

You have a calming, almost hypnotic effect on people, with a quietly compelling manner. Genuinely empathetic, you enjoy drawing them out. This encourages others to trust you instantly, which also means they let their guard down. Any surprise that psychologist, trial lawyer, and talk-show host are leading Virgo Nine professions? Medicine is another forte; you have just the right mixture of compassion and objectivity to be a successful surgeon, albeit the type who blasts the Stones in the operating room. Your dramatic flair and dry wit make you a superlative actor. Any meet-and-greet occupation such as nightclub entertainer or restaurateur is right up your alley as well.

Money runs through your fingers. You're accustomed in living in style and you love picking up the bill for your twenty closest hangers-on. Nor can you resist a friend in need. Try to put a little aside every month, preferably in a hard-to-reach place.

The ♍9 Potential

You're a strikingly amiable, approachable human being, which endears you to everyone. You're the ideal confidant, with a natural gift for getting people to open up. You have a marvelously sneaky, playful wit, at odds with your rather stylish yet proper appearance. You can also tap into your psychic ability and become a medium not for raising ghosts and purging poltergeists, but rather for chasing away the nagging hobgoblins of insecurity that affect us all.

FAMOUS VIRGO NINES

Ricki Lake	9/21/1968	Samuel Goldwyn	8/27/1882
Colonel Sanders	9/9/1890	Jane Curtin	9/6/1947
Bill Murray	9/21/1950	Phil Jackson	9/17/1945

LIBRA

●

♎ • 1
Libra One
"The Active Artiste"

♎+	1+	♎-	1-
Polished	*Pioneering*	*Vain*	*Self-Centered*
Glamorous	*Trend-setting*	*Underachieving*	*Domineering*
Attentive	*Energetic*	*Self-absorbed*	*Flashy*
Dapper	*Assertive*		

Even if you're not conventionally attractive, you're the Cunard of dreamboats. You possess an indefinable aura, that *je ne sais quoi* that most mortals, mouths agape, call striking or just plain old-fashioned glamorous. You avidly pursue anything that makes you healthy, wealthy, and wise; your concern with beautifying yourself and your surroundings may come across as vain, but you know you're here to project your positive self-image to others.

One pushes Libra to realize its Cardinal assertiveness. You're a battler, though your weapon of choice is cajolery rather than threats. You can bring someone around to your point of view, expending no more energy than lifting a glass of bubbly to toast your new venture together. If necessary, you're able to express your anger better than many Libras, which is actually quite healthy for all your relationships. Meanwhile Libra's refinement and One's rational approach ensure the scene will rarely be stormy and melodramatic. (You abhor being dragged down to the knock-down-drag-out level of fighting.) And you'll always listen, of course, to their side, even if you have no intention of compromising your principles or agendas.

You have a salon mentality and enjoy bringing the right people together at your undoubtedly palatial home. You're a big party planner, whether a small, intimate dinner for your twelve closest friends and business associates, replete with place cards, or an Oscar bash for one hundred with ballots and a huge pot. Of course, you select the guest list with maximum care. You're aware that business is best transacted in a pleasant environment; the bonus is that it makes socializing a write-off.

Love, Sex, and Marriage

You're a dashing dilettante with your choice of prospective partners. Settling down becomes a priority for you, since it's one less thing you can check off on your busy schedule. Anyway, who can keep all the names straight? Your Libran need for partnership and One need for primacy make finding your equal a number priority. You want a true give-and-take, but relationships are never 50/50; if the seesaw teeters to 52/48, it offends your sense of what's right. Like all Librans, you'll run a hundred-yard dash from confrontation. But you can't run away from your own emotions. Every so often, you'll feel anger, mistrust, jealousy—all of which come into conflict with your view of The Way Things Should Be. Still, the cool, rational approach actually works best with you. You like to discuss problems like reasonable adults; throwing vases and slamming doors will never be your style.

As you mature, you learn to look beyond the surface appeal and see the person within. But on some level, appearances, deceiving as they may be, do count in your world. Everything, including your mate, is designed to show off your undeniably superior taste. Your partner for life must also be intelligent, witty, charming, and refined: essentially your mirror image. He or she must play the role of social, supportive spouse to the hilt; after all, a party can only be as successful as its cohost.

Money and Career

Whoever first claimed "Image is everything" must have been, or been burned by, a Libra One. You know how to mold bodies: consider cosmetics, fitness, fashion, plastic surgery, and photography (you bring out the contrast of light and shadow and every angle, whether of architecture or cheekbones) as potential bonanzas. Don't ignore politics; your combination of tact and authority has tremendous public appeal and, more important, helps broker or break deals. Knowing how to present yourself doesn't hurt; you could also mold other careers as a media consultant or policy adviser. Thoroughly at ease in the power structure, you can play everything from diplomat or social secretary to acidic chronicler of the latest hip scene.

You enjoy spending money; you see it as a sign of not only success but power. You're a thoroughbred clothes-horse, though the closest you get to a real horse is probably Polo Ralph Lauren. You're on intimate terms with every chic boutique salesperson and salon hairstylist on Fifth Avenue and Rodeo Drive. They know what you like and also provide a most reliable source of information.

The ♎1 Potential

You possess an almost eerie ability to transform yourself into the flavor of the moment. It's that soft, gushy Libra side commingled with the dynamic One influence. You're a tasty dish that everyone wants to taste, and don't you know it. You excel at introducing people, making contacts, and initiating projects, not only for yourself but your very large, immediate, ever-expanding circle. The old saw about a stranger being a friend you haven't met yet is your credo; well, some of them are relegated to acquaintance status. You can't have time for *everybody,* though you certainly try.

FAMOUS LIBRA ONES

Alicia Silverstone	*10/4/1976*	*Sting*	*10/2/1951*
Suzanne Somers	*10/16/1946*	*Truman Capote*	*9/30/1924*
Charlton Heston	*10/4/1922*	*Elizabeth Hurley*	*10/6/1965*

♎ • 2
Libra Two
"The Deft Diplomat"

♎+	2+	♎-	2-
Balanced	*Diplomatic*	*Vacillating*	*Indecisive*
Well-mannered	*Sociable*	*Inactive*	*Timid*
Prudent	*Companionable*	*Overdependent*	*Quarrelsome*
Adaptable	*Compassionate*		

Being a Libra Two endows you with double the charm, grace, tact, and appreciation of beauty and justice both Librans and Twos possess in abundance. Indeed, you're one of the most pleasing packages anyone's likely to run across. No one is more adept at the art of apparent compromise. You'll nod, flatter, and cajole, knowing instinctively where to give in on minor details to ensure you achieve your ultimate goal. In the midst of a heated policy debate, you'll wait for an angry silence, then sweetly, tentatively offer, "You know, I might have a solution." And you'll make everyone else feel it was their idea to begin with in the bargain(ing).

Sometimes those carefully calibrated scales feel more like a seesaw. Your greatest fear is that you're a mere people pleaser. You can inwardly torture yourself: are you genuinely sincere, generous, and openhearted or do you simply act that way because you want people to like you? Well, let's put it this way: you *are* obsessively giving—and anyway, we all want to be appreciated! That misplaced guilt can only create a reservoir of repressed anger and frustration.

Truth is, you're so scrupulous that even your own highly developed value system can come into conflict. You adore luxury, yet disdain frivolity: do you buy that mink or donate your Christmas bonus to PETA? You can be equally indecisive—sorry, fair and balanced—in choosing a restaurant ("well, A's closer to the theater, but B has that hot new chef; of course, C's ambience is more pleasant, though D has a better prix fixe menu. . . ."), so imagine what intellectual and emotional cartwheels a major life choice triggers. Still, for all your sweetness and light, you're ready, willing, and able to make war in order to preserve the peace, since you're more concerned with reaching the right conclusion than with being right. You'll sooner walk away from otherwise happy relationships or profitable alliances than sacrifice your convictions; you secretly smile at the astounded look on people's faces when they discover for the first time how surprisingly stubborn you can be.

Love, Sex, and Marriage

Oh my, do you listen, making the appropriate grunts of affirmation and dispensing sage advice when the seventeenth friend calls that day to bitch and moan. Obviously this makes you mighty appealing as a partner. And an equal partner you must be, in all your relationships, to be truly happy. You're just as afraid of intimacy as anyone else, fearing your identity will be subsumed in your partner's. That's why you need an equally sensitive mate, but one more in synch with life's practical side. You can become quite dependent, and if you're not careful, co-dependent.

You relish each small detail of dating, remembering the first box of chocolates, even fondly recalling the first silly tiff over which movie to see. You love long drives to absolutely nowhere; let's pack the picnic hamper with champagne flutes and the second-best china and skedaddle! Emotionally you're the same way; you see life with someone as an endless journey. You don't mind tangents or side routes and can exceed the speed limit or slow to a crawl. You're generally content to let your partner dictate the pace, and become easily attuned to his or her rhythms. Ironically, this makes you seem so obliging and easygoing that people project their needs—and fears—onto you, but you'll manage to draw the line where they can take advantage.

Money and Career

You realize "all the world's a stage," and whatever your career, will assume the roles of actor, politician, and good-will ambassador. For all your diplomatic skills, you're best off negotiating behind the scenes since overt confrontations or backstabbing office politics on a daily basis fray your nerves. You'll often gravitate toward an artistic or even athletic career that allows you to express your deep feelings or at least burn off that considerable nervous energy.

You appreicate little niceties, preferring hospitable surroundings, and will set aside part of your paycheck to buy a delicate miniature watercolor or seventeenth-century Buddha that you can contemplate when you need to relax. You'll ensure that your work space, even the smallest cubicle, is a peaceful oasis and home away from home, with your favorite mug, African violet pot, and whimsical decorative touches that softly whisper, "Me."

The ♎2 Potential

Take a cue from Nike and JUST DO IT! You can grab that brass ring and swing from it as artfully as any gymnast. You're so concerned with everything being fair and right that you can cause yourself untold suffering. The truth is, the world isn't always fair, and you can't change that. Focus on those areas of your life where your sense of balance and harmony really can make a difference. The choice is yours: eternal indecision or a muscular sense of justice. Learn to do what makes you happy first. Only by taking initiative and making decisions will you satisfy both others' needs and your own, encouraging everyone to understand one another's point of view.

FAMOUS LIBRA TWOS

Julie Andrews	*10/1/1935*	*Kevin Sorbo*	*9/24/1958*
George C. Scott	*10/18/1927*	*Paul Simon*	*10/13/1941*
Greer Garson	*9/29/1908*	*Marie Osmond*	*10/13/1959*

♎ • 3
Libra Three
"The Inspired Socialite"

♎+	3+	♎-	3-
Sauve	Convivial	Social-climbing	Scatterbrained
Artistic	Easy-going	Fickle	Flirtatious
Gracious	Artistic	Superficial	Sycophantic
Discriminating	Romantic		

You may be a social butterfly, but ah, what iridescent colors you flash as you flutter about. Gracious and gregarious, you're a born raconteur and effortless networker. You have impeccable taste and a keen eye for beauty. There's no denying you love the high life; you can be easily seduced by *la dolce vita.* The wealthy, powerful, and merely famous hold an eternal fascination for you. Though you'd never admit it, you're an avid gossip-page reader; *Vanity Fair* isn't just your favorite magazine, it's your lifestyle choice. You're an incisive observer of the social scene and sharply feel the disparity between classes and stations in life; as fellow Libra Three F. Scott Fitzgerald wryly noted, "The rich are different from you and me."

You're fittingly Gatsbyesque, reinventing yourself for each new crowd, a chameleon who adapts to any given situation. Those who enviously watch you smoothly negotiate a party may find your gift of gab and penchant for flattery hypocritical, sniping you're a social climber, even a parasite. You're not. But if you can't say anything nice, you don't say anything at all, well aware you catch more flies with honey than vinegar. Besides, you genuinely look for the positive side, and no matter what, contribute an aura of style, class, elegance, and a wicked wit to your surroundings.

You can reach Himalayan heights without huffing or puffing; at the very least you have the most fashionable oxygen mask. No Trappist monk, you know how to enjoy the trappings of a lavish lifestyle. Most important, you want to share the spoils with others, especially your one and only. After all, it's much more fun sipping champagne from someone else's slipper. Well, as long as it's glass and hasn't been worn yet.

Love, Sex, and Marriage

In romance, Libra Threes float on fluffy little clouds. You believe in the ideal of courtly love; only you could transform that stripper at a bachelor(ette) party into a medieval troubadour serenading the crowd with ballads. You equate old-fashioned with glamorous. You'd gladly trade in that three-piece suit for a waistcoat or petticoat, while camisoles and bodices (that rip easily, of course) intrigue you. Without even trying, you radiate a fragile, ethereal charm that makes men and women alike want to rush to your aid; in a world where most people prefer playing the shining knight, regardless of gender, you're coyly content to play the damsel in distress, no matter how politically incorrect the role has become.

Loneliness threatens you; you ache for someone to bounce ideas off of and act the straight (wo)man at parties. If you're single, you probably have a date every night of the week; you should learn how to be alone with yourself. Needless to say, you pamper your amour du jour silly. And the sex? Wait, it's always "making love," since you manufacture an aura of romance around an obvious one-night stand. Anyway, a Libra Three probably invented foreplay. You perform the act so exquisitely, it's practically torture, like being teased with thousands of feathers on every erogenous zone simultaneously.

Money and Career

Libra Threes are naturally attracted to the best things in life; you're all too aware they're not really free, as the song claims. Anything that puts you among beautiful objects and beautiful people is a potential gold mine: acting, fashion, interior design, celebrity biographer, gossip columnist, and hairdresser to the stars top the list. You're driven to succeed so you can lavish yourself and loved ones with lovely little trinkets. You could even become rich by proxy; those attentions could pay dividends in a hefty inheritance. But if you don't have money or real estate, it doesn't really matter. You know that as long as you're a witty conversationalist, there will always be a place at the dinner tables of the rich and famous. Just take care; shopping *is* your favorite form of exercise. Money can run through your fingers as they walk through the Yellow Pages.

The ♎3 Potential

You're both the perfect host and the ideal guest, with a remarkable gift for bringing taste, wit, and style to any gathering. So why restrict yourself to the social and professional arenas? Don't waste that ability to create beauty and harmony wherever you go on superficial pursuits. Use your talents to help others. You can throw the ball where the prince meets his Cinderella while donating the crown jewels to charity. Or by chronicling celebrity doings, you can satisfy people's hunger for gossip, yet with your acute insight, help them understand that all that glitters is not gold. As the original golden boy and girl, who'd know better?

FAMOUS LIBRA THREES

Gore Vidal	*10/3/1925*	*Gwyneth Paltrow*	*9/28/1973*
Groucho Marx	*10/2/1890*	*Montgomery Clift*	*10/17/1920*
Helen Hayes	*10/10/1900*	*Johnny Mathis*	*9/30/1935*
Samuel Taylor Coleridge	*10/21/1772*	*Niels Bohr*	*10/7/1885*
Thelonious Monk	*10/10/1918*	*Lillian Gish*	*10/14/1896*
Barbara Walters	*9/25/1931*		

♎ • 4
Libra Four
"The Practical Dreamer"

♎+	4+	♎-	4-
Persuasive	Stable	Waffling	Lazy
Discerning	Diligent	Mooching	Contrary
Even-tempered	Ethical	Manipulative	Too busy
Equitable	Systematic		

You can juggle several projects while dealing with four blinking phone lines, three yapping Chihuahuas, two miserable teenagers who flunked chemistry *and* cheerleading, and one irate mate who can't find the remote control. You stay the course and go with the flow, no matter how choppy or whitecapped it may be. Four stabilizes the Libran oscillation and vacillation; instead of a wildly pinging EEG, with Himalayan peaks and valleys, yours gently undulates like a rippling pond. You convey the same tranquillity and grace under pressure in every situation. You weigh the pros and cons, evaluate each side, and examine every angle before pronouncing judgment. You strike a balance between truth at all costs and seeing the world through rose-colored glasses. You never lie, but you can sidestep issues adroitly when your interests are at stake. Then you play one party against another to buy time. You're hardly indecisive, but instead can be decisive about so many important conflicting matters.

For all your style and love of tradition, you have a daffy side. You'll use that Chippendale chair as an ironing board, or top the Louis XVI marble commode with issues of *Architectural Digest, House and Garden,* and *GQ.* You don't like anything or anyone cheap and vulgar, though you can tell a pretty mean dirty joke with an absolutely angelic expression. You deserve a halo for your cool, calm, collected, composed manner in an emergency. You handle nuclear attack and your baby's diaper rash with equal poise.

Love, Sex, and Marriage

Four calms the typical Libran flits and flutters. You don't believe that love makes the world go round, merely that it makes the ride enjoyable. Oh, you can be swept off your feet by a grand passion; but once your head reaches the clouds, your feet are firmly planted again. You're loving, attentive, and sincere, but you don't let fantasies interfere with the daily grind. You won't sit by the phone waiting for the call, or cancel dinner with friends because your latest squeeze dialed at the last minute. In fact, you hate games: playing hard to get, making yourself unavailable. Please! You're open, straight forward, and eternally surprised others aren't.

Just because you're dating doesn't mean you've made a lifetime commitment. You *are* willing to make a commitment to discovering what's there, follow it through. You're too busy to date several people at a time; what's the big deal, spending a few months getting to know someone, finding out if this is the right one. You know everyone has intimacy issues; let's deal with them when they arise rather than freak about moving in together after five dates. You figure if you worry too much about the past and future, you won't enjoy the present.

Money and Career

No one surpasses you at fostering a spirit of teamwork; even a chief executive Libra Four knows how to set an example by rolling up the sleeves and sweating. Nothing fazes you. You're a genius at throwing off someone's equilibrium with a carefully calibrated plan of attack; your questions seem so innocent, yet you're sizing up the competition. Equally nimble with your wit and hands, you're a clever designer of anything from furs to furniture. You bring inspiration and perspiration to all your undertakings. When your Libran enchantment and creative ability meet your Four structure, they result in a blissful artistic pairing, whether in acting, writing, singing, or dancing. Your work is stylish yet accessible, that rare commercial and critical hit. That same critical eye is fitting for scientific research: you see the simple elegance of the electron. You're a strong, capable leader in politics and business; and your strong, capable body is built for endurance sports.

The ♎4 Potential

There's no pinnacle you can't attain. You're blessed with the invincible duo of Libra charm and Four pragmatism. The former opens doors, the latter keeps you in that cushy leather catbird seat. You never seem to lose your cool, remaining steady, unruffled, and annoyingly disarming, making your points with firm charm. Your scales are beautifully balanced; that equableness and equilibrium set an example for everyone you meet. Don't be surprised if you end up baby-sitting the world, including the adults, or at least holding their hands through life's thunder and lightning.

FAMOUS LIBRA FOURS

Sarah Ferguson, Duchess of York	10/15/1959	Will Smith	9/25/1968
		Michael Crichton	10/23/1942
Margaret Thatcher	10/13/1925	Martina Navratilova	10/18/1956
Tim Robbins	10/16/1958		

♎ • 5
Libra Five
"The Global Glamour-puss"

♎+	5+	♎-	5-
Social	Easygoing	Inconstant	Unfocused
Witty	Versatile	Frivolous	Self-indulgent
Fluid	Alert	Shallow	Discontented
Fluent	Vivacious		

You could have been the model for those adorable photos that come with the wallets you buy at the five-and-dime: you know, the dimply baby on the bearskin rug, the smiling mom or dad who clearly never needed orthodontia. Even as an adult, people still want to go gitchee-goo to you. You

look as if you'd be ready to hug, cuddle, and giggle at any
moment, and you would be. Even you'd admit you have
your live-for-the-moment gadabout side. You can bait and
bat your lush lashes at the world with abandon. You stroll
about as if you were in your own personal sixteenth-century
castle, transported and painstakingly reassembled from Bur-
gundy, performing every task with élan. But anyone or anything that hems you in sends you hurtling out that rapidly
descending heavy iron gate—or you'll shut it in his or her
face.

Your style, perhaps even your upbringing, might be described as preppy-bohemian. You enjoy straddling the world
of high society and downtown arts, even though you may
joke that you sometimes feel saddle-sore. You need to be
surrounded by an entourage that shares your sense of fun
and the offbeat. You love throwing parties almost as much
as attending them; you seem born to socialize, with the exceptional gift of making the smallest talk seem vitally important. You're so ubiquitous, it's like trying to keep track of a
pinball, the way you keep pinging and ponging about. You
may seem like a flibbertigibbet, but you listen carefully and
soak up every last detail. Your photographic memory and
insatiable curiosity fill the shelves of your inexhaustible store
of knowledge; you're just as comfortable and erudite discussing etiquette as etymology.

Love, Sex, and Marriage

Biology, especially anatomy, was probably your favorite
subject as a teenager. By the time you attended sex education classes, you had probably already devoured every book
on the subject, from the *Kama Sutra* to *Everything You Always Wanted to Know About Sex but Were Afraid to Ask*.
Needless to say, you were never afraid.

Sometimes your sheer likability, curiosity, and atten-
tiveness make people think you're making advances; they
mistake your natural courteousness as a pass. Since you are
so swooningly charming, be aware of the signals you might
be sending out, otherwise your courtliness can get you involved in situations you regret. Although you like to play

the field, one stallion or filly inevitably plays the favorite; after some dallying and shilly-shallying, you place the bet. Common ground is vital—and you cover lots of territory. Continual growth, evolution, change, and development form the key to unlocking your potential for a happy, continuing relationship. You make a thoughtful, imaginative, even zany lover. You come up with offbeat gifts, bringing your lover for his or her first pedicure and facial .. or skydiving experience.

Money and Career

You succeed in all the glamour professions, such as film, theater, dance, fashion design or retail, art direction, painting, music, magazine editorial, cosmetics, interior design, and public relations. In fact, you're a promotional whiz; ideally you'd like to publicize the trendy new clubs and restaurants, but your fertile imagination could make fertilizer seem fashionable. Or you could get a stand-and-pose, meet-and-greet job such as maître d', resort operations, or boutique manager, preferably at some velvet-rope type of place currently in vogue. You dislike routine, but your inquisitiveness and insight contribute to a fulfilling career as a teacher, investigative reporter, or psychoanalyst.

Be careful about placing all your nest eggs in one basket. You like comfort but can fritter things away on the road to Zanzibar or whatever exotic call strikes your fancy. You should diversify if you want to hold on to your holdings. Put a little aside for that rainy day, because in your case, it could be the kind of flood declared a national disaster. It doesn't take much to restore your good spirits: a shopping spree, theater tix (preferably sold-out), foie gras, et al.

The ♎5 Potential

You're the supreme arbiter of taste and fashion. Funny, civil, charming, and attractive, you define smart and hip no matter what your background and education. You're incredibly discriminating, yet democratic, too, believing you can learn something from just about anyone. Still, you could easily be the one standing at the door of that hot new boîte deciding who gets in. It may be annoying, but your instincts are infallible. But then, you would know the right crowd for a heavy-metal slam-dancing club and a society cotillion.

♎ • 6
Libra Six
"The Dreamy Dramatist"

♎+	6+	♎-	6-
Peaceful	Unselfish	Manipulative	Self-righteous
Resolute	Artistic	Procrastinating	Susceptible to
Altruistic	Loving	Self-absorbed	flattery
Cooperative	Responsible		Domineering

As the prototypical Libra Six, John Lennon, sang, "All we are saying is give peace a chance." You idealize love in all its forms. You're equally passionate about justice, with a keen sense of responsibility to humankind. Very often you set an example for the rest of the world through the partnerships you form. You're a remarkable inspiration to others; despite your dapper, dashing appearance, you're capable of backbreaking work for a cause or person you love, agreeing with yet another Libra Six, Friedrich Nietzsche, that whatever doesn't kill you makes you stronger.

Your intense idealism is frequently disappointed, and you can retreat into a profound depression. But you don't like being in a funk, and being an essentially social creature, will put on your favorite CD, dance around the room in your underwear, and *voilà!* your optimism is restored. You have a touching, naive faith that everything happens for the best. You retain a wide-eyed wonder that life even arose to begin with. Your vision is both new-fangled and old-fashioned. You

realize that a greater sense of values—whatever those are—
was instilled in bygone years, yet recognize that traditional
concepts of morality are in a constant state of flux, and that
our increasingly technological global society where anything
is available by pressing a key has rendered many comforting
homilies obsolete. Not for you those dark sci-fi renderings
of the future. You want spacious, gleaming cities straight
from Jules Verne and H.G. Wells, married to a Norman Rockwell fifties-sitcom existence in which every problem is
solved by fadeout: *Leave It to Beaver* that *Father Knows Best*.
Yet when adversity strikes, no one could be more intrepid
or inventive. No matter how patrician your background, you
always step up to the front line of the fray.

Love, Sex, and Marriage

You're such a catch that you unfortunately attract self-
seeking types who want to be taken care of. But you need
TLC and protection just as much. You want someone who'll
appreciate and reciprocate the love and respect you offer.
Yet the combination of Libra and Six sets such high standards that you may remain single or end up in the divorce
court.

Your love transcends the intellectual; you don't just discuss your feelings, you show them, and even put them on
display. Your loved ones can expect plenty of PDAs, not to
mention hand-squeezing and footsie under the table. You
shower them with compliments and even when you find
fault with their appearance or behavior, usually offer firm
encouragement rather than carping criticism. Remember that
marriage is not an escape hatch, and don't imagine that you
can change your partner for the "better"; no one can fix
things for another person.

Money and Career

You're a tenacious, snarling bulldog when it comes to
defending your own beliefs. Although the very core of your
being seeks peace and goodwill, you can go to battle for
those principles. A perfect example and amusing paradox is
Alfred Nobel, who used the earnings from inventing dyna-

mite to fund the prizes named for him. This zeal makes you an inspiring general, military or spiritual, who leads by example such as fellow Libra Six Dwight D. Eisenhower; an able ambassador, eliminating cultural, ethnic, and sociological boundaries and limitations; an inspirational unforgettable teacher (whose life could be turned into a movie); and a hellacious minister or orator, whose sermons describe current conditions in such incendiary terms that hellfire seems like a breeze by comparison. You're blessed with a soft, devotional quality as an artist who moves millions. And because you recoil from strife, you could explore becoming a marriage counselor, couples therapist, even sex surrogate!

The ♎6 Potential

A Libra Six needs love, pure and simple, and recognition of his or her efforts. Resist the temptation to play the martyr or keep an emotional ledger, in which you compare how much you give to how much you receive in return. You're almost preternaturally sensitive; what others call nuance has all the subtlety of a Mack truck for you. You're attuned to a higher frequency; you regretfully concede that it's pitched too shrilly for most human beings, yet you strive to modulate it so everyone can hear its message of harmony.

FAMOUS LIBRA SIXES

Christopher Reeve	9/25/1952	T.S. Eliot	9/26/1888
Eleanor Roosevelt	10/11/1884	Bryant Gumbel	9/29/1948
Heather Locklear	9/25/1961	Jesse Jackson	10/8/1941

♎ • 7
Libra Seven
"The Elitist Democrat"

♎+	7+	♎-	7-
Eloquent	*Analytic*	*Snobbish*	*Aloof*
Cordial	*Discriminating*	*Chameleonesque*	*Suspicious*
Literate	*Civilized*	*Aloof*	*Secretive*
Refined	*Forward-thinking*		

Once upon a time you carefully looked under your bed for spooks, goblins, and boogey-men. You poked about with a broom until you were satisfied that nothing would go bump in the night, and settled down to a deep, dream-laden sleep. You still check the closets, and with your acute radar and ESP, will be the first to offer proof that UFOs exist. You're a believer; they *are* out there. You're a fabulist who wants everyone to have fun, but you're profoundly serious; your typically Libran appreciation of life's finer things is primarily cerebral.

There's no greater miracle to you than bonding with another human being. You pine for a soul mate with whom to share your life; *compromise* is not part of your romantic vocabulary. Your continual search for perfection is the loveliest side of your nature, but it often isolates you. You over-idealize love to the point that no one could possibly meet your standards. Yes, you long for a beautiful home and a caring partner, but remember Libra is an intellectual air sign, and Seven a lone-wolf logician. You probably expound more about *l'amour* than anyone around, but even you have to admit it remains mostly talk. You adore the idea of passion, but hate the messiness that love ultimately brings to your life.

If the romantic in you is frustrated, you offer your munificent imagination to the fortunate world at large. During your search for companionship you won't neglect other social opportunities. You also cherish the lively, stimulating company of good friends. Unlike many Sevens, you like being the center of attention, but you're selective about your audience. You're masters of social observation and wits of dangerous charm; everyone clamors for an invitation to your parties, since the A list makes a beeline to your home.

Love, Sex, and Marriage

You require a quiet yet smolderingly sexy lover—but not too fiery. You tend to go for the ornamental first: someone who wears the right clothes and wears them well. You generally have a physical ideal, but when intimacy issues crop up, can magnify perceived faults out of all proportion; suddenly that scar you found sexy and full of character becomes a hideous disfigurement.

You want sex to be transcendent, magical, mystical, even esoteric. You might indulge in Tantric sex or explore yoga positions. You lead a rich fantasy life, but nothing so clichéd as Tom Cruise or Liv Tyler sprawled invitingly on the divan. You want to be transported to another world, another plane entirely. You imagine yourself in exotic settings and love experimenting with your lover, encouraging and incorporating his or her fantasies. But above all, sex must be a spiritual connection that transcends the purely physical.

Money and Career

Your work must satisfy your soul, expressing your innermost feelings. The artistic fields are your surest road to success, on a personal and professional level. Even your light comedy has dramatic flair; people identify with your creations since you touch their most primal emotions, making them roar with laughter and cry with compassion. You're just as content to run the show as a patron or cultural maven, taking pride in discovering fresh, exciting talent. The sciences also appeal to your logical mind. Of course, mathematical equations take the romance out of astronomy, and dissection takes the fun out of anatomy, but you're aware of the valuable role research plays and ardently promote progress of any sort. Social work and psychiatry are also marvelous choices, as you listen and analyze as well as anyone.

The ♎7 Potential

You're a dream weaver. It isn't just your own gift for fantasy, it's your ability to unlock the hidden child in everyone. You make people believe that anything is possible. Never let your own search for the impossible dream disillusion you. Remember your unwavering faith and longing for a better world are contagious. Even the most cynical Libra Seven fervently prays for a new, improved humankind, and steals a look at the stars wondering if maybe, just maybe, another, more highly developed civilization holds the answer.

FAMOUS LIBRA SEVENS

Jim Henson	*9/24/1936*	*George Gershwin*	*9/26/1898*
Fran Drescher	*9/30/1957*	*Michael Douglas*	*9/25/1944*
Susan Sarandon	*10/4/1946*	*Angela Lansbury*	*10/16/1925*

♎ • 8
Libra Eight
"The Jaunty Jurist"

♎+	8+	♎-	8-
Fair-minded	*Realistic*	*Acquisitive*	*Aggressive*
Philosophical	*Authoritative*	*Extravagant*	*Workaholic*
Courteous	*Accomplished*	*Exploitative*	*Materialistic*
Equable	*Understanding*		

Libra Eight is a winning-through-intimidation combination of Miss Manners and Captain America. You fight for truth, justice, and the International way, with the American Dream thrown in for good measure. You possess an uncanny aptitude for sizing up the opposition, and act accordingly. Generally your honesty will win out, even when it's not in your best interests, though you can resort to unscrupulous means to attain a scrupulous end. Conversely, you're an unrelenting, unyielding force when you're convinced of your side, a promoter of the "might makes right" dictum.

You're solidly humanist and probably liberal in your views. It saddens you that ours is a world in which ethnic or special-interest-group agendas have come to supersede basic human rights. You understand all too well the need to take pride in our heritage and identity and find a sense of community and belonging. Still, you wonder why we can't be human beings first, and Azerbaijanis or Zoroastrians second. Possessing pride and principles in abundance, you can turn a small-scale matter into a full-scale boycott, knowing that cause does indeed have an effect on others. You actually hate upsetting the apple cart, but you'll vigorously debate the difference between apples and oranges or abstract versus reality, perhaps only to defend your right to free speech.

You're forever absorbed in various projects, since you're not content with fewer than five irons in the fire; dating and courtship run a poor second during a particularly hectic, frantic, frenetic (any adjective ending in *tic* will do) week. But you'll move several Alps to make room for your love life; you're happiest when involved with someone, though your partner may not be enthralled with your appointment calendar.

Love, Sex, and Marriage

"Each man kills the thing he loves," wrote Libra Eight Oscar Wilde. You're a serious romantic, and your emotions are not to be trifled with. Like Wilde, you'd be willing to go to prison for your love, the world be damned. Indeed, part of you secretly wants to be compelled to offer proof of your love; what better way than a public trial?

You prefer to focus your attention on one person; after all, you're already juggling multinational corporate dinners and international art movies with friends on your calendar. You don't mind if your intended sees other people, as long as everything's up front. You can't fault him for being foolish, and you expect him to come to his senses. Once you've established firm footing, however, you put your foot down more possessively. Marriage is a long-term investment that must pay dividends; because of your numerous social and professional engagements, a long engagement suits you. You might be perfectly content with the three-nights-per-week arrangement for years. But often your significant other becomes restless, wondering when and if the relationship will move forward. That's usually when problems crop up. This is natural; remember it takes two to tango, and you're a conversational twinkle-toes. Talk through the issues, don't be discouraged, and tell your partner what you really feel.

Money and Career

You change jobs rather frequently, especially when younger. You want to explore so many options, and have so much curiosity and zest that it takes you a while to hit your stride and discover your calling. Once you formulate your plan, you're driven to succeed. You seek personal, professional, even political gain in all your endeavors. Money, comfort, recognition, and community standing are of paramount importance. You're highly sensitive to your work environment; if you don't get along with your co-workers or if the job description doesn't live up to its promise, you have no qualms about seeking something more challenging. You're particularly skillful at manipulating public opinion. You might wangle a job at a grass-roots movement where you get paid to coordinate rallies. Labor organizer, media guru, and attorney also appeal to you. In an office situation you're a benevolent bureaucrat, but you find paper pushing off-putting. Your penetrating mind makes you a persuasive writer; social injustice, of course, might be your great theme, but it's usually in the guise of biting satire.

The ♎8 Potential

You're a revolutionary philosopher, whose broad-minded tolerance can be a beacon for the world. People can actually see those scales of justice, and you're the radiant fulcrum. You make your medicine go down easily with your natural grace, bracing wit, and impressive intellect. Best of all, you never give up: if you've converted one, then you're not content until that individual has shepherded three or four apostles for the cause.

FAMOUS LIBRA EIGHTS

Timothy Leary	*10/22/1920*	*Mickey Rooney*	*9/23/1920*
Chevy Chase	*10/8/1943*	*Melina Mercouri*	*10/18/1915*
Jim Palmer	*10/15/1945*		

♎ • ❾

Libra Nine
"The Activist Actor"

♎+	9+	♎-	9-
Urbane	*Charitable*	*Shallow*	*Dissipated*
Humanitarian	*Spiritual*	*Escapist*	*Thoughtless*
Cultured	*Creative*	*Indecisive*	*Demanding*
Peaceable	*Attractive*		

A Libra Nine sports an almost messianic complex: you believe you have to save the world in order to justify your existence! You want to transport people to another level, whether of reality or the imagination. You exist to provide inspiration; your vision could be liberating either a nation or the sexual mores of an entire generation. Ever thought of yourself as a combination Gandhi and Brigitte Bardot, your fellow Libra Nines? They make quite the odd couple, but then you've always felt in your element with an oddball lot. Think about it, though. The bodacious Ms. Bardot embodied the latter, sparking millions of adolescent fantasies. And today she's making headlines and headway with her single-minded underdog crusade for the ethical treatment of animals. As for the Mahatma, he almost single-handedly vanquished the British Empire.

But don't canonize yourself quite yet. Yes, you tirelessly battle corruption, organize literal and political cleanup campaigns, champion causes, stump for harmony and brotherhood. But your idealism is never so excessive that you lose touch with reality. There's always a touch of the performer grandstanding for the audience in your words and deeds. But back to your qualifications for sainthood. Some Librans can be class-conscious, but you respect people who work hard to get where they are, overcoming adverse circumstances. You're scrupulously aware of the need to balance your spiritual and artistic growth with the practical necessities of life.

Even if you don't actively seek the spotlight, it just seems to locate you like a police searchlight. Once there, of course, you don't mind even the harshest glare, not to mention the paparazzi's popping flashbulbs. If anything, this inspires you to perform even more selflessly and efficiently. You know the value of publicity and you have implicit faith in your ability to project just the right image to the public. And yes, you do like to receive credit; you have a becoming modesty that is approximately 99 percent genuine and 1 percent show.

Love, Sex, and Marriage

You're primarily sensuous, not sensual; you love with your mind, for all your slinky, slithery sexuality. Since you project a combination of cool refinement and restrained intensity, no matter how married you are, opportunities will always flirt with you. If single, you certainly don't lack for willing candidates, but you let most of them down easily, their love not so much unrequited as unrequired. You've got your priorities: you're here for humanity first, loved ones second, and yourself about ninth.

Which doesn't mean you're an inattentive or uncaring lover. You're tenderly concerned for your partner's welfare and dole out plenty of hugs and kisses. More than most, you tend to identify with your lover's feelings, which sometimes makes you unsure of your own. You're actually quite romantic in an old-fashioned sort of way, often waiting beyond the infamous third date to consummate the relationship, and deluging the datee with attention. That's true during the courtship stage and after you're happily wedlocked, key long since thrown away. It's the in-between part—dragging you to the altar—that can be difficult. But since you're usually attracted to an assertive partner, that's sooner rather than later.

Money and Career

Well, if you can't be an actual role model or sex kitten,
you still have plenty of options to ensure your message is
heard and acknowledged. Since you so adroitly take society's pulse, you could act as a public relations consultant or
media guru—if you believe in your product, of course. As
with any Libra or Nine, the performing arts beckon. You
could be a publisher or producer who introduces groundbreaking new artists. Psychology and medicine, especially
alternative forms of healing like acupuncture and homeopa-
thy, allow you the one-on-one hands-on contact you also
enjoy.

The ♎9 Potential

Sounds idyllic, doesn't it, a Utopian vision: everyone living
in peace, listening to one another's point of view? Unfortunately, life is rarely like that. Libra Nines spend much of
their time and energy ensuring the scales don't tip too far;
someday those scales need to fall from your eyes. Something's gotta give—as in learning to establish a true give-
and-take in all relationships, from marital to professional.
On second thought, remain in your blissful ignorance. We
need you armed and ready to fight the good fight. Who
knows? With you leading the way by opening your eyes,
arms, mind, and heart, the world might just become the
joyous love-in you envision.

FAMOUS LIBRA NINES

Jimmy Carter	*10/1/1924*	*James Clavell*	*10/10/1924*
Madeline Kahn	*9/29/1942*	*Dwight Yoakam*	*10/23/1956*
Angie Dickinson	*9/30/1932*	*R.D. Laing*	*10/7/1927*

SCORPIO

●

♏ • 1
Scorpio One
"The Stable Adventurer"

♏+	1+	♏-	1-
Thoughtful	*Bold*	*Callous*	*Selfish*
Tenacious	*Direct*	*Brusque*	*Inflexible*
Ambitious	*Inventive*	*Skeptical*	*Impatient*
Constructive	*Independent*		

Direct and to the point, you seldom mince words when in the pursuit of—well, anything your little heart desires. And you started pursuing what your heart desired at a young age, much to the delight and chagrin of parents and parishioners. Favorite childhood question: why? Second favorite: why not? No particular subject fascinated you more than any other because you wanted to know the why and how-to of Absolutely Everything. A somewhat exhausted family cheered as you got your diploma and headed off to college. Mixed with their pride was the relief that now someone else, someone in the university's ivy-covered halls, would be expected to provide you with answers.

Early in the game, you realized that the kind of questions

that kept you up at night had no nice neat or even *available* answers. In fact, sometimes the so-called experts weren't as much help as you expected such scholarly elders to be. Since you aren't the type to leave a stone unturned or re-source untapped, the truth slowly dawned: it was up to you to venture into the uncharted territory and get those answers for yourself! You would take the lead and give everyone else the answers when you found them. Faster than you could say, Daniel Boone (also a staunch get-it-done Scorpio One guy), you'd signed up for grad school, or started throwing seriously large stones wrapped in newly discovered legal loopholes at the latest road block in your progress, maybe even at that bleeping crystal corporate ceiling.

A quick wit and sharp come-back opens and closes doors at the speed of light. No matter. You have a resiliency and tenacity to succeed that make you a much sought-after ally. Naturally, you're pleased when the public at large recognizes you to be one of the sharpest pencils in the box. Not that YOU ever doubted it for a moment, but it is nice to get that appreciative confirmation.

Love, Sex and Marriage

Love and sex, sex and love, hmmm—what's on the menu today? Can I have both? Hmm—but what if I don't want both? These questions are undeniably important but become moot when the chemistry starts to churn. You will have a relationship your own way by mixing healthy doses of sizzle and sweet until the Real Thing comes along and smacks you over the head. Once the cherub's arrow hits your heart, you stubbornly try to stick to a logical list of "Perfect Mate Quali-ties" for—oh, about an hour or so. Then you change the list to match the fascinating lover you simply can't live without.

Family ties do matter to you and whatever else you might add or subtract from the perfect mate list, you keep family values at the top and non-negotiable. You want a family of your own and expect to raise the precocious tots with a partner. Should children not actually make an entrance into the home picture, you find that out in the world, you're quite adept at challenging young minds and encouraging curiosity and intellectual growth. Meanwhile, you and the love of your life spend quality time traveling the globe or sitting together snug and secure by the fire reading the latest best seller.

Money and Career

Rich is better than poor, but there is so much more you want to do besides make money. Starting out, you might get the pursuit of a career mixed up with earning enough money to put a roof over your head and heat the place in the winter. Once you figure out that working and coin of the realm do matter for Basic Survival but that you want more than that, it gets progressively easier to earn what you need for fashionable togs and Dom Perrignon and have a plus honest to goodness career.

Be a professional—a professional almost anything. You like admiring glances and relish the respect of others. Because you have an extraordinary mind, you feel more productive when challenged by puzzling problems. Finding solutions is almost as much fun as getting your own way and you know how satisfying that is! Big money may not ever be the primary motivator. You're about so much more than money, but when you decide you do want more than the average bear, especially for things like enlarging the family den, you have no problem making it happen.

The ♏1 Potential

Friends count on you and with good reason. You come through for them and, eventually, you figure out how to do that for yourself, too. An innovative thinker, you turn people on to their own potential and show them how to view life through a different lens. You lead them down new mental tracks, and persuasively suggest how to consciously create the future and still enjoy living life one day at a time.

You teach us all of this by example; by how you live. Sure, what you have to say is instructional, and sometimes inspiring, but it's what you **do** that hands us the key to unlock our own inventive streak. We might not follow your particular star, but thanks to you the rest of us know how to pick out a star of our own, and how to pack up the buggy and get going.

FAMOUS SCORPIO ONES

Lauren Hutton	*11/17/1944*	*Larry King*	*11/19/1933*
Maria Shriver	*11/6/1955*	*Kevin Kline*	*10/24/1947*
Sally Field	*11/6/1946*	*Carl Sagan*	*11/9/1934*

♏ • 2
Scorpio Two
"The Gracious Executive"

♏+	2+	♏-	2-
Energetic	*Gracious*	*Skeptical*	*Indecisive*
Compassionate	*Supportive*	*Self-critical*	*Shy*
Tenacious	*Persuasive*	*Intense*	*Nervous*
Quick-witted	*Conscientious*		

It isn't that you don't know what you want, you just want to make sure before you play the winning card that the outcome will be the best for everyone concerned. You don't worry so much about yourself; you can recover from any false step or wild-goose chase that seemed like a good idea at the time. But the others around are standing close by, and if the results are goop instead of glitter, you don't want anyone else to get slimed. In those cases, if the reward is great enough, you detach and go it alone.

It started when you didn't tell Dad one of your teeth had fallen out because you wanted to see if the Tooth Fairy would really visit if Dad didn't know. You continually test the waters. You don't consider yourself the secretive sort, but there are enough of them stacked in your personal closet to fill a small file cabinet. Besides, you're a private person and don't like anyone mucking about in those classified files, or helping out when you'd rather do it yourself.

Other times, when you might be developing a new hybrid rose, you do the research, and experiment, but then consult with experts. Sticking with it is the way you've always done things, especially since you know that formula works. And you can switch from scientist to diplomat with ease.

Honestly, you would like to shower your family with gold and keep getting silver dollars from the Tooth Fairy forever. But you do find a way to make your own glitz, find love, and inspire others through your wonderful gift of being all things to all people.

Love, Sex, and Marriage

Getting your attention is the first challenge any would-be heartthrob has. You're often blind to pensive, speculative looks and warm smiles. You interpret them as "friendly" overtures and are surprised when confronted with an invitation to a concert and dinner. When you're uncertain there's anything romantic going on here, a good-night kiss can dazzle you in that warm and funny way you like to be dazzled.

You're sensitive and strong, and your affections are not to be trifled with. You play for keeps and prefer the married life. Love and friendship are vital to sensuous sex and a solid marriage. You intend to have them both and are open about your expectations with the object of your affections. As a parent, you enjoy every age and stage of your young one's progress from birth to adulthood and often become better friends as adults. That's also when you turn the tables and surprise your mate by suggesting a whole new lifestyle when the nest empties out.

Money and Career

Attracted to the law as much as medicine and entertainment (though not necessarily in that order), you examine ways to pattern your life. Work is an essential and it can put you where you want to be in the world. You could write epic novels like two other famous Scorpio Twos: Margaret Mitchell and Robert Louis Stevenson. Maybe *Gone with the Wind* or *Treasure Island* isn't your style, but you do have much to say, and an eloquent way of saying it.

Money is a teeter-totter that slips to extremes on a regular basis. As much as you would like a constant cash stash, it doesn't turn out that way, what with the trip to visit ailing cousin Jack or the dollars you wired to Janie at college for an emergency. You aren't a soft touch, but you can be counted on. When the need is money, you figure out later how to replace it, just as you always have.

The ♏2 Potential

The quiet, refined side of you is reflected in the way your home is decorated. Those fortunate enough to be a guest are instantly acquainted with what matters to you most—friends, family, the Little League trophy for son Derek, the kindergarten diploma for daughter Mary, and fresh-cut flowers to bring one of nature's gifts inside. Whether the dahlias stand in a jelly glass or an elegant lead crystal vase, they add just the right touch to make the place a home.

Indecision and insecurity could cripple you as you go from one extreme choice to another. Finding an acceptable balance of sweetness and light with gritty self-determination is the challenge of younger days. Responsibilities weigh heavily—enough to account for a rebellious moment or two that you get to live with forever. No matter. Through the process of doing what you have to do, you find yourself and blossom into a wonderful person who's a treasure to know.

FAMOUS SCORPIO TWOS

Whoopi Goldberg	11/13/1949	Claude Monet	11/14/1840
Jane Pauley	10/31/1950	Roy Rogers	11/5/1912
Hillary Rodham Clinton	10/26/1946	Prince Charles	11/14/1948

m, • 3
Scorpio Three
"The Enterprising Romantic"

m,+	3+	m,-	3-
Constructive	Imaginative	Shrewd	Scattered
Curious	Quick	Impulsive	Verbose
Practical	Sociable	Aggressive	Extravagant
Enterprising	Expressive		

After having yet another E-mail returned from the Black Hole Monitor of cyberspace, you decide independence is highly overrated and, with nostrils flaring, dial the help desk *one more time.* Before the hold music launches into the next movement of Vivaldi's *Four Seasons,* the phone is answered and you marvel at how sweet you sound between clenched teeth. A master of communication, you're good at pumping up a friend in need or helping Auntie Mae decide to buy the rose carpet for the bedroom instead of that stuffy tweed thing.

The endless reel of pictures in your head bounces between the practical and the imaginative. If there is an entertaining way to get the drudgery done, you not only find it, but show others how to make the trick work for them, too. A bleeding heart, you aren't. You stop long enough to share a trade secret or two, but fully expect everyone to make their own way.

Learning to tie your shoes like the big kids took persistence and patience, both of which you were born with, so you kept at it until you got it right. This is the cornerstone of your approach to everything important. You know you might not get it right the first time, and might have to ask for help, but being the professional old soul that you are, you see it through. The grown-ups think you're such a level-headed and serious child until you're overheard telling the dog a story about elf princes and goblins.

It comes as no surprise that you cheer for Godzilla in the rubber-monster classics. You understand the misunderstood, can coax the best from people, and put a positive spin on any message you deliver.

Love, Sex, and Marriage

Winning your heart isn't easy. You're a generous friend and creative playmate, but slipping a ring on your finger takes stamina. Not the let's-wear-out-the-sheets kind of stamina (though that is helpful), but the mental dexterity and fortitude to stay with you through the projects and campaigns. Not that you wouldn't give a chance to a charismatic suitor with a basket of daisies over his arm and a Ferrari parked at the curb. It's just that you need much more than window dressing for the long haul.

Falling in love is easy for you, but marriage is too important to take lightly. An eternal child yourself, you enjoy connecting with young people. Family is a serious venture and one you don't want to miss, and won't once you find the other perfect parent for this setup. Protective of both mate and offspring, you manage to juggle it all like a pro!

Money and Career

Money plays a big part in determining the career(s) you choose. You view each job you take as a stepping-stone to something else—from money for a vacation in faraway Spain to a cushy chair of your own on the board of directors. You never take your eye off the ball, and you can manage several bouncing balls at the same time. That's a talent that puts bread on the table and keeps you from missing the next opportunity.

Chances are you perform multiple jobs and tackle several careers, but those that are the most fulfilling let you be more than PC Clone #45 of 50. If that is where you start, you don't stay there for long. Your ingenious way of problem solving, ability to interface with any and all personality types, and practical approach make you a logical candidate to snatch from the pool. Keep your eyes open for the inevitable mentor.

The ♏3 Potential

Your temperament is nicely balanced between male and female, left and right brain, which gives you the potential to make any fantasy come true and still keep a grip on reality. You believe in the power of love, myth, friendship, and family. You know for a fact that determination isn't rated highly enough. In the process of getting what you want, you give back much more to those you meet along the way.

Spinning your wheels isn't an activity you like, but you fall into the Going Nowhere Fast Zone more than you care to admit. Shut out the multitude of distractions to get out of that rut and start moving again. Save your valuable energy for skiing down snow-covered mountains, gazing at the star-filled sky over the desert, or enjoying a sparkling waterfall. It isn't just roses you need to smell; you must reconnect with Mother Earth to be inspired!

FAMOUS SCORPIO THREES

Jodie Foster	11/19/1962	Ken Griffey Jr.	11/21/1969
Jamie Lee Curtis	11/22/1959	Glen Fry	11/6/1948
Winona Ryder	10/29/1971	Robert F. Kennedy	11/20/1925

♏ • 4
Scorpio Four
"The Dynamic Master Builder"

♏+	4+	♏-	4-
Courageous	Practical	Suspicious	Undemonstrative
Energetic	Determined	Willful	Too Busy
Executive	Logical	Blunt	Needs Proof
Ambitious	Good Hearted		

So you dreamed you were having tea with Mickey Mouse, Madame Curie, and Bill Gates, an odd group—and you wonder, What? Why? Maybe you're on the brink of a lucrative discovery in a trailblazing kind of way like these famous

Scorpio Fours. Ever notice how people either get out of your way or join you when you latch on to a starburst of an idea? That's because they know you are going to *do* it, and keep at it, regardless of the bumps and twists in the road from here to there.

Okay, so no one at Microsoft wears Mickey Mouse ears (do they?) but it's as much a fantasyland for techno-whizes as the Magic Kingdom is for kids young and old. Undeniably the six-foot mouse and bespectacled software mogul know how to earn a buck—make people happy! Give them what they want before they even know they want it!

Mingling inspiration and perspiration is your secret formula. You like tangible results, which is why you got that paper route at age ten to buy your first set of skis and join the ski club. Some teachers see you as industrious while others watch you drift through their class. You *are* learning, all the time, but not necessarily how to conjugate "to be" in French.

Though you undoubtedly ventured into the workaday world at a young age, you might not find your footing, personally or professionally, until long after the ink on your college diploma (if any) dries. More important than titles or degrees, you intend to live life your way and quickly learn how to flatten out the bumps. First and foremost, you are your own best friend and never intentionally shoot yourself in the foot. A more faithful and staunch friend, there may never be; and you well know about the rewards and the costs of everything you do, including relationships.

Love, Sex, and Marriage

Since age three, you've been drawing houses, a hobby that has grown into a serious portfolio of architectural plans. You might not have a clue who's going to live there with you, but you are a bit old-fashioned when it comes to providing the roof for you and yours. Sex and the psychic realm are often intertwined for you, and while you might act on a physical attraction, it won't turn serious unless there's an element of the unusual woven throughout.

A practical dreamer, you delight your partner with imaginative ways to explore each other's erogenous zones. Even after the initial rush of passion, you manage to breathe excitement and fire into the relationship. You get mighty distracted by business, but make a conscious effort to schedule time for sex games as well as Junior's softball game. You want it all and know if you can just schedule it right, you *can* have it all.

Money and Career

Whatever you do for work must be fun; that's your kind of fun, which might not be anyone else's. You believe in progress and hard work. As an employee, you won't last long if the boss doesn't recognize how hard and brilliantly you perform. As the employer, you hire people who are enthusiastic about the work, and you get along fine as long as they wholeheartedly join the team.

You're a straight shooter; beating around the bush and keeping things under wraps drive you crazy. Though you love a good mystery and do well in any area that requires research and logic, you warm up to people who say what they mean and mean what they say.

Money is a vital part of why you work. Sure, you like doing what you do and might work when you don't need the money, but you expect payment for the effort, and often work well beyond retirement age by choice.

The ♏ 4 Potential

A true Scorpio Four has Borg tendencies: "Resistance is useless, you will be absorbed." You believe so completely in your ideas, discoveries, and methods that you simply have to get everyone on board. The truth is you do have amazingly good ideas.

It would be easy to let work consume your life, even with a loving family and terrific home. Make sure you have an office in that home and parameters around the volume of work that follows you there. Dynamic and knowledgeable with an easy grin and predisposition to want to like everyone, you provide inspiration and tangible tools for improvement to those you mentor. And by the way, don't listen to anyone who tries to pigeonhole you as a particular type. You've got multi-faceted potential!

FAMOUS SCORPIO FOURS

Demi Moore	11/11/1962	Bill Gates	10/28/1955
Meg Ryan	11/19/1961	Will Rogers	11/4/1879
Roseanne Barr	11/3/1952	Bryan Adams	11/5/1959

♏ • 5
Scorpio Five
"The Worldly Wanderer"

♏+	5+	♏-	5-
Devoted	Freedom Loving	Blunt	Restless
Energetic	Networker	Impulsive	Fickle
Quick-witted	Curious	Secretive	Hasty
Constructive	Resourceful		

From the first time you walked into the big kids' book section at the neighborhood Library, you've known you wanted to meet everyone everywhere. Travel has a mystical quality about it that calls you to the far corners of the earth. Perhaps from Connecticut to Australia, Montana to Ireland, and then to Florida. Even if it's from the City to upstate, or Boston to the Berkshires, you won't let grass grow under your feet. There are far too many wonderful and exciting things out there to experience.

That lusty thirst of yours for life certainly gives Mom plenty of opportunities to curse you with the hope that you have six children just like you. You do, of course, and they pop wheelies on their tricycles just as you did, with the same occasional mishap. You know they have to figure out this whole cause-and-reaction thing, and you hope they do it as quickly as possible before they break anything important. Fear has never kept you from doing anything you ever thought was worthwhile.

You're a staunch and stable friend, and getting to know

you is easier than it looks. You don't think you're unap-
proachable, but that dynamic whirlwind of activity is somewhat daunting. You make the most of those be-my-friend
overtures; it suits you to meet new people. They're all so
interesting.

Love, Sex, and Marriage

A connoisseur of the better things in life, you enjoy the
same in the dating game. As much as you love to wander,
you need a solid honey by your side. Nothing replaces having someone you can count on or who believes in you. To
win your heart takes considerable energy on the part of any
would-be lover. Does he hunger for adventure as much as
he lusts for your body?

This is not an idle question because many of your goals
are centered around seeing and living in various parts of
the world. Family is equally important to you, and you're
completely prepared to pack up the tots and teens to come
with you wherever you roam. What better way to teach the
young about where they live? And you demand the utmost
fidelity from your partner.

Money and Career

Money is seldom a problem for you other than making
the last payment on the sailboat or the exercise gym you
bought last year. Wealthy or not, you believe in work and
seeing something tangible for your efforts. If you're not employed in the travel industry, a close second preference is
physical fitness, or arranging trekking expeditions that include you as the host, of course.

You enjoy owning a business and like to be involved
about wrist-deep. Providing service and working with interesting people are high priorities for you whether you're an
employee or the employer. You've been known to stay at
a low-paying job because you were working with friends
and/or learning a lot. Part of your personal security comes
from having some money tucked away that's yours and
yours alone. Whether you have to work or not, if not ac-

tively traveling, you will work—where else can you meet travelers such as yourself to swap tall tales with?

The ♏ 5 Potential

Though you don't sugarcoat the truth, you rarely share your keen insight unless appropriate. And when you do, your words cut straight to the heart of the matter, maiming or praising whatever is in question with astonishing accuracy. Having experienced so much yourself and with your insatiable thirst for knowledge, you have uncanny insight into your fellow man.

Sometimes that quick tongue of yours goes on a rampage and cuts the wrong man down to size. But even then you have your reasons—perhaps a personal slight or explanation for unfair behavior that you never got. That doesn't mean you're wrong, but before making a venomous comment, make sure you aren't cutting off your own nose to do so. But even then, what you have to say is usually dead-on. You provide the rest of us with a collective conscience and a running commentary of facts and speculation and we need to hear it.

FAMOUS SCORPIO FIVES

Kate Capshaw	*11/3/1953*	*John Cleese*	*10/27/1939*
Billie Jean King	*11/22/1943*	*Dennis Miller*	*11/3/1953*
Georgia O'Keeffe	*11/15/1887*	*President Teddy Roosevelt*	*10/27/1858*

♏ • 6
Scorpio Six
"The Dazzling Detective"

♏+	6+	♏−	6−
Daring	Responsible	Aggressive	Self-sacrificing
Focused	Artistic	Secretive	Domineering
Practical	Nurturing	Critical	Jealous
Curious	Idealistic		

At the top of your to-do list is love, followed by love, followed by (you guessed it) love. You don't live for love, you understand, but in a crazy world like this one, surrounding yourself with it is essential. Loving friends, devoted family, upbeat co-workers—if you have any say about it, are all one big happy family. Not that you're all sweetness and light— *au contraire,* love is pleasure *and* pain; you know it for a fact firsthand. You are a thoughtful, constructive counselor when there are pieces of a shattered dream to pick up and help glue back together.

As you make the rounds of the office with an encouraging word for everyone, another part of your brain sees everything (Joanne isn't wearing makeup, the picture of Julie's main squeeze is gone, Jeff has herbal tea instead of coffee in his cup), evaluates, and updates your mental files before reaching your own office door. A friendly smile on your lips, there's another layer to your complex personality, the shrewd competitor, always on the lookout to improve, change, and transform the future in your image.

A divine partner and aggressive adversary, you bend over backward to help others get it together to be productive. Should others mistake that concerned cheerleader countenance for a naive bubblehead without a clue of the bottom line, you curtly set them straight. This involves everything from tossing them out on their ear to beating them at their own game. However you act, your intitial reaction is painful—after all you've done for them, how *could* they?

Somewhat of a health nut, you border on being a fusspot about what you will and will not put in your mouth. Life is precious, and keeping your body a finely tuned, healthy machine is a responsibility you don't take lightly. You won't be happy unless you feel as energetic physically as you do mentally. Besides, you want to stay thin to wear those kicky fashions!

Love, Sex, and Marriage

For all your lofty love ideals, your first love is your opposite—exciting, but short-lived. Because a family is important, you eventually narrow the dating-game parameters to marriage prospects only. Vows in front of an altar aren't as important to you as living with a partner who loves you in spite of your imperfections and who endeavors to live up to the high standards you set.

Sex gets better and better as love deepens and fidelity is assured. You eagerly explore the mysteries of love and lust when you know you are loved, and are willing to try almost anything to heighten the experience. When it comes to pleasing and being pleased, you can switch from seduced to seducer with ease, much to the delight of your playmate.

Children play a vital part in your idea of marriage. Those born to you are lucky enough to have a friend for life who will, in spite of any shortcomings, always love them.

Money and Career

History fascinates you almost as much as surgery, the ministry, the chemistry lab, and the entire beauty industry. And on the side you write a book, or many books, from how-to to historical romances to cookbooks, while sharing not only recipes but also personal philosophy. So motivated are you to educate and improve, that you make a brilliant educator and fascinating theorist. Besides, you can make anyone look their best, and that takes talent.

Remember to keep a balance between the private and professional aspects of your life or you keep second-guessing priorities continually. Money is one such priority. You enjoy having it more than not having it, but have never been misguided for more than a nanosecond about the value of spending all your time making big bucks and having the home crew become strangers. You make it as you need it, and alternate between big spending and major investments.

The ♏ 6 Potential

You expect the best from people and are skilled at drawing the positive traits to the forefront of the most pessimistic person. By finding the slighest kernel of an idea, you can prod others into stretching beyond the confines of the box to fulfill their own promise. Nothing pleases you more than that, except perhaps watching your own son be presented with a scholarship to a college he didn't think he could win.

A tiger on the playground or in the boardroom, you let no one get away with wantonly attacking you or yours or a pet project that you *know* will work. Be careful that in your intense rebuttal you don't sear too many egos or burn the bridge completely. Since you never like to leave any loose ends, it will make closure more complicated. Of course, there are those who do need an expert singeing from time to time to see the world the way it really is instead of the way they want it to be. (Ooops, is that too close to a nerve?) Because you know how blinding this illusion can be, you're an expert bubble burster who conscientiously sticks around to pick up those pieces.

FAMOUS SCORPIO SIXES

Goldie Hawn	*11/21/1945*	*Ted Turner*	*11/19/1938*
Brenda Vaccaro	*11/18/1939*	*Michael Landon*	*10/31/1936*
Bonnie Raitt	*11/8/1949*	*Simon LeBon*	*10/27/1958*

♏ • 7
Scorpio Seven
"The Practical Perfectionist"

♏+	7+	♏-	7-
Energetic	*Perfectionist*	*Skeptical*	*Secretive*
Compassionate	*Intellectual*	*Self-critical*	*Argumentative*
Tenacious	*Analytical*	*Intense*	*Suspicious*
Quick-witted	*Private*		

When you first learned that the earth travels at one thousand miles per hour, you raced home to see if the goldfish had been flung out of the bowl from the speed. Max and Maxine were okay swimming peacefully around the bowl, blissfully unaware of something so scary as science. The next day you learned about gravity and walked home wondering if we'd all get sucked into the center of the earth. All this knowledge was such a burden in the fourth grade. Now it delights you to discover new and useful information.

You might not admit it to your hairdresser or lover, but there's a competitive streak in you a mile wide. Every now and then the aspiring ladder climber pops out and you fantasize about leaping to the podium to accept your award for cutting-edge research into the mysteries of mating rituals of goldfish. What next? A monastery to make wine and meditate? As tempting as it sounds, you have other fish to fry (no, no, not Max and Maxine—they're family).

The lone-wolf pose suits you every now and then, but you also use it as much to withdraw to sift through new facts and regroup before getting back in the game as you do to truly detach from the pack. There are those times when you need quiet moments in the garden to contemplate the beauty of a tree and analyze the intricate patterns of life. Other days you use the retreat to read a romantic novel or jot private thoughts in a journal.

Knowing as much as you do, you wonder why sometimes you still have problems you can't solve. No one has all the answers, not even you. But with your keen intellect and practical determination, it certainly seems as if you do to the rest of us.

Love, Sex, and Marriage

The cool, reserved facade masks the passionate heart of a willing lover. So skilled are you at keeping your attraction under wraps that you might give your intended a little warning before slipping him your hotel room key. Not that he won't be there. Few can resist what you promise because of all your eyes imply. But fair is fair and you always want the cards on the table before you hop into the Jacuzzi with someone, don't you?

Marriage may have to wait until later—you have so much to do. Of course, you change your tune if someone on the same wavelength comes along. You do so love a mystery, and if another intellectual in just the right package appears, you plan to unravel the mysteries of life, and each other, forever.

Money and Career

Philosopher, scientist, psychic, surgeon, all suit you. Instead of choosing, you're likely to be all of the above and more. Acting is second nature to you since you've got a multilayered personality and can easily choose one aspect or another to fit any occasion. A natural detective, you use charm and observation to get to the bottom of a knotty tangle. Hunches work for you when you back them up with facts in hand, and as competitive as you are, you learn how to get those facts early in your career.

Recognition for your efforts is important and money is only one form of it. Though you have more of it stashed away than most who know you would guess, you know how to make a buck last and can live simply or in swank style just as easily. As long as you have your electronic gadgets and books, and a selection of food to put on the table, you're happy. Whether you're head of the department, an artist on Hawaiian shores, or the entrepreneur, doing and learning from what worked and what didn't, learning from experience is what it's all about.

The ♏ 7 Potential

You get started early, trading childhood toys to perfect skills that enable you to hit the ground running at a tender age with no regrets. Satisfying your curiosity and researching the mysteries of the universe provide more than enough challenge and excitement for you. You have the ability to bring together disparate facts, logic, and intuition, and weave them together to provide fresh and useful information for the rest of us.

There's a fine line between experiencing all life has to offer firsthand and jumping off the deep end. Think long and hard before taking a step in a direction with no U-turn lane, no matter how enticing the hook might be. And should you venture into territory that threatens to swallow you up, reclaim your identity and write a book to warn off the others. With you, nothing is wasted. Knowledge is power, and to not succeed is only a setback (never a failure). As long as blood is pumping through your veins, there's a chance of success, and that's enough to keep you and the rest of us inspired.

FAMOUS SCORPIO SEVENS

Bo Derek	11/20/1956	Bruce Jenner	10/28/1949
Kate Jackson	10/29/1948	Dylan Thomas	10/27/1914
Julia Roberts	10/28/1967	Françoise Voltaire	11/21/1694

♏ • 8
Scorpio Eight
"The Stylish Traveler"

♏+	8+	♏-	8-
Patient	Authoritative	Suspicious	Workaholic
Determined	Global View	Inconsistent	Impersonal
Constructive	Endurance	Ambitious	Indecisive
Quick-witted	Capable		

Nothing is ever cut-and-dried. Even the simplest cut diamond has a multitude of facets to reflect the light. People are like that—multifaceted, durable, and glorious. The good guy isn't completely good any more than the bad guy is thoroughly bad. Yes, there are a few wackos who might be, but not in the "look at that guy sitting at the table by the plant in Starbuck's window" sort of way. Not the players in the circles you usually run in. It could be true if you decide to make it your life's mission to clean up those other circles; Scorpio Eights are proficiently skilled to do so.

Picking out a new diamond is more to your liking. A little reward for a job well done is always in order, whether it was for losing those ten pounds (again) or snaring the million-dollar-deal for your profoundly grateful CEO. So you can't afford a diamond; that doesn't stop you from purchasing grade A pavé crystal to reflect the sparkle of success. You well know the difference between failure and success and can't even count the number of times you've picked yourself up to dust off your derriere before plunging forward on another tack.

Failure isn't a word you use—so final, so depressing! Besides, who in their right mind would ever admit to not being able to learn from their mistakes? Certainly not famous researcher Dr. Jonas Salk, spent his later years searching for a vaccine to slow the spread of AIDS infection, and who successfully invented the polio vaccine earlier in his career. Sure, he found a lot of ways that didn't work, but eventually he found the way that *did* work, and saved the lives of millions from polio. His dogged persistence is part of every Scorpio Eight.

And if there's fun to be had along the way to reaching the finish line, you find it. Like now. With your new pavé teardrop necklace aglitter, you walk back by Starbuck's window to find that adorable brunette is still reading the newspaper, slowly sipping his coffee, and the other chair at that cozy table is still vacant. Are all the Universal vibes going your way today or what?

Love, Sex, and Marriage

The relationship starts in Australia when you meet a fellow American who immediately switches on the hidden fantasy file you keep so well concealed. As you compare passport stamps and swap border-crossing stories using foreign accents and languages, you check out the bare third finger on the left hand. Your eyes are stuck on the curve of a muscular calf but manage to focus on the clear blue eyes and luscious smile to catch the punch line of the story in progress.

Waiting for the MTA or TWA, it doesn't matter. A meeting like this doesn't come along very often. By the time he pulls out his laptop computer and flips it on in response to a question you've posed, the only thing left is the "I dos" and designing a home with separate offices and a room set aside for a nursery. That and delicious bedroom games, of course.

A healthy skeptic, you love the way you met, but there's no rush to make it permanent. Plenty of time to meet his mom and dad, and kid sister Annie, and to make sure the fit is right for the future you envision. Better safe than sorry, even in the romance department, eh? "Where have you been all my life?" is really more likely to come out as "What have you done so far?"

Money and Career

Respect is as important to you as the green stuff, but you do so love the sound of "stock options," and "upping your bonus percent." No mercenary, you must be making a solid contribution for the good guys to be happy in your work. Jobs that fit like a glove are reporter, educator, executive, artist, or any job that involves travel. Even touring with a rock band (as someone onstage, of course) suits you as long as the applause and pay are right. Money comes and money goes in an endless cycle for Scorpio Eights.

An astute judge of character, you interview propsective employers as thoroughly as they interview you. Likewise employees. You can spot potential and never miss an opportunity to watch it bloom. Current and former employees often thank you for hiring them and credit you with opening doors for them at just the right time. You were only doing what a responsible manager does, and are pleased to be able to help others succeed as you have.

The ♏ 8 Potential

Your first goal at the tender age of five was to own Disneyland. Okay, it wasn't for sale, but that doesn't stop you from thinking big for the rest of your life. You're tougher on yourself than anyone else could ever be. Once you set a high bar, you actively chip away at obstacles and complications to get results. You inspire others to believe in themselves, and seldom expect anyone to work as hard as you do.

Lighten up and spend an afternoon whale-watching with your niece occasionally. The workaholic buzz gets hollow if that's all you ever hear. Even a spouse can't compete with your devotion to work, and shouldn't have to, right? Besides, when the wheel turns and you experience a string of high highs and low lows, you need the loving support of the family you love; the family you knew you needed to keep from being an aimless drifter instead of the first-class investigator/deal maker that you are.

FAMOUS SCORPIO EIGHTS

Mary Hart	*11/8/1951*	*John Philip Sousa*	*11/6/1854*
Princess Grace Kelly	*11/12/1929*	*Pablo Picasso*	*10/25/1881*
Loretta Swit	*11/4/1937*	*Martin Scorsese*	*11/17/1942*

♏ • 9
Scorpio Nine
"The Mystic Manager"

♏+	9+	♏-	9-
Practical	*Compassioante*	*Forceful*	*Detached*
Energetic	*Impartial*	*Moody*	*Careless*
Tenacious	*Charismatic*	*Ambitious*	*Needs Approval*
Smart	*Performer*		

Before you knew it was unusual, you were happy to confide that your imaginary friends visited you for tea every afternoon. They were as real as the air tea you poured into tiny enamel teacups with red roses on them. So real, in fact, you knew whether you were drinking Darjeeling or orange pekoe, and which song Darla, who wore the funny hats, sang as you poured the air tea. This was your first taste of the intangible realm and its precious guidance and inspiration that you receive on a regular basis through the years.

The first time you heard about reincarnation, it answered questions you hadn't even asked and slid puzzle pieces together you hadn't realized you were collecting. Whether you kept it to yourself or told the world, you immediately recognized its value and learned as much about it as you could. Scorpio Nine General George Patton credited his military strategic skills to several lifetimes spent on the battlefield, but not every Scorpio Nine is so quick to go on public record about such stuff.

You wouldn't think of giving the credit for enhancing those life skills to anyone else, and may never acknowledge the spiritual connection you've discovered to anyone else. It doesn't matter. The important thing is that you are open to experience any and everything in life in your quest to make the days you have on earth count for something.

A private person, you do enjoy having an audience. As a result, even if you aren't performing under hot stage lights, you become a leader in your own right. People respond to you when you get up to speak. Your ideas, however unusual, get everyone thinking more about the possibilities of the future than the events of the past.

Love, Sex, and Marriage

Performance is important to you—you even approach the dating-courtship-marriage thing with a careless air that belies the intense drive you have to make every moment perfect. A generous lover, you're as creative in the bedroom as you are onstage. When you fall in love, it's completely, and you don't hesitate to reveal to your partner the vulnerable side you hide from everyone else. Your love is unconditional, though you might appear to be impersonal or detached at times.

Find a mate who isn't rattled by a continually ringing

phone and doorbell. Befriending a stranger in need is as natural to you as inviting the entire office home for dinner and a game of touch football. And consider the quests that take you away from the home fires for weeks at a time. Even when you're home, you get lost in your own thoughts and projects and need a secure partner who understands and approves of what you do.

Money and Career

Your captivating smile enchants audiences large and small. From Danny in the next cubicle to the executive staff upstairs, you garner unilateral support without opening your mouth. Good thing, because on any given day you have the choice of a dozen possible ventures to be achieved. You do equally well as an employee or a boss. You prize a well-oiled team, and fit in well when you share the same objectives. Otherwise, you prefer to do your own thing, such as write a provocative novel or construct beautiful buildings.

Compassion for the underdog gives you remarkable insight into the human condition—valuable knowledge to succeed in any areas that attracts you. At home in front of an audience, you have the dramatic talent to complement your shrewd perceptive ability. Interestingly enough, you are as technically oriented as you are creative and can earn a fine income whatever you decide to do. The combination of creativity, curiosity, and technical savvy keep you a willing worker long after friends have retired.

The ♏ 9 Potential

The choice to be famous or infamous is yours, but life is easier once you accept that you won't be allowed to blend in with the crowd or shuffle off to anonymity. Knowing that what you do *is* noticed makes you think twice before taking action; at least it could be a safety net for you if you let it. You have multiple opportunities to do big things, but the choice is yours to go for it or not.

Like other Nine combinations, you seldom meet a stranger. As a Scorpio Nine, you have fine-tuned reception for such events and use those déjà vu feelings to identify the subliminal (or past life) connection you have with the person you just met. Since nothing is allowed to stay the same, people enter and leave your life via a cosmic revolving door. Yet the contact, however brief, is meaningful, sometimes overwhelming, and always memorable.

FAMOUS SCORPIO NINES

Linda Evans	*11/18/1942*	*Rock Hudson*	*11/17/1925*
Dale Evans	*10/31/1912*	*Burt Lancaster*	*11/2/1913*
Mackenzie Phillips	*11/10/1959*	*Kurt Vonnegut*	*11/11/1922*

SAGITTARIUS

•

♐ • 1
Sagittarius One
"The Fearless Philosopher"

♐+	1+	♐–	1–
Energetic	*Inventive*	*Impulsive*	*Headstrong*
Enthusiastic	*Original*	*Fanatical*	*Iconoclastic*
Open-minded	*Self-starter*	*Blunt*	*Overbearing*
Fun-loving	*Daring*		

Dr. Livingstone, I presume? As a kid you were splayed across the carpet with an atlas almost as big as you, poring over maps and memorizing world capitals; you still keep up-to-date with the latest name and leadership changes. The siren call of exotic places beckoned, Timbuktu to Kalamazoo. You exemplify the Sagittarian fascination with adventure and curiosity about different cultures. For you, life is like an air-conditioned motor coach, without prattling guide and fixed itinerary. Even an uncharacteristically timid Sagittarius One takes risks, but more in the manner of a small child entering an abandoned house on a dare.

An individualist and rebel, you abhor living according to societal restraints and delight in violating taboos. One thing you won't tolerate is limits. A true maverick, a Sag One archer lives life at full gallop, resisting anyone who attempts to rein you in; you'll throw anyone who tries to saddle you with too much responsibility that isn't of your own devising. You know where you're going and you're playing Pied Piper to the rest of the planet.

Nothing is more important than those shining goals and ideals. You're not opportunistic, but you know when to seize opportunity that presents itself. No one sells him or herself better than a Sagittarius One. It's so convincing precisely because it isn't a performance. Your faith in yourself is so unshakable that you can make even the most outlandish idea sound plausible. No wonder the prototypical Sagittarius One was Walt Disney, who brought out the child in us all and truly believed "It's a small world after all."

Love, Sex, and Marriage

You value your independence and that of others. You offer—and would prefer to receive in return—devotion, loyalty, commitment, mutual respect and support, sharing adventures and goals, a good raucous debate now and then, continual curiosity about life, and passion (on any number of levels). If you don't marry, it's not necessarily because you're afraid your freedom will be curtailed (though like all archers, you're a prime exponent of the "don't fence me in" philosophy of relationships). You're aware that sometimes you must go it alone, pick up at a moment's notice and travel, and you can't bear to make promises you know you can't keep. Especially earlier in life, that may be a revolving door to your bedroom.

You should try to focus your love life and get it out of the way, so you can concentrate on doing your own thing (once you've discovered what that is, of course). You require a steady mate who doesn't get in your hair yet knows exactly how to ruffle it when you're ruffled, preferably someone with a strong career of his or her own. You want someone smart, sharp and stylish, who can stand up to you in a debate and stand in for you until you arrive at the latest see-and-be-scene soirée.

Money and Career

There's nothing Mickey Mouse about your ambitions. You're likely to change careers or diversify your field of operation. Behind that twinkle is serious, steely business. You won't stop until you've made that dream become reality. Despite being a high-minded philosopher and deeply caring person, you're capable of sacrificing people to your ideals. Your energy and eagerness move mountains (or at least re-create them on your chosen spot!).

You're a pioneer and couldn't stay long in one place; being behind a desk is stultifying. Of all people, you need to determine your own special line of work and start your own business. Not that any profession is denied you; you attack your job with driving enthusiasm. Your competitive instinct means success whether you become an able athlete, boffo business tycoon, or canny comedian. You love making people laugh, so your piercing wit comes in handy as a writer or performer. As your powerful presence makes people snap to attention, politics and the military are other possible vocations.

The ♐1 Potential

Your sparkling Sagittarius One humor and serious idealism seek to improve humankind's condition in unique ways. You're the original dream weaver, and you don't drop a stitch. But you never step back and admire your handiwork, because you're already working on a new pattern. Think of some of those classic Disney songs: "When You Wish Upon a Star" and "Whistle While You Work." They might just as well be your mottos as you cheefully knit the world closer together.

FAMOUS SAGITTARIUS ONES

Noel Coward	12/16/1899	Benjamin Disraeli	12/21/1804
Sammy Davis Jr.	12/8/1925	Patty Duke	12/14/1946
Jean-Luc Godard	12/3/1930	Teri Garr	12/11/1949

♐ • 2
Sagittarius Two
"The Mellow Maestro"

♐+	2+	♐-	2-
Striving	*Supportive*	*Thin-skinned*	*Extremist*
Tolerant	*Charming*	*Undisciplined*	*Nervous*
Imaginative	*Intuitive*	*Brash*	*Procrastinating*
Innovative	*Sincere*		

A tender soul, you weave a poetic spell wherever you go. Openhearted and open-handed, you set yourself up for many a fall, but always fall back on your rich imagination and unshakable faith that things will work out. You have an incurably romantic streak, which is often manifested not on a personal but on a private, creative level. You channel your emotions into the piano or the paintbrush, but your shyness won't always allow you to share your gift. Your closest friends might be surprised to learn you're a wickedly deft pen-and-ink caricaturist or can play a Chopin étude with both precision and feeling.

Your artistry extends to your inner circle. Your love will relate an anecdote of your experience stomping grapes in Tuscany at a tiny family vineyard; though not a storyteller yourself, you can't resist embellishing it with unique touches or telling details only you observed that bring it to life. The sad-eyed waif hiding behind you whose parents scolded her for trying to join in because she was too small. The fat, jolly uncle singing arias in a booming tuba baritone and scooping up cupfuls as he danced the tarantella through the vat. When someone interrupts to ask why they don't just sell the grapes to a bigger vineyard if they lack the machinery, you say the wine is just for private use, remind them that's not the point anyway, and make a note to throw in a lecture on the world's increasing dehumanization later. You believe everyone has an interesting life story to tell, and feel you should play the wandering minstrel of old, singing the praises of Everyman.

You're philosophically mawkish, listening compassionately as total strangers spill out their hopes, dreams, and fears. You become terribly sentimental about people's paths in life. You want to walk alongside them, chattering about the scenery and chatting up the locals you meet, as you take the voyage. For all your buoyancy, you're a wounded sparrow indeed when your wings are clipped. You need supportive friends, not so much for balance as ballast.

Love, Sex, and Marriage

Commitment is not a four-letter word to a Sagittarius Two. You're not into casual sex; you're looking for someone who can bolster your self-esteem, respect your individuality, won't tramp heavily through your dreamworld in muddy combat boots, and will always be there to caress you when something disappoints you. Sure, you're fiery as all get out and know how to keep the flames of passion stoked for a long time, but that's the point: companionability and intellectual/emotional compatibility are vital before you warm up those sheets. You'll set the bed aglow with a steady blaze, since your Sag side is sexually experimental and your Two side is sensitive and attuned to others' needs.

For a relationship to work over the long haul, you need to feel in touch, that you have shared interests and goals; then you'll gladly portage through any rough spots. You're often diffident in your advances and need someone with the right teasing yet loving touch to elicit your trust. Once burned, quadrupled shy, you must curb your fatalistic streak and lower your expectations, if not your standards.

Money and Career

With your vivid imagination and affectionate personality, you can become an admirable artist, actor, healer, mystic, minister, theologian, philosopher, professor, painter, poet—take your pick. You make a surprisingly good fighter when you believe in the cause, and your fire often thrusts you into the role of reluctant leader. But your ardor always carries the day with your troops. Actually, you're a dazzling writer or director of breadth and vision. You're irresistibly drawn to epic and/or romantic subjects of course. Your touch is gossamer-fine and silken-smooth.

Between the glad-handed Sagittarian influence and the Two's thrift, you'll probably be impulsive about money, giving it away one minute, regretting it the next. Hmmm. Better let your partners handle the accounting.

The ♐ 2 Potential

You exist to bring life's lyrical side to light. You have a subtle, rarefied charm and appeal. Your looks, style, and manner are all utterly memorable. When you overcome your natural reticence, you become a vocal, inspirational leader, helping others discover the more sensitive, artistic side of their natures. Don't hold yourself back for fear of being hurt or misunderstood; you have greater strength and willpower than you realize until your convictions are tested.

FAMOUS SAGITTARIUS TWOS

Kenneth Branagh	*12/10/1960*	*John Paul Getty*	*12/15/1892*
Kirk Douglas	*12/9/1916*	*Cicely Tyson*	*12/19/1933*
Kim Basinger	*12/8/1953*	*Frank Zappa*	*12/21/1940*

♐ • 3

Sagittarius Three
"The Winsome Wanderer"

♐+	3+	♐-	3-
Cheerful	*Expressive*	*Impractical*	*Flighty*
Optimistic	*Creative*	*Fickle*	*Profligate*
Clever	*Merry*	*Gabby*	*Unstable*
Idealistic	*Inspirational*		

You feel like Tinkerbell, spreading magic dust, and pleading with the world to clap if it believes in fairies. In your case, though, the fairies are your beliefs, causes, and ideals, and you yearn to find fellow travelers. Curious, bouncy, and jaunty, you bound up to total strangers, chattering inces-

santly and asking personal questions. Okay, you're tactless.
A true Sag Three never intends to hurt anyone; you'll inno-
cently tell your best friend her face looks like a chipmunk
thanks to those extra five pounds. You're inevitably shocked
when she pouts; you were just trying to be helpful, and
besides, she looks kinda cute with her cheeks puffed out!

You'll be just as eager for excitement and novelty at eighty
as you were at eight. Retire? You? You'll never settle down
to canasta, pinochle, and mah-jongg at some cookie-cutter
Sunbelt condo. Despite your seeming Sagittarian restlessness, you possess a highly spiritual side, which tugs at you
from all directions. Until you find a target for your bow and
arrow, you'll always feel you're missing out on something.
Fortunately, your glass always remains half full, if not
overflowing.

Guileless and irrepressible, you can laugh at yourself,
even your most outrageous mistakes, which endears you
to everyone you meet. That happy, happy-go-lucky attitude
makes you lucky. You always seem to get the break, stum-
bling onto the right place at the right time, meeting that VIP
by sheer chance. You have an almost naive faith in yourself,
not to mention the Great Dane of underdogs, and can't resist
betting on long shots; you're often right. You might seem
irresponsible to some. It's not that you lack direction, but
rather that focusing on one thing makes you feel claustrophobic. You need tangents, avenues of mental escape, and
plenty of balls to juggle. If anyone scolds you for being
impractical, you do your patented "Reality? What's that?"
routine, impishly grinning your way out of a potential
drama.

Love, Sex, and Marriage

Every time you fall in love, it's like slipping on a banana
peel: just when you least expected it, there you are on your
derriere with a goofy grin! You always assume in your
charming, naive way that this is it, this is the one. Even if
it's not, you're far too optimistic to remain in the dumps
after you've been dumped. While your heart may never be

broken, it's seen its share of hairline fractures. Yet its beat remains strong and sturdy.

You're solicitude itself—when you're there. You rarely realize partners do a slow burn as you juggle all the irons on your fire; put them on the back burner once in a while and you stand a better chance of happily-ever-aftering. You can overwhelm potential lovers with your inexhaustible energy; buzzing about like a hyperactive mosquito, you can be a nuisance and draw blood when you least intend to. Calm down, Cupid. Remember that if you pepper your target with daily phone calls, one of two things might happen: you'll drive your intended away or frighten yourself off.

Money and Career

No one conveys as much enthusiasm and sheer delight in a project initially as you do. The problem is getting you to see it through. You have no trouble handing over the reins of authority to someone else; in fact, you have little interest in the end result, because you're already off on another journey. Obviously this makes a regular nine-to-five job anathema. You're best off working in fields that permit a flexible schedule. Public relations or marketing would be perfect: think of all those parties you can throw and the people you can meet and introduce. Though your own date book is filled with illegible scribbles and cross-outs, you'd make a superb social secretary, caterer, bridal consultant— anything that allows you to dip into your Filofax and spend hours on the phone.

Money? Hey, it's only paper. But you'd better make piles of it, since you're easy prey for prodigal kids, ex-wives, or lost-lost acquaintances down on their luck. You just can't bear to see a dream deferred and will bankroll even the most outlandish projects just to give someone's sagging spirits a boost, even if it means going bust. Still, money usually materializes when you need it; you've never questioned the source of your almost mysterious good fortune. Even in the most dire straits, that otherwise fair-weather friend you lent a grand turns out to have saved something for a rainy day.

The ♐3 Potential

Your greatest gift is your infectious love of life and people. In your zeal to understand everything, don't overcommit yourself, making promises you can't keep. Good intentions aren't enough; they must be backed up by resolute action. We all have an inner child, but you need to get in touch with your inner parent for guidance. When you've decided what you want to do, you're a genius at convincing everyone in your orbit to help. Whether it's cheering people through a dreary task, cajoling megabucks out of tightwads for your favorite cause, or putting on a clown show for the orphanage, you were meant to remind people that things could always be worse, and if we'd just pitch in together, they could suddenly get a whole lot better!

FAMOUS SAGITTARIUS THREES

Jeff Bridges	*12/4/1949*	*Margaret Mead*	*12/16/1901*
Jane Austen	*12/16/1775*	*C.S. Lewis*	*11/29/1898*
Dave Brubeck	*12/6/1920*	*Bill Pullman*	*12/17/1954*

♐ • 4
Sagittarius Four
"The Audacious Auditor"

♐+	4+	♐−	4−
Honest	*Hearty*	*Inconsistent*	*Overworked*
Humorous	*Nature-loving*	*Self-absorbed*	*Contrary*
Honorable	*Methodical*	*Hotheaded*	*Undemonstrative*
Zesty	*Persevering*		

Life for a Sagittarius Four is a constant search for a balance between grounding and the feeling you've been grounded. You're an intense workaholic, even though you may loathe your job and the daily grind. But it's your nature to find the ideal in everything; you see the beauty even in drudgery, though you grumble, groan, and gripe as much as anyone about ruts and routines. You're not fooling anyone: your friends and associates immediately notice your perseverance, and dedication. That's true of your home life as well. Your spare weekends are filled with painstakingly restoring your house, a standing tennis game (where you run your opponent ragged), and an adult extension course in The Art of the Wok.

Through it all you sustain yourself with your lively, often ribald, sense of humor. You're the Pavarotti of the pratfall; kids love your athletic derring-do, somersaulting over sofas. Despite your deceptively cheerful, industrious facade, you're surprisingly sensitive. Should others anger you, even if you acknowledge deep down they were right to confront you, you can turn off for life. To be fair, few can get an accurate read on you. You're quite the paradox: an obsessive planner who thrives on routine yet bores easily. This impels you turn projects around as quickly as possible so you can move on. Intensely idealistic early on, as you grow older you instill a more practical view of both *l'amour* and your career ("Who, *moi?*" you say, grinning).

As a result, people marvel at your ability to bounce back after every setback. There's no obstacle you can't surmount. You're like those clown punching bags: no matter how many times you get decked, you'll come up smiling, a steely, determined look in your eye. You tirelessly wear down anyone who gets in your way; eventually your opponents back down out of respect and sheer awe.

Love, Sex, and Marriage

You're rather elusive in romance. You want to settle down, but you don't want to settle. You want a home, yet you want freedom, and you often find yourself in some unsatisfactory combination. You labor mightily to make it work, but if it doesn't, you wriggle out, bloody but unbowed, and put it behind you without a thought or a scar. As a result, you're rarely burned, but you sure have been singed a lot! If you've been disappointed, you're skittish; you use your job or your manifold other social commitments as excuses to avoid dating, let alone relationships.

Once someone learns the right approach, leaving you to your own devices, showing the exactly right balance between attention and dismissal, your ears perk up even as your hair stands on end. Suddenly you're saying the vows you vowed never to say again. This time you're determined to see it through, and having learned your own lessons, you probably will. And hey, marriage isn't such a bad idea, after all. Someone cooks dinner while you're at the office, has a bottle of wine waiting, and massages you in all the right places. Hmmmm.

Money and Career

Boy, are you quick with your hands and your words. You make a super sports car or computer technician, software consultant, urban planner, geologist, fabric manufacturer, or engineer; indeed, you thrill to the challenge of building actual bridges and tunnels, which fulfills your need to forge connections on a realistic level. Very good at evaluating situations, you rarely make a false move or investment. Financial planner or CPA are other vocations where you can put your considerable tools to use. Your wit and whimsy can also lure you into the arts. You have real presence as a performer; few can take their eyes off you, either on film or stage. You certainly upstage the other actors—unintentionally, of course. Your writing is similarly distinctive, notable either for its visionary or down-to-earth quality.

The ♐ 4 Potential

Living proof of human resiliency, you set a fine example for others, using healthy doses of humor and practicality to see you through the rough spots. You're a dependable friend, showing up with posies and peppermints every day at the hospital when Rita gets her face lifted and lifting Joe's spirits during his divorce proceedings with a pair of tix to the sold-out Bulls-Knicks game. You're never down in the dumps or down for the count for long, and you spread that message even when you're spread thin.

FAMOUS SAGITTARIUS FOURS

Brad Pitt	12/18/1963	Tina Turner	11/26/1938
Woody Allen	12/1/1935	Larry Bird	12/7/1956
Frank Sinatra	12/12/1915	Mary, Queen of Scots	12/16/1542

♐ • 🜄

Sagittarius Five
"The Nervy Navigator"

♐+	5+	♐–	5–
Spontaneous	Adventurous	Reckless	Restless
Expansive	Communicative	Outspoken	Fickle
Exploratory	Progressive	Tactless	Irresponsible
Ebullient	Outgoing		

At heart, every Sagittarius Five is a time traveler, in search of new worlds, not to conquer, but to defend, for the moment, until you're off on the next adventure. You're a swoony action hero, even if your exploits are limited to rescuing the neighbor's kitty from the elm tree. It doesn't surprise you that the noble immortal alien Highlander (aka Duncan MacLeod) is a Sag Five. You'll roam the world geographically and spiritually before you're through, and don't really care where you're going: it's the journey itself—the lessons you learn and the people you meet along the way—that matters.

You're a rare Sagittarius Five indeed if you haven't at least contemplated eating fugu (the potentially deadly blowfish sushi), skydiving, bungee-jumping, running with the bulls at Pamplona, or being locked in a Lakota sweat box to discover your animal spirit guide. You're too smart to play chicken or Russian roulette for real, but you do take risks. Even as a kid you hated sitting still. No hobbyhorse for you: you zoomed off on that tricycle at warp drive while your mom screamed, "Don't turn the corner!" At ten you rigged a glider and jumped off the roof, convinced you could fly, breaking your wing in two places. Wow, how cool having the entire class sign your cast! Now it may only be your ideas taking flight, but if you crash and burn, well, that's life.

You're reallly an old-fashioned traveling salesperson, with a suitcase full of ideas and ideals to peddle to the world. You actually thrive in chaotic conditions. Think about it: so many possibilities, unanswered questions, endless horizons. And no restrictions! Thanks to that hunger to see and do everything (preferably by the time you're thirty, of course), you'll never feel limited. The world's your oyster, with plenty of pearls of wisdom to collect.

Love, Sex, and Marriage

You're a rolling stone that gathers no moss, though you do gather plenty of amorous momentum. No one could hope for a jollier boon companion, when you're around (which isn't often). You lust after a traveling companion with the same wanderlust; if there's a fork in the road, you take it, shouting, "See ya later and we'll compare notes." Since you're so avid for all sorts of experiences, you have a roving eye, mind, and hands. You thrive on the sheer romance and the danger of being caught, having probably entertained more than a few fantasies of nooky in the elevator or airplane rest room.

Although you intend to be circumspect, you rush in where love is concerned. You pin on the third date, marry on a whim by the eighth date, marry again on the rebound because that nice person you met at the blackjack table in Reno seemed so simpatico. You think of monogamy (if you think of it at all) as an intriguing idea, perhaps worth experimenting, but not your ideal. You're not incapable of fidelity, but it isn't high on your priority list. You consider it impractical; "It's just sex, not love" could be your mantra. You're often happy juggling several affairs at once. You want a challenge, after all, and availability can be a turn-off. But find another dashing, emotional-white-water-rafting sort, and you might just try running the rapids of marriage for keeps.

Money and Career

The market for superhero(ine)s being somewhat limited, you flourish in any activity that doesn't tie you to a desk, such as flight attendant, or better yet, pilot; real-life explorer; journalist, especially war correspondent; and PR flak or even travel agent, specializing in adventure and ecotourism, natch. A stand-up sort, if you can't land a job that takes you to exotic climes, your next choice would be to stand up for someone's rights: indeed, you'd want to overhaul the justice system. Consumer advocacy, defense lawyer, labor organizer, or special-interest-group lobbying is right up your alley.

Money runs through your fingers, especially if there's a new gadget or an Antarctic cruise on sale. You'd be first on the waiting list for the moon shuttle, coughing up the hundred grand even if it means a second mortgage. For all that, you always land on your feet, able to sweet-talk a loan or a raise that keeps your head above water and your new kayak afloat.

The ♐ 5 Potential

Temper your restlessness, both real and spiritual, with a greater consideration of others as individuals: remember, even explorers requre a home base from which to operate. Cultivate a greater sense of responsibility. Everyone needs roots to anchor them; it doesn't mean losing your freedom. You crave understanding and companionship as much as anyone, but you must learn it can't always be on your terms. Sacrifice a little spontaneity; don't suddenly take off on a trek to Tibet at the last minute, forgetting you promised to attend *Madame Butterfly* with your sweetie. Consult other people occasionally and check their schedules. Work assiduously toward your goals—once you've identified them. Then you can travel the world and share your discoveries on both the personal and universal levels.

FAMOUS SAGITTARIUS FIVES

Bette Midler	*12/1/1945*	*Little Richard*	*12/5/1932*
Don Johnson	*12/15/1949*	*Ray Liotta*	*12/18/1955*
Friedrich Engels	*11/28/1820*	*Liv Ullmann*	*12/16/1939*

♐ • 6
Sagittarius Six
"The Electric Educator"

♐+	6+	♐-	6-
Supportive	Idealistic	Insistent	Overidealistic
Cheerleading	Philanthropic	Outspoken	Unreasonable
Open-handed	Straightforward	Reckless	Self-righteous
Joyous	Warm		

Six is the number of duty and responsibility, and Sagittarius the sign of philosophy, idealism, and moral truth. The combination is heady indeed. Extremely patriotic, you're the type who could turn guerrilla if invading troops threatened your family and community, but your sharpshooting and sniping are usually verbal. You're fanatical about your belief system. No, you're not the kamikaze or bomb-planting terrorist sort, yet your zeal carries you far (and sometimes far off the mark). You don't merely like or dislike, you adore or abhor. No moderate, you lean so far left or right you could teeter over if you're not careful, either wrapping yourself in the flag or burning it as an activist. They're two sides of the same coin, of course; you simply have a powerful sense of duty, honor, and ethics—which may not always be mainstream, as the concept of individual civil liberties is usually dear to even the most conservative Sagittarius Six. The chain mail and hairshirt you wear are mighty uncomfortable and woefully unfashionable. But you intend to lead by example, your stamina, willpower, and work ethic unquestioned. Still, you're hardly a puritanical role model. You can blast off at inappropriate moments, shooting from the lip when frustrated. You despise toadies, sycophants, and hypocrites. You're the type who'll out that closeted politician because you think it's the right thing to do. After all, you'd never hide anything yourself. When you're younger you may be more revolutionary, getting arrested at protests, saving everything from the ozone layer to the baby seals.

You need to feel that the entire world is your home and every person in it part of your extended family. You willingly take on the role of Big Brother or Sister to everyone you meet, but can't hack the discipline part; behind the "love, honor, obey me" mentality and stern looks, your elastic face melts into Silly Putty. You just can't hide your emotions; they steal across your countenance like a kid trying to open his presents on Christmas Eve.

Love, Sex, and Marriage

Between the Six penchant for commitment and responsibility and that Saggie impulsiveness, you've mapped out the next fifty years after your first date. Any place you hang your hat is home, but unlike many Sagittarians, you're unafraid to move your entire wardrobe. You don't mind the ranch house, the 2.3 kids, the PTA meeting (all right, the diapers had better be disposable—there are limits, after all). It's a sure bet you have an RV packed and ready to go; you simply take your family along for the ride, imbuing them with the same sense of adventure. You're an ideal parent; you take your kids seriously and take pride in their accomplishments, yet revel in their all-too-human foibles, too, sending in that candid moment of Billy splattered with the tomato/peanut butter/cola concoction that just exploded from the blender to *America's Funniest Home Videos*.

You have your emotional baggage, but have learned when to check it while traveling with someone. You've also learned how to scan others' valises with your X-ray insight. But you consider the luggage valuable: as long as people don't keep it under lock and key, it represents our journey of self-discovery. What could be more exciting than that?

Money and Career

A true humanitarian, you're concerned first and foremost with others' welfare, and like to see the results firsthand. Whatever your field, it had better get you out *in* the field. You're naturally attracted to social work; as a physician or nurse, you'd boast a wonderful bedside manner, gently flirting and coddling. Maybe you'll invent a new line of home products that you can pitch as the only pyramid that really does work. As a manager, you know exactly when to praise them or provide an incentive. The ministry or military are other avenues where you feel you can make a difference.

You wear your heart and your art on your sleeve; you're a writer or performer of charm and accessibility, mining the everyday for your gentle humor. If you want to get out of the house, you could run select tours, like visiting the wine country, or go on the lecture circuit as a self-help guru. If you want to stay at home, your hospitality could lead you to build a B&B. Interaction with others is paramount to your happiness.

The ♐ 6 Potential

You project both wit and warmth. People feel they can confide in you and that you'll offer both sage counsel and a quick quip to cheer them up. You're an advocate of the power of positive thinking. You illustrate your point with anecdotes that go straight to the listener's heart and the heart of the matter. Guard against becoming too narow-minded in your credos; you're generally quite tolerant in the abstract, but can clash with people with dissenting opinions. Agree to disagree; though you won't stop preaching and pitching, now, will you?

FAMOUS SAGITTARIUS SIXES

Caroline Kennedy Schlossberg	11/27/1957	Dick Van Dyke Joe DiMaggio	12/13/1925 11/25/1914
Charles Schulz	11/26/1922	Sinead O'Connor	12/8/1966
Steven Spielberg	12/18/1947		

♐ • 7
Sagittarius Seven
"The Animated Analyst"

♐+	7+	♐-	7-
Original	*Truth-seeking*	*Absentminded*	*Sarcastic*
Knowledgeable	*Studious*	*Foolhardy*	*Distant*
Curious	*Mystical*	*Insensitive*	*Picky*
Specialized	*Civilized*		

Resisting anything humdum, you don't follow the beat of a different drummer, you establish it. Sagittarius Sevens are optimistic cynics, forever deliberating whether the glass is half empty or half full. Nonetheless, you're endowed with a deep faith, not necessarily in organized religion, but that things will work out for yourself and the world at large through a combination of research and good fortune. You want to make your mark; you feel it's your mission to share your philosophy of life with others. Chances are you'll be thrust into the public eye early, often by forces outside your control, and you feel your life has been predestined in some way. Certainly you're fascinated by Fate as a concept, without becoming a fatalist.

Still, you can pity yourself. It seems as though most people simply lack your insight, wisdom, faith, and lust for knowledge. Alas, you may be right, which is why you play so vital a role, whether in your community or with your loved ones. You genuinely question where our ultimate responsibility lies: to ourselves, to our loved ones, or to the world at large. You understand all too well that humanity is a series of communities, each seeking its own identity and sense of belonging, which inevitably come into conflict.

As a result, you're a bona fide news junkie; keeping in touch with current events amounts to a mania. Though you have your backpacking side, you want CNN in your hotel room and papers in five languages representing eight ideologies delivered every morning when you travel. For all your love of the outdoors, big business, and socializing, you need the occasional retreat to commune with nature, taking long

tramps through the woods. You burn off steam in such solitary activities as biking, jogging, and working out; you do
your best brainstorming when you get those endorphins
flowing.

Love, Sex, and Marriage

Those high ideals and visions can cause you to forget the
practical side of life—and love. When you're younger, you
sometimes confuse "hey, hey in the hayloft" for a permanent
liaison, but usually focus on loftier pursuits by your thirties,
when you discover life isn't just one long amusement-park
ride. Suddenly you realize you can be more effective if you
settle down in more ways than one. When Sagittarius Sevens
learn not to equate freedom with lack of commitment, you
carefree roamers make splendid domesticated partners, but
you'll always believe on some level that a house is not a
home.

A clinging vine is like poison ivy. You'd lead a double
life if you could. No, not bigamy, just separate jobs, separate
friends, separate lives on many levels; when they overlap,
grand. Your significant others had better respect that when
you're in "save the world" mode, you can't be bothered. On
the other hand, you welcome spontaneity and the unexpected, even sexually. You want an educated and exploratory mate. Not cheating, mind you; the "don't ask, don't
tell" approach, or better yet, an "open relationship," which
satisfies your code of honor and honesty, allows you suffi-
cient illusion of freedom and control. Besides, you don't
want to hurt your partner—and you're not so sure you want
him or her to enjoy the same independence.

Money and Career

You're a speedy thoroughbred in the workplace, trotting
out one dizzying, dazzling idea after another, leaving your
rivals in the dust as you gallop past. You demand a vocation
that will utilize every ounce of your intelligence and commitment. Lecturer, professor, archaeologist, anthropologist, econ-
omist, and theologian are job descriptions that appeal to you.
Satire is a particular forte, which lends itself to your becom-

ing a newscaster, political correspondent, critic, or writer of bountiful, unlimited imagination. Politics is probably your primary ambition, because you have to feel you're making a difference or you become disillusioned. The only drawback is stumping on the campaign trail: There are only so many babies you can kiss and hands you can shake before you need to curl up with a good book; you've been meaning to reread Kant's *Critique of Pure Reason,* Malthus's *Essay on the Principle of Population,* and Paine's *Common Sense.*

The ♐7 Potential

Your trenchant mind and burning idealism can light the world on fire. You're a dangerous adversary, able to bury someone with a crushing one-liner; your zeal is commendable, but sometimes you have to remind yourself that people are human beings first and platforms second. You exist to move, shake, rattle, roll, and rock this planet with your fiery speeches and disarming combination of earnestness and lightheartedness.

FAMOUS SAGITTARIUS SEVENS

John Kennedy Jr.	*11/25/1960*	*Winston Churchill*	*11/30/1874*
Emily Dickinson	*12/10/1830*	*William Buckley Jr.*	*11/24/1925*
Chris Evert	*12/21/1954*	*Abigail Adams*	*11/23/1744*

♐ • 8
Sagittarius Eight
"The Steadfast Strategist"

♐+	8+	♐-	8-
Honorable	*Ambitious*	*Thoughtless*	*Workaholic*
Frank	*Useful*	*Argumentative*	*Braggardly*
Dynamic	*Capable*	*Blunt*	*Indecisive*
Energetic	*Nonjudgmental*		

Admit it: you Sagittarius Eights would be lost without your Day-Timer and Filofax. Jog with the dogs at 5 A.M. Read the local paper and *Le Figaro* and the *London Financial Times* (delivered daily) over decaf and granola. Flirt with the co-worker down the hall. Sell the board on your latest project, then lunch with a headhunter from a rival firm. Call Aunt Frieda to wish her happy birthday: who has time for cards? Make a mental note to yourself to buy Aunt Frieda a computer and get her on the Internet. E-mail that proposal for the new magazine you want to launch. Squash game with that obnoxiously obsequious junior partner. Attend a cocktail party to save the Paraguayan rain forest, then pop in on three board meetings: a tenants' coalition, an breast cancer fundraiser, and that groundbreaking theater company whose work marries Kabuki and flamenco techniques. Every so often you have a free night—and you're amazed that no one thought to invite you to their birthday party or give you that spare ticket to *Carmen*. Can you blame them? they figure you already have plans and probably aren't home!

No one will ever take this centaur for a ride, since the naïveté and optimism of Sag are counterbalanced by the Eight's common sense and perceptiveness. You should keep a rein on your emotions; bide your time, no matter how much you champ at the bit to change the world. You'll always be an ardent champion of the underdog, but as you grow older, you do become more comfortable and corporate, if not downright conservative, preferring to change the system from within. Still, even as CEO, you can spout off how the world is run by economics and class structure. When you travel—and you will, throughout your life—suddenly you go from hostels and one john per floor to the Ritz (or its nearest local equivalent).

You could well become a socialite-climber, quite literally. Though you often make scads of money, you resist being pent up in your penthouse, so boom, you're financing a trip to scale Everest. Why? everyone asks. Because it's there and you're a globetrotting gladiator! Just remember that money could be easy-come, easy-go and go easyon your impulse throttle.

Love, Sex, and Marriage

Truth be told, you're too busy for dating—unless an escapade is dumped right in your lap. But you don't regard

marriage as a prison. It's all a matter of negotiation. You
have to draw up a contract with yourself guaranteeing X
number of dates per month while you're on the New York–
London–Bonn–Kathmandu route. Your potential partner
had better be as busy as you are, and learn to time his or
her business trips with your own for maximum interaction.
Must've been a Sag Eight who first boasted, "I give great
fax."

You have a healthy, vigorous, but erratic libido, easily
channeled into other outlets like rock or corporate ladder
climbing. Still, when you get around to it, you're the Energizer Bunny of sex: you keep going and going and
going. . . . You're not opposed to the idea of kids, but with
your busy schedule, you know they'd grow up spending
more quality time with a nanny and your personal assistant,
and you just don't think that's fair.

Money and Career

You climb the ladder of success assiduously, yet the view
from each new rung dissatisfies you. You don't fear the
heights, but others' backbiting, desk banging, and general
screaming seem to increase in direct proportion to the height
of your office building. You find the corporate jungle a
steamy, insect-infested place—and love hacking through it.
You'd never find it easy to downsize your company, even
if you know it will save more jobs and money in the long
run. Despite such qualms, you're an excellent businessperson. You can gauge public opinion in your sleep. You
take yourself very seriously, yet have the gift for appearing
nonchalant in the public eye. Jurist, politician (in the opposition), political analyst, spin doctor, and CEO are your natural
eminent domains.

You learn how to dot your *i*'s and cross your *t*'s and gain
mastery of the Xs and Os of corporate fiance as you reconcile your almost Marxist ideals with your capitalist bent. Regardless, you donate more than your share of time, money,
and energy to various charities, causes, and campaigns. Just
remember the money isn't always there, so beware casually

dumping a million shares of IBM while skiing a fresh dump of powder in Utah.

The ♐8 Potential

You could actually show the socialists that capitalism isn't as evil as they fear, when everyone pitches in and a determined effort is made to match people's skills and interests with their jobs. If someone whacks your nose out of joint, don't cut it off to spite your face. Balance your unparalleled honor with realism; choose your battles as carefully as you do your causes.

FAMOUS SAGITTARIUS EIGHTS

Andrew Carnegie	11/25/1835	Jane Fonda	12/21/1937
Ty Cobb	12/18/1886	Nostradamus	12/14/1503
Dick Clark	11/30/1929	Betty Grable	12/18/1913

♐ • 9
Sagittarius Nine
"The Artistic Adventurer"

♐+	9+	♐-	9-
Trenchant	Compassionate	Unrealistic	Critical
Solicitous	Creative	Undisciplined	Demanding
Broad-minded	Charitable	Capricious	Egotistical
Agreeable	Liberal		

A Sagittarius Nine is a high horse indeed, the Triple Crown winner of moral rectitude and humanitarian activism, designed to sprint to the finish line, through not in a cold sweat or dead heat. You have a killer instinct, knowing just when to make your move during the stretch run. Others may think you're dawdling or doodling; they're in for a shock when you pull ahead by a nose at the wire. You do enjoy that photo finish flair! But even when you ride rough-shod over others' feelings, you somehow emerge with your image as the white knight or fair maiden intact. That's because you believe chivalry isn't dead, buried, and decomposing—not while you're here! At least you have a sense of humor about your inviolate code.

You're a deep thinker and an absurdist at the same time, who could probably make existentialism both comprehensible and funny. You have a broad range of interests and can discourse on them for hours at a dinner party, interspersed with your anecdotes about getting married on skis in full bridal regalia and repeating your vows in astronaut suits at NASA. Not to mention a litany of your pet peeves and causes.

Truth is that even though you're probably not conventionally religious, you belong on a pulpit. You can't help but share your views on everything with everyone you meet. You're a fire-and-brimstone preacher when you believe in something; even avowals of your atheism will be put forth with evangelical zeal. You *are* superstitious about karma or whatever you call its equivalent. "Do unto others" sounds like a good idea, anyway, until they try to undo *you* in some way, that is. And believe it or not, you never break a sweat and can squeeze in enough downtime for a whole golf game and wine tasting!

Love, Sex, and Marriage

Although Nines usually point others to the high road, Sagittarians are always emotional rescuers. You long to ride in and save someone from an unhappy marriage or a destructive life. The pattern of your infatuations is predictable. It's all very innocent at first, quite noble and high-minded: no impure thoughts, just friends. You listen compassionately as they tell you how misunderstood they are. You convince yourself that their mate doesn't appreciate them. But *you* do: you'll cherish them.

Alas, once the damsel has been saved, the dragon vanquished, and you have to settle down to the humdrum routine of patching up the chain mail and polishing the sword, uh, silver, the excitement fades. A clever partner will learn how to read your moods, and make him or herself unavailable, well, scarce, with his or her own projects.

Money and Career

Your individuality is your greatest asset and liability in the corporate world. You're a natural salesperson, so smooth and funny at the business dinner, which keeps you out of the doghouse when you rant and rave about poor working conditions, the fact that you haven't received a raise in three months, or how your job sucks because you have to suck up so much. Like any Sagittarian, you want a post that involves travel. News correspondent, the diplomatic corps, or adventure tour operator will do. You can be an author or artist of rare penetrating insight; as an actor, your performances will be thoroughly original—you also know how to pick roles that showcase your talents and will appeal to popular sentiment.

You have exquisite taste and will probably spend megabucks amassing an impressive wine cellar and Native American pottery collection. Since you enjoy the good life and a good debate, you generally associate with people in higher income brackets with equally high-minded ideals.

The ♐ 9 Potential

Charismatic and kindly, you have only to discover your own personal gospel and spread the word. You're an incisive observer of human nature, with a slightly cynical, off-kilter wit that keeps people on their toes. You're a great pal, enjoying sharing your latest interests with everyone in your circle. You're easily bored, and sometimes dismiss people with whom you think you have little in common. You may be right, but you'd be surprised how much you'd learn if you listened when nothing is apparently at stake.

FAMOUS SAGITTARIUS NINES

Garry Shandling	*11/29/1949*	*Jimi Hendrix*	*11/27/1972*
Louisa May Alcott	*11/29/1832*	*Richard Pryor*	*12/1/1940*
Beau Bridges	*12/9/1941*	*Mary Martin*	*12/1/1913*

CAPRICORN

●

♑ • 1
Capricorn One
"The Tenacious Trailblazer"

♑+	1+	♑-	1-
Diplomatic	*Inventive*	*Lonely*	*Stubborn*
Resolved	*Courageous*	*Unforgiving*	*Domineering*
Reliable	*A Leader*	*Ruthless*	*Inflexible*
Wise	*Direct*		

It's not that you ever expected to be famous; you just do what you want to do, what you think is right for you, and voilà! There you are, standing out in front of the crowd. The stuff of legends is in your veins: Martin Luther King Jr., Kit Carson. Famous or infamous, à la the notorious Capricorn One Benedict Arnold, there's no hiding for you. From the first fist of fudge you snitch from the plate cooling in the kitchen at age five, to having your private notes for a sensitive business deal fall into the hands of the opposition, there is little in life you can actually get away with. You learn to be careful.

Caution doesn't stop you from taking a gamble when the perceived gain is greater than the potential loss. You're determined to come in first, and politician that you are in any game, you manage to take charge *almost* any time you want. The inspirations you have today, as out there as they seem, history judges to be a voice of your times. Somebody has to be the first one to speak up.

If you suffer from a lack of confidence, even intimate friends won't know. How could they tell the difference between your normal reserve and aloof withdrawal? They can't and won't, unless you make an out-of-character decision and tell them. You plow through the anxiety on your own, and eventually start moving forward again. As persevering as you are, you abruptly end any plan or cut loose any pal that is holding you back.

With a reverence for the traditional, you're a fountain of ideas about how to improve the future. Digging for details isn't your strong suit. But even before swilling down your first cup of coffee, you can open minds to new ideas and point the way to Shangri-La. Everyone wants to be on your team because they know a winner when they see one.

Love, Sex, and Marriage

You know a good thing when you see it, too—trim figure, crowning-glory hair, and lots of common sense. "Now, there's one attractive couple," people say when you two walk into a room. Since you don't consider yourself so good-looking, you gravitate to prospective partners with more head-turning potential than you have. But you're not the shallow sort, you want more than to look good together, you also want a buddy who believes in you and your dreams.

Family is important to you, and though you may enjoy your children more as adults than little ones, you wouldn't be happy without them. Marriage is a step you don't take quickly. Okay, you might impulsively pop the question, but that's only after hearing every word on the grapevine about your lover and checking him out from tipsy halo to toes. You expect respect in public, and passionate bedroom games in private. With your magnetism, you always have a choice of partners.

Money and Career

Money is the first consideration in every move you make. Experience teaches you that if you don't track every penny, the golden goose stops laying those valuable eggs. Besides, you prefer to buy the best, and while you might shop for a bargain eighteen-karat bracelet for your sister's sweet-sixteen party, you always buy the best quality you can. You know you and yours deserve the best.

You work hard for your money, and believe in your ability to manifest promotions and better jobs. If you aren't holding the reins at work, you must at least be revered as the resident expert to not scan the want-ads every day for something better. Designer, engineer, dentist, politician, jeweler, musician, art dealer or manager are all perfect spots for you to earn a good living and be well satisifed to boot.

The ♑1 Potential

You have strong visions of how to make improvements, usually against tradition, on a grand scale or one on one. People are willing to follow you; they understand the logic of your ideas and respect your awesome ability to get things done. With you in front to lead or behind to push, you encourage others to perform miracles.

All work and no play makes you tired, tired, tired. Lighten up! You can't inspire anyone when you've been living on junk food delivered to the office, or not had a full night's sleep since you can't remember when. Use your executive ability and inventive ideas to lead by example and get more done in less time that you thought possible.

FAMOUS CAPRICORN ONES

Janis Joplin	*1/19/1943*	*Humphrey Bogart*	*12/25/1899*
Tiger Woods	*12/30/1975*	*Brandon Tartikoff*	*1/13/1949*
Simone de Beauvoir	*1/19/1908*	*Rosalind Cash*	*12/31/1938*

♑ • 2
Capricorn Two
"The Aspiring Ambassador"

♑+	2+	♑-	2-
Ambitious	Tactful	Stingy	Timid
Dependable	Supportive	Workaholic	Moody
Organized	Gracious	Fatalistic	Extremist
Generous	Conscientious		

There are at least two sides to you. Not that anyone would actually say you were two-faced, so stop that sensitive flush before you start smarting about the nerve of some people. You have to admit that you can lead colleagues on a merry chase for today's itinerary. With your multilayered agendas, it's hard to know what's necessary and what are pet to-do's you want to dip your artistic hands into. To get to pick what you want to do, you spearhead the delegation of tasks with a smile.

Efficient, yet sensitive to everyone's needs and whims, you nimbly lift a heavy load even at your own expense. You fully expect a round of give-and-take and are stunned to find out not everyone plays by the same rules you do. When that happens you slip away to lick the wounds in private. Sometimes it *is* proper to sulk alone, but not for too long. Learn the art of collaborative confrontation and you can vanquish adversity and keep everyone's self-respect intact, especially your own.

Taking the stairs two at a time on your way to a meeting puts you at the boardroom table first to soak in the vibes of the place before the big players arrive. No matter where your name falls on the company's organizational chart, you never feel like a big player. You see your role as the Good Sense Glue to hold the group together to focus on the collective objective.

"Doing the right thing" is no hollow motto for you, but words to live by. The definition of the right thing changes frequently, depending on the situation. You dig deep to offer ways to make it a win-win for everyone, but when you can't, you ensure that you and yours come through the flames okay. Hence the root of the "more than two sides to the complex you" tales making the rounds.

Love, Sex, and Marriage

Few can penetrate the tough shell that houses the heart of a beguiling romantic. You search for the Prince Charming on your personal wave length—the fellow with enough brains to read a spreadsheet and enough guts to punch a hole in the thick wall of unavailability you've built around your vulnerability. Even with a shallow fling here and a near-miss engagement there, you never give up hope that Mr. Right will come knocking.

Marriages are built on partnerships, and partnerships start on the playground, the gym, and at the office. Mixing business with pleasure is a must because you live at work as much as you do at home. You've been known to blur the line between the two, so please remember to lock that office door with its smashing park view from the eighteenth floor before you sweep your sweetie onto the mahogany desktop to indulge your mutual desires.

Money and Career

With an astute hunch, you surprise competitors by stopping a deal in motion to study the possibilities thoroughly. Of course, you want to make big bucks, but more than money, you crave the accompanying accolades to validate the achievement of becoming the best in your field that you can be. Expect to have a few different careers in your life as you alternate between the workaday professions and many creative interests.

You manage employees with ease, and provide them with every tool needed to perform. All you expect in return is a job well done, acknowledgment for acting as mentor, and respect for your privacy. You also envision money and first-class bennies to be a reward, and once you find out about the bonus plan, you figure out how to get in on it.

The ♑2 Potential

A gatherer of facts, you do the research and have the intuition to be a reliable forecaster of trends and outcomes. A practical visionary, you share insights when appropriate and always with someone near and dear. Gracious in spirit, you soothe a worry with a kind word and a folded fifty-dollar bill—no questions asked. The paycheck is important, but you never neglect friends or family in the process of earning one.

To make your own spirits sparkle, retreat from the daily grind to beautiful surroundings on a regular basis. Ink "time alone" into the schedule every month or so, and don't let anything come between you and your date with yourself. Teach others to be sensitive to timing, pay attention to details, and listen to their intuition to pursue the prizes that will make them happy. Others have seen you do it, so they know your special formula works, and look to you to share the secret recipe.

FAMOUS CAPRICORN TWOS

Pat Benetar	1/10/1953	A. A. Milne	1/18/1882
Jane Wyman	1/4/1914	Edgar Allen Poe	1/19/1809
Shelly Fabares	1/19/1944	Vidal Sasoon	1/17/1928

♑ • 3
Capricorn Three
"The Imaginative Manager"

♑+	3+	♑-	3-
Sensible	Creative	Jealous	Extravagant
Conventional	Sociable	Nervous	Cynical
Particular	Imaginative	Brooding	Scattered Effort
Diplomatic	Expressive		

Thank goodness you had a practical fairy godmother as a young tot. She and the Tooth Fairy left you hard cash and fanciful dreams that put your tiny feet on Imagination Lane in search of fun and fortune. Even after you come to terms with the fact that pixie dust won't make you fly, you keep the glittery bottle and a sunny-side-up smile. If there is a way back home from Oz without ruby slippers, you will find it. Magic or no, there's always a way.

Youthful effervescence stays with you even after retirement. Besides fanning your charisma, it's a fountain of ideas and energy. That energy, complemented by the stash of functional data you've acquired about how to get on in the big, wide world, lets you remain active long after college pals have hung up their track shoes.

Whatever career track you choose, you use those creative talents and gut feelings to imprint your personal stamp on the endeavor. Self-expression is your lifeblood, and no job or relationship lasts long if it doesn't give you the freedom to do your own thing. You always make it to the finish line, but you do resent being told how to get there.

As quick as you are, you can easily switch from one activity to another yet, you never give up on favorite quest. If something isn't working out, you simply set it aside for a while. The first chance you get, you go back to see if it might fly this time. You don't believe any effort is wasted. The treasure may be yours years later, but it happens only because of your particular brand of persistent magic!

Love, Sex, and Marriage

You know about all the different kinds of love—the forever-and-ever kind, the right-now kind, and the tantalizing tango kind who's got your full attention as he handles that sculpted physique like the sensuous instrument it is! You wouldn't say no. In fact, the glint in your eyes says you're figuring out how to make it happen. It's not that you're a no-tell-motel girl, but there are some sumptuous morsels simply too good to pass up.

As the resident romantic, you know not every mating dance ends up in "I love you" or "Hey, let's do the happily-ever-after thing," but that doesn't stop you from grabbing a partner and stepping onto the dance floor. In love, you sometimes go to elaborate lengths to endear yourself to a prospective partner, but you are much too sensible to let the game get out of hand. Since you're a child at heart forever, little tykes and big teenagers are drawn to your side. If you decide to do the family thing, you find your offspring a delightful wonder.

Money and Career

As long as you can curb extravagant spending, you can have the stocks and savings you want. Not only do you believe in the hard-work ethic, you also know that if you do it the right way and never give up on yourself, the sky's the limit—even when it comes to money. Your so-called unrealistic view of the world has worked for you over and over again. The best opportunities come through friends and occasionally a synchronistic meeting with a stranger. And it's especially helpful to have your network of influential friends you can call to make it so for you.

You like to run your own show, but are a patient ladder climber. Disciplined, you watch and learn as you create and do. By the time you are offered the lead, you are ready for the part. Remember the tales of another Capricorn Three, Horatio Alger? That's a legacy to live up to, which on some psychic wave you already knew, didn't you?

The ♑3 Potential

The unbeatable mix of Capricorn's down-to-earth good sense and persistence mixed with Three's creative talents and artistic flair make you an unbeatable combination in business and pleasure. You are a thoughtful person with the ability to be an amazing success once you pick a particular direction. Like a bumper car bouncing through life, your resiliency is inspiring.

Knowing you is a profitable and happy experience; everyone who joins the party in progress at your place is made to feel welcome and valued. Don't let stress pop your temper valve or turn you ruthless. Stay focused and positive. Celebrate achievements and make light of it when the bottom falls out. With your enthusiasm, executive ability, and fixed focus, you'll be back on top in a twinkling or two.

FAMOUS CAPRICORN THREES

Katie Couric	1/7/1957	Kevin Costner	1/18/1955
Maggie Smith	12/28/1934	David Bowie	1/8/1947
Tracey Ullman	12/30/1959	Lloyd Bridges	1/15/1913

♑ • 4
Capricorn Four
"The Persevering Perfectionist"

♑+	4+	♑-	4-
Aspiring	Persistent	Conceited	Too Busy
Competent	Constructive	Nervous	Lazy
Organized	Even tempered	Impatient	Stubborn
Particular	Practical		

From the first castle you built with chunky wood blocks or snappy, bright Legos, you have never outgrown the joy of watching a Huge Something be built from Nothing. In those days a building-block project could take days or weeks, depending on the patience of parents and the pounce-swat-grab action of Chaucer cat, the tiger gold opportunist who liked to hang out in your room. Chaucer made you furious when he knocked over your version of a medieval palace, but also taught you that anything can be rebuilt, and it usually comes out better than the first attempt.

You think big but nurture those ginormous goals in secret, lest the cold, callous criticism of others casts a hint of doubt to undermine your determination. A realist, you start small and study world-class achievers to learn how to be competitive—athletes, songwriters, actors, entrepreneurs, and knights in shining armor. The resulting chain of successes startles those who underestimate you, as many foolish adversaries do. You have staying power.

Few will ever know how disciplined and ruthless you are with yourself, nor will anyone convince you *not* to be hard on yourself. Yet you go out of your way to let others know

you accept them just as they are with words of encouragement or an approving smile. You dispense humor to break
tension, and give a hug to show you care. Then you slay
the dragons to keep the kingdom safe. Oddly enough, you
don't expect the same in return from anyone, but once in a
while you think it sure would be nice.

Determined to achieve certain goals since childhood, you
experience setbacks in moving to the front of the line, but
know these are only delays in getting there. You evaluate
in detail the whys and why-nots, then take up the task once
more. In spite of all the effort and hard work, no one is
more surprised than you when they hand you a Grammy,
an Oscar, or the keys to your own castle.

Love, Sex, and Marriage

Red-blooded lust flows through those veins hidden under
the gray gabardine suit. Looks alone don't create chemistry.
It's a combination of substance and sex appeal that has to
be just so before you make a move. Outside the bedroom,
you want qualities in a mate such as appropriateness and
high standards. Inside, anything goes with an eager playmate who loves you. You delve into straightforward sex and
playful with a lover who has the right mix of brains, wit,
and guile to explore the kinks. In addition, you expect your
partner to keep up with you between the sheets and out.

You tend to marry early in life and fully expect the marriage to last forever. Should you find yourself divorced, once
you've come to terms with it, you actively seek another
spouse. Children provide that whimsical view of the world
you sometimes miss. You enjoy your own kids, and make
a responsible parent and a loyal partner to count on.

Money and Career

You learn astute business skills through trial and error.
Luckily, you are cautious enough to not gamble your entire
nest egg on a "sure thing." Well, at least not without a winning prospectus and safety-laced contract involved. When
you do get knocked down, you're dazed to think you over-

looked anything that could have backfired. But then you take a deep breath and plan the next move.

A doer, you must be involved in the planning and execution of projects in order to be happy in your work. You aren't the ivory-tower type, but will go it alone if you have to. You prefer a staff of smart, solid performers to help you get things done your way. Truly you aren't bossy or hardheaded, but you do know exactly what you want and the most efficient way to get it. You do well in accounting, engineering, manufacturing, construction, archaeology, law, education, and the arts.

The ♑4 Potential

You always have a backup plan or two. Primarily an optimist, you take pleasure in proving gloomy Guses wrong. There is always a way to get to the finish line, unless, of course, you decide you don't want to *get* to that specific finish line. Diligent and discerning, you are a steadfast friend and scrupulous ally.

Strive for balance between the professional and private parts of your life. No one can be brilliant all the time without pleasurable diversions, not even you. Enlarge your inner circle of friends and let them offer a helping hand when you need it. There *is* time to do everything and go everywhere you want—you simply can't do it all and have it all at the same time.

FAMOUS CAPRICORN FOURS

Val Kilmer	*12/31/1959*	*Dolly Parton*	*1/19/1946*
Howard Stern	*1/12/1953*	*Clara Barton*	*12/25/1821*
Jason Bateman	*1/14/1969*	*Chad Lowe*	*1/15/1968*

♑ • 5
Capricorn Five
"The Reliable Risk Taker"

♑+	5+	♑-	5-
Conscientious	Versatile	Cautious	Reckless
Down-to-earth	Curious	Awkward	Hasty
Economical	Adventurous	Ruthless	Restless
Generous	Resourceful		

The metal-flake blue four-by-four that you drive indicates the free spirit beneath the conventional everyday clothes. When the five-o'clock whistle blows, you and your honey will be on the beach for a quick swim and a long walk on a sandy shore searching for sea treasures. If he or she can't make it, there's shopping pal Jenny or sweet Aunt Joan just a cell phone call away to share the ocean's beauty with you.

Because you're an organized adventurer, you manage to pack in a chunk of unstructured moments alongside the mandatory meetings, presentations, and phone calls. Monday the beach, Tuesday the bowling league, Wednesday aerobics, and Thursday a private meeting with you-know-who to do you-know-what. All that and you still manage to attend Grandma's birthday party, and transport Keith's science project to school.

Not a dyed-in-the-wool overachiever by any means, you simply schedule equal time for work and play. You readily accept that most of the day is already spoken for out of necessity, and you do more than just make the best of it when it comes to punching the clock. You observe and take calculated risks to advance your position and plump up your paycheck. As long as you don't get too impatient, the plan pays off and keeps your services in demand.

Even your effervescent energy runs out sometimes and forces you to make tough choices between the boating regatta and finishing the proposal for the Becker account. Just the thought of sacrificing fun for work is enough to rejuvenate your batteries. If there's a way to make it all happen, you find it. On those rare occasions when you can't, you're

sensible enough to remember where your bread is buttered
and reschedule the fun for later.

Love, Sex, and Marriage

Your head might swivel around to get a better look at a
to-die-for physique as it glides by, but you introduce yourself to the one holding a guide to Maui and no ring on the
finger. Shared interests, a ready laugh, and an attractive
smile are enough to lure you closer. Sex and having a good
time depends as much on a meeting of the brains as it does
the bodies. Okay, so you've sown a wild oat or two in your
day but when you settle down, that's over and even those
memories fade.

A mate by your side who stands ready to travel on a
moment's notice or take up parachute jumping with you is
the right match for the forever thing. When you two start
talking children, the hard rock and roll turns to conventional
classic. You want only the best for those little guys, and
with you two for parents, they learn not only how to get
on in the world, but also how to shoot the rapids, hold a
job, and keep strong family ties—the same as you do.

Money and Career

Money isn't the only thing, but with the taste you have
for Dom Perignon and ski trips to Aspen, it helps to know
how to make a lot of it. During the lean times that come to
us all, you don't waste any time sitting around and pout-
ing—you buy Korbel and drive the family to Vermont for
winter fun. Just because you work hard for your money
doesn't mean you're stingy with it; you pay the bills first
and put aside a bit for vacation.

Though you like a dependable routine at work, you need
variety within the routine to be happy. You do well in businesses related to machinery, manufacturing, entertainment,
law, tourism, newspapers, and journalism. Since you like to
investigate new items on the cutting edge, and always have
a new idea to promote, people are curious about what you
have to say.

The ♑5 Potential

When you share your practical philosophy, your smooth presentation and worldly air capture an audience of one or one hundred. You didn't ask to be influential, but you are. Your view of being conventional and pushing the boundaries at the same time is unique to other folks. They see you weave adventure and responsibility into a workable lifestyle and want to try it, too.

Be cautious enough to weigh the risks with the excitement of conquering new territory, and consider those lining up behind you to follow before you load up your gear and head out. A physical person, you have a habit of overestimating your endurance and how fast you can snap back. Never lose that youthful enthusiasm for the next foray into the unknown—you never know what's around the next corner.

FAMOUS CAPRICORN FIVES

Benjamin Franklin	*1/17/1706*	*Betty White*	*1/17/1922*
James Earl Jones	*1/17/1931*	*Susan Lucci*	*12/23/1950*
Denzel Washington	*12/28/1954*	*Barbara Mandrell*	*12/25/1948*

♑ • 6
Capricorn Six
"The Ambitious Idealist"

♑+	6+	♑-	6-
Industrious	*Nurturer*	*Suspicious*	*Self-righteous*
Realistic	*Loyal*	*Domineering*	*Moody*
Fearless	*Idealistic*	*Critical*	*Self-sacrificing*
Resolute	*Responsible*		

Today when you casually lean over the copy machine to tell a co-worker you've been having visions and hearing voices, her first response is, "Find out anything useful?" Not so for mystic Capricorn Six Joan of Arc, some 580 years ago. Sure the voices made her "special" and she got to be a

Chosen One, which we all know from watching *Star Wars* and *Mortal Kombat* is as much a curse as the chance to be a superhero. The good news is that your copier sidekick isn't going to schedule a trial, then burn you at the stake because she's sore about the miraculous victory you won in the Hundred Years War.

Okay, so you don't swashbuckle around contemplating strategy to win an impossible war. Instead you stroll around the forty-second-floor offices with a determined "I've got a vision of my own" look on your face. Everyone doesn't have to know the vision is a size-six you in a hot red dress or that you've decided to get that graduate degree no matter what it takes.

Just because you're an idealist doesn't mean your idea of "perfect" is the same as anyone else's. Sure, some people carry the same banners to improve the environment and raise smarter kids, but not everyone wants to give up chocolate and fat. No matter, changing the world starts with you. Even if you *do* become a crusader for a cause, keep your wits about you when it comes to making sacrifices; remember dear Joan!

Let a tolerant heart and strong moral code guide you to show the rest of us that what we do day to day does make a difference. With your sincerity, you could chose a song instead of a sword to lead us, and we'll listen.

Love, Sex, and Marriage

There's an image wrapped in a misty rose cloud of the family you imagine. You play the dating game by multiple rules designed to select the perfect mate from the herd and still appear to be the "I just want to have fun" single kind. Love, sex, and brains are important, but you don't expect a three-in-one package to magically appear. The selection process takes time, and can be a delicious quest.

So you call the faithful stand by guy on Wednesday night and leave for work the next morning from his place. But at Thursday lunch, you contact the Possible Bridegroom and invite him to dinner. You're amazed to find that both these men could fill the bill for the till-death-do-you-part thing.

Assuming, of course, each is also drop-dead gorgeous, your mother loves him as much as your boss does, and the sheets sizzle when the two of you slip between them.

Money and Career

Loyalty isn't just a word to you. You fully expect the office troops to pay attention and stick with you through thick and thin. When moving from one job to another, you like to take a trusted colleague or two with you to the next employer. No problem, since you routinely inspire others who find you hardworking, intelligent, and downright chipper to be around. Whistling while you work is more fun with a group you know.

Your career vision is about being valued for what you do, for enlightening, uplifting, and making a bunch of bucks in the process. Should you land in a drudgery-filled job with cheerless co-workers, you quietly post off a sharp résumé to about a million places and find a new place where your vision, strategy, and get-it-done-the-right-way attitude can be appreciated.

the ♑6 Potential

Being a cosmic parent makes you an easy target, but then what decent parent isn't misunderstood by those they try to nurture, prod, kick, and coerce into doing what's best? The Right Thing is always obvious to you, but you might not do it or maybe you take a questionable path on the edge of right to get there where you want to be. That's because you believe the results can justify the means. Be prudent with this sort of justification as it could land you nowhere.

Words of encouragement fall freely from your lips. You urge everyone to have a direction to travel, to see how far they can go, to try. Good advice for yourself, too. Don't get so bogged down in appointments and promises that you lose sight of your own hopes and dreams. Nothing makes you prouder than to spearhead a project that brings solid benefits to people you care about. And you know what? The feelings are usually mutual. They are just as proud that you made it happen, too!

FAMOUS CAPRICORN SIXES

Kirstie Alley	*1/12/1955*	*John Denver*	*12/31/1943*
Yvette Mimieux	*1/8/1941*	*Cary Grant*	*1/18/1904*
Sissy Spacek	*12/25/1949*	*Isaac Asimov*	*1/2/1920*

♑ • 7
Capricorn Seven
"The Selective Specialist"

♑+	7+	♑-	7-
Generous	*Intellectual*	*Reserved*	*Shrewd*
Reliable	*Articulate*	*Workaholic*	*Suspicious*
Organized	*Analytical*	*Cautious*	*Aloof*
Persistent	*Seeks Solitude*		

Still waters run deep. Your sultry eyes framed with lush lashes promise volumes and miss nothing. They are the portals to your soul and your sharp scientific mind. Not all Capricorn Sevens are bona fide shout-it-from-the-rooftop psychics like Jeanne Dixon, but she does represent the combo well. Perhaps you should warn the unwary considering cultivating an intimate relationship with you that it will be an unusual ride.

A private person, you enjoy a fine meal and interesting conversation, but won't spill the specifics of the Australian deal or details of your love life over spinach salad and stuffed mushrooms with a friend. You drink a glass of deep red Merlot, ask questions, listen attentively, and laugh. You offer praise or constructive criticism as appropriate, but what you don't do is talk about yourself.

Friends who have known you since Miss Inga's first grade class are amazed at how many miles you've traveled to follow your own guiding star. You would have been self-conscious if you had realized that was what you were doing. What you accomplish takes some effort, and unwavering focus to understand a trying childhood or to assess whether a current relationship is worth working out. You seldom recognize such tangles as obstacles, just a difficult knot or two to work through.

You don't always get what you want, though when you don't, it seldom ruffles your feathers. You fall back, study, and regroup before revving up for another fearless run for the gold. Easygoing but with steel resolve, you're a constant surprise to everyone around, including yourself.

Love, Sex, and Marriage

Sharing your lover's solitude for the long haul is no trip you sign up for lightly. Candidates have got to do more than appreciate your gorgeous gams or figure out how to push the hot-hot-hot button. Well, okay, that part does work for exhilarating sex that's a far stretch from the veil-and-satin-shoes date. Sensitivity, sex appeal, and smarts are a start, but giving you your own space is *the* top requirement. A busy life of his own and a spectacular smile don't hurt either.

You select friends just as carefully as you do a housemate and think of them as family, in addition to or instead of the folks back home. Small children are great when they belong to someone else, which you realize by about age thirty. If you hop into parenthood young, you do your duty with enthusiasm and make a fine job of producing independent, intelligent offspring. Given the choice, unless you have a big house and employ a nanny, parenting isn't an experience you need in order to make your life complete.

Money and Career

Your bank balance is nobody else's business. In fact, you prefer a separate account from your spouse. Sure, you pay more than your half of the expenses (and probably earn more than half), but you don't like the idea of anyone else having ATM access to your money any more than to your secret thoughts. Saving and spending are often out of balance, but somehow you manage to have what you need to pay the rent.

The big boss is puzzled when you turn down a promotion, but how could he know that you run a thriving breeding kennel for dalmatians on the side or just finished penning your fifth book? That's because you prefer to keep the many different phases of your life separate. Eventually, even if you resist, you're the best paid assistant in the company with a desk outside the CEO's office, and everyone considers you worth your weight in gold.

The ♑7 Potential

You're critical of the work you produce; your drive for perfection makes you continue to enhance and improve your skills. By the time you're done, you're more of a technical expert than the teacher who instructed you. You have a gift for stripping away the trappings and pointing to the essential issue. It's a skill that unnerves some and enthralls others—that and the interesting way that very few events surprise you when they happen.

Pursue mystic interests, develop psychic skills, and schedule alone time every day to reflect, read, and write. Keep track of friends who matter, because those precious intimate ties are crucial connections not easily replaced. Don't jeopardize future happiness with too many secrets. Show others how to get up to speed by sharing what you learn. The message you send is a simple but powerful one: If I can do this, so can you!

FAMOUS CAPRICORN SEVENS

Dyan Cannon	*1/4/1937*	*Mel Gibson*	*1/3/1944*
Joan Baez	*1/9/1941*	*Stephen W. Hawking*	*1/8/1942*
Mary Tyler Moore	*12/29/1937*	*Muhammad Ali*	*1/17/1942*

♑ • 8
Capricorn Eight
"The Practical Philosopher"

♑+	8+	♑-	8-
Industrious	*Global View*	*Selfish*	*Impersonal*
Realistic	*Ambitious*	*Pretentious*	*Workaholic*
Fearless	*Capable*	*Critical*	*Materialistic*
Resolute	*Arbitrator*		

Calculated risks are the name of the game, and not just with respect to the career and roof over your head. Oh, no—we're talking about the quick way you say, "I can do that" whenever something interesting is up for grabs. Whether stitching the first flag for a fledgling new country like Betsy Ross, or popping off on an Alaskan wilderness jaunt for fun, you aren't someone who likes to get left behind. In fact, you like to lead the pack or be one of the top dogs, with recognition as such. Not at all stuffy, you're a marvelous friend, and when you achieve those sky-high goals, you share the booty.

You don't expect the world to pay you homage because you're Mr. and Mrs. Jones's darling offspring, you are the model for the "10 percent talent and 90 percent perspiration" idea. Immediate plans are always kept flexible, but the long view is to be successful and make mucho moola. Unless you get sidetracked by too many personal missions, you make that plan a reality.

Once on top, wherever that might be, and you've been amply rewarded, you divvy up the wealth in various forms. You're a patient teacher and wise counselor; your advice and direction are there for the asking. An expert at playing devil's advocate, you don't give advice unless asked, and when you do, your practical words are laced with ideals of freedom and spiritual well-being.

Underneath the casual clothes is a wise old soul who through firsthand experience can tell you what and what not to do. You have as many unbelievable highs as you do lows, and every stage in between. It's this worldly wisdom that makes the rest of us sit up and listen attentively when you speak.

Love, Sex, and Marriage

Life is too short to spend with someone who doesn't make you happy, so you don't. There's a long litany of pertinent items to review before popping the question or untying the knot, but even if you can't find logical justification to get hitched or be cut free, you do it anyway when your heart is screaming: yes, yes, yes. Your brain doesn't have *any* argument that can drown out that ardent wail of your heart.

You strive to be politically correct in an offbeat way. Usually it has absolutely nothing to do with actual politics or law, but with people. You've even been known to be a voice of the people. The right spouse, then, has to let you go your own way when you hear such a call, but is able to reel you back home when you spend too many days pursuing justice or the perfect wine. Sex is another matter, but as you well know, it's delicious with or without the ceremony.

Money and Career

A master organizer, you have unlimited potential when doing work you love. You always hold the big picture in mind, and need at least one assistant to handle the mundane tasks.

You have the same passion for making money as you do for everything else. Besides wanting a mountainous pecuniary pile to fall back on, you also want cash at your fingertips to spend as you see fit. A true humanitarian, you aren't hung up on anyone else's status, only your own. With your ability to accumulate wealth, it's difficult to deal with limited resources during one of those inevitable downturns. That's when you beat yourself up and worry about those who depend on you. Even standing at the Pearly Gates, when you hear others mutter that they shouldn't have worked so much, you think you *could* have worked a bit harder, could have done it better or accomplished more. Don't be so hard on yourself for playing hooky and chasing pleasure. Remember the Nobel Prize or Emmy already sitting on the mantel at home and be happy.

The ♑8 Potential

You have a firm belief in your ability to accomplish and improve. Whether you wind up as CEO of a major corporation or step out onstage with guitar in hand, you have the ability to touch people, to inspire them by example and through the countless down-to-earth good deeds you do. You also generously share your wisdom and laughter freely.

A sincere thank-you from one you've helped puts you on top of the world, but it's a surprise if anyone say you are their hero. You like a full life and get absorbed in whatever you do. With a penchant for sensuous, tactile pleasure, watch your diet and marshal your energy output. Your gift is to show us what to do, how to do it, and caution us not to overdo it. Remember to take some of your own advice once in a while!

FAMOUS CAPRICORN EIGHTS

Naomi Judd	1/11/1949	Lorenzo Lamas	1/20/1958
Diane Keaton	1/5/1946	Jack London	1/12/1876
Diane Sawyer	12/22/1945	Rudyard Kipling	12/30/1865

♑ • 9
Capricorn Nine
"The Diligent Showman"

♑+	9+	♑-	9-
Persistent	Generous	Brooding	Impersonal
Conscientious	Compassionate	Critical	Self-interested
Ambitious	Performer	Nervous	Inconsistent
Pragmatic	Charismatic		

Quicker than you can say, "Hey, Rocky, watch me pull a rabbit out of my hat," there you are, hat in hand up on stage, a ringer for Bullwinkle the Moose, another Capricorn

Nine. Getting on the stage is easy, but staying there is another story. Only a hint of rejection throws you into a thirsty-sponge student mode, searching for a way to hold your audience spellbound. You knew you had the performer's flair when Granny didn't scold you too seriously for tap-dancing on the teak dining room table at two years old; she was such an appreciative audience.

So you practice, observe, and think about how to make it big. Following in the footsteps of other famous Capricorn Nines—Paul Revere, the silversmith-turned-patriot; the missionary scientist Albert Schweitzer, and entertainer Elvis Presley—you never stop testing your limits and trying new ways to make it better. Maybe you don't hit the mark on the first or fifteenth try, but just like the Moose, you eventually *do* pull a rabbit out of your hat.

Along with the showmanship charisma is the caution to not take yourself too seriously. You have the power to see your name up in lights, or grace the cornerstone of an office building, or to be remembered by scores of second graders who will never forget you. Little did the youngsters ever guess that your glib, fanciful stories showcased ironclad ethics in a way to create a firm foundation of their own.

As a teacher, you can be very demanding, but also shower generous praise when it's due. Yes, students remember that you taught them much more than music theory or mathematics. Classroom teacher, movie star, or idea man at corporate headquarters, you are always onstage, so take care to present a favorable view for the world to see.

Love, Sex, and Marriage

In love, you take a long time to trust another person with your private thoughts. It's important to have someone to believe in you, but finding that soul mate to wear your ring is a cautious undertaking. Though you might hop into bed in response to one of "those" looks across a crowded room, marriage is a different matter. You very much believe in wedding bells, and know that a good marriage is as much about compatible intellect as it is about emotions and sex.

Speaking of the Passionate You, performance matters to

you in bed and out. A considerate lover, you are kinky in a conventional sort of way but can nimbly acquiesce to your bed partner's preferences. The Right Match is someone who can play seductive games and shares your fascination with career and how the world works. That's the one you invite to share your private château.

Money and Career

As extravagant as you are cheap, you have unlimited earning potential, but always worry that the bank account will dry up tomorrow. A money manager or a super piece of software would help ease the worry by tracking the income and outgo. It's not that you can't live within a budget, but you feel as if you're either in financial survival mode or lavishly wealthy. Since you could earn, lose, and earn back several fortunes in a lifetime, take whatever help you can get to be disciplined and in the know about cash flow.

More comfortable in a crowd than one on one, you do well as a manager, executive, producer, or on your own. You do fine managing just yourself, but enjoy the process more with a staff of your own to help make deadlines and field phone calls, besides offering valuable advice.

The ♐9 Potential

Generally self-confident, you do need the occasional pumping up before you trot out a presentation to a new client. You may think it's out of character for you to ask for help, but no one else does, and they stand ready, hoping for the chance to quell your butterflies. Focus is sometimes difficult for you, but only because you are constantly bombarded with new ideas at the rate of a thousand or so an hour.

You might not consider yourself a visionary ready to lead the masses, but don't be surprised when others use such adjectives to describe you and your accomplishments. You always want tangible results, which makes you proficient at taking your brainstorms and translating them into reality. Sounds like a simple thing to do, doesn't it? But the rest of us admire you tremendously for being able to do it.

FAMOUS CAPRICORN NINES

Ethel Merman	1/16/1909	Paul Revere	1/1/1735
Diane von Furstenberg	12/31/1946	Jim Carrey	1/17/1962
George Burns	1/20/1896	Anthony Hopkins	12/31/1937

AQUARIUS

•

≈≈ • 1
Aquarius One
"The Progressive Pioneer"

≈≈+	1+	≈≈ -	1-
Leader	Bold	Extremist	Aggressive
Diligent	Independent	Tactless	Inflexible
Generous	Decisive	Aloof	Willful
Sociable	Innovative		

Standing in front of the candy counter, quarter in your chubby child hand, you knew what sweet you wanted before stepping up to the glass. "That will be one pecan divinity, please," you say and place a shiny quarter on top of the high glass display case. If Mom smiled at the seriousness with which you conducted this transaction, you never noticed—you were intently watching your precious purchase be dropped into the bag and you were sure to flash a smile at the sales clerk as she handed it to you.

Mom had no idea that this was just one first step in a larger master plan called "taking control of your own life." You intend to know how to do any and everything for yourself; you do so hate depending on anyone else. You figure that the faster you can learn how to take care of yourself, the quicker you can get on with living your life they way you want. Even as a youngster, bold ideas whirl in your head. Maybe not ideas like Susan B. Anthony wanting women to have the right to vote. But then, when it comes to politics and social injustice you can be a bit naive, my dear, and you make even that work for you. After having the reality thrown in your pretty face, your glassy-eyed optimism turns into diamond hard resolve to change that harsh reality.

What starts out as the ability to learn quickly and the need to make your mark could turn into a crusade. Futuristic ideas that could become tomorrow's norms fascinate you and you do your best to spread the innovative concepts around. You're honestly more interested in planting a seed here and there than you are in sticking around to water the plant and watch it grow tall and straight. There are plenty of other capable people to do that and besides, you have other forests to plant elsewhere.

Love, Sex and Marriage

Your idea of a bedroom romp involves plenty of conversation and laughter. In fact, some times, you'd rather have a lively debate than hit the sheets. You relish making love, make certain you know your partner's turn-ons but more importantly you want them to know yours. And when it comes right down to it, that's what you like best—the direct approach with games and mysteries left at the door. You pick up the conversation afterwards and talk through the wee hours.

Having a family is important, but only if it doesn't tie you down too much. Hire a nanny or housekeeper or find a partner who relishes the Mom role with or without your constant physical presence. Otherwise, you might want the rethink the whole children/family thing. Anyway, you're not in any hurry to tie the knot and don't mind if the neighbors wonder who the gorgeous guy is that stops by your place every Thursday night. You have your secrets, and your enjoy those tantalizing moments. And once you figure out how sex-for-pleasure works, you can relax in a relationship and enjoy the dance.

Money and Career

Unless your name is close to the top of the company org chart, you aren't a happy worker-bee employee. You will work for forty + hours straight on your own project or idea, but have difficulty being a "just do it and don't-ask-any-questions" drone. To prosper you need acknowledgment, and an occasional kind word about what a genius you are.

There isn't any problem you can't solve, when you decide you *want* to. You instinctively know how to find new solutions and are always ready to try unusual approaches, often tossing aside the entire procedure used by the guy who had the job before you. You enjoy having a savvy group of people around to bounce ideas off and make money with, but you like it better if it's your voice that has the last word and divvies up the budget for raises.

The ≋1 Potential

You have a sharp, photographic memory, but before you put a stage act together and head for Vegas to dazzle the slot-machine crowd as Wanda the Amazing, think about better ways to use such a skill. You see things as they are, and also as you believe they *could* be. So what if you sometimes get the two confused. Use the could-be view as the outline to make improvements—large and small—to benefit yourself and the rest of us.

Be careful not to withdraw too far from the very set of friends who inspire you and can urge you on to greater heights. Too often, you decide to remove yourself from the fray to play lone-wolf and do such a thorough job of it that reestablishing yourself into the fold becomes a daunting effort. Of course, there is always a place for you to sit at any table you might choose, but honestly, rather than be with strangers, isn't it nicer to be with those who know you secretly crave pecan divinity? Besides, sticking with those who know you and love you anyway saves so much time on your way to becoming a genius, doesn't it?

FAMOUS AQUARIUS ONES

Christian Dior	1/21/1905	John Hurt	1/22/1940
Ayn Rand	2/2/1905	Somerset W. Maugham	1/25/1874
Ann Jillian	1/29/1951	Lou Diamond Phillips	3/2/1952

≈ • **2**
Aquarius Two
"The Reserved Aristocrat"

≈+	2+	≈ -	2-
Determined	Persuasive	Secretive	Moody
Cooperative	Patient	Radical	Shy
Generous	Supportive	Quarrelsome	Worries
Eloquent	Gregarious		

From the moment you debuted in your recital for Ms. Rafferty's tap-dancing class, you knew you had a split personality, and wondered if it was just you or if anyone else did. Or maybe it was later as you wandered around a college campus puzzling why everyone else seemed to be on a different wavelength? Whether the realization happens at six or twenty-six, it could hamper your progress until you figure out that everyone else isn't different, it's you!

Yes, it is a big deal, but catch your breath quickly, sweetie, because beneath the insecurities, you have a brilliant mind to develop. Choose one idea from the passel of possibilities within your reach and watch it grow. Please just try it. Oh, you can have a hard head sometimes, dear Aquarius Two, and use it to hide your shyness or play for time—anything to delay the decisive act of picking a direction and leaving the dock of the familiar. So what if you're bored to tears and have a burning desire to go, do, and comquer. You think you will be safer here and then pow! Everything right here is yanked out from underneath those cute little tootsies, leaving you scrambling to make the same sorts of adjustments and changes you were tyring to avoid.

Deep below the layers of anxiety is the flame of Ambition.

You just "know" how to do it right, but are afraid to come right out and declare yourself especially if it seems far-fetched, in case you end up on the evening news. Life would never be the same again, but then it never is anyway. Procrastination is a lovely hiding place, but turns you into a crusty curmudgeon if it stops you from being all you can be. Remember this especially at those times when you're criticized from departing from the norm and showing us that intuitive genius of yours.

Love, Sex, and Marriage

It's not that you aren't interested in marriage; in fact, you like to have someone to trade stories with, to compare strategies about how to scale a cliff, and to play with under the bright blue Grand Bahama sun. You need the wide-open spaces as much as the togetherness and can't imagine finding such a kindred soul out there. Stop worrying; with your magnetic powers and psychic vibes you can pull a candidate into your path from a million miles away.

Home and hearth is a place to revive creative juices and enjoy quiet times with a spouse. Sex may be a separate issue from the other reasons you got married, but you honestly are more turned on with someone you love. This area takes chemistry plus a secure connection to enjoy to its fullest. No matter how wonderful the union and sex might be, you won't hesitate to dissolve the whole thing and start over if personal freedom becomes an issue.

Money and Career

Money isn't your game. Sure you want the privileges and bags of gold that come with the deal, but first you check the contract to see if you get top billing. Your dreams aren't about power, but you wouldn't mind calling the shots or applying your creativity. If you have enough free time you could write a symphony or such on the side.

You perform better with the approval of others, so even if you do decide to go solo in the work world, develop a network to stay in contact with those who are like minded. Praise from strangers is one thing, but acknowledgment from peers and competitors is the ultimate trophy. The dearest friends in your life come through the work that you do— no, not the time-clock part that puts food on the table, but the work that pays for your creations and introduces people who believe in you enough to write a check for what you produce!

The ≈≈2 Potential

With the many gifts you have, it's no wonder that you keep moving onward and upward every single day. You constantly find ways to improve ideas and want to be recognized as a professional in your chosen field. The spotlight isn't always where you want to be, but you do want to feel its warm glow sometimes.

Balance is a difficult state to achieve. You tend to switch from extremes—between insecurity to overconfidence. Likewise, in your personal and professional life, it's all of either one or the other. Try to balance both, lest you slip off the deep end into the workaholic, crazed artist who hasn't a clue of how to live up to responsibilities regardless of the rewards. You are gifted, and loved for the gracious, generous spirit you willingly share. Remember, it *is* love that makes the world go around.

FAMOUS AQUARIUS TWOS

Morgan Fairchild	*2/3/1950*	*Wolfgang Amadeus Mozart*	*1/27/1756*
Isabel Perón	*2/4/1931*	*Michael Jordan*	*2/17/1963*
Eartha Kitt	*1/26/1928*	*Philippe Candelaro*	*2/17/1972*

≈ • **3**

Aquarius Three
"The Pragmatic Idealist"

≈+	3+	≈ -	3-
Eloquent	*Expressive*	*Insecure*	*Extravagant*
Generous	*Romantic*	*Naive*	*Verbose*
Sociable	*Sociable*	*Withdrawn*	*Scattered*
Independent	*Creative*		

No one notices how skillfully you dance around the mulberry bush until he wants a direct answer. "Will you go to Vermont with me this weekend?" The Artful Dodger hat pops on and the smoke screen of soothing words starts as you busily glance at your watch a thousand times, then make apologies and vanish—to somewhere out there with the other wizards.

It's not that you're all image and no substance, but you do talk a lot and avoid giving out many personal details. As a young adult, you take special care to avoid being pigeonholed or pinned down, with the exception of when the conversation is particularly intriguing or there's a certain magical air about the person attempting to do the pigeonholing. You want to keep open the option to change. If you haven't figured out what you want to do with your life yet, how can you tell anyone else? Sure, you want to be a star, musician, writer, a baker, a candlestick maker. You may work in your chosen craft at a young age, but you don't buy in to anything as a career until you've been doing it for many moons.

Your ability to dart from your own social class to a foreign culture or to the complete unknown can be intimidating. Seldom do you let a little thing like lack of skill keep you from saying yes when asked if you can ride a horse bareback. How hard can it be? Twenty-four hours and two busted buns later, you admit to yourself that you might have been a tad optimistic. A quick learner when motivated, you go from novice to expert rapidly, but even you aren't an instant pro at everything. Don't forget you also need focus,

because all it takes is an enticing invitation to share a jug
of wine in the butterfly-filled fields to turn you in a different direction.

Love, Sex, and Marriage

You adore exploring the unknown and are an eternal romantic, a ripe candidate for the *M* word. As youthful a spirit
as you are, you enjoy being attached to another, and having
someone to share the whole darned journey with. Should
you shy away from early involvement with a live in lover
it may be much later in life before you venture into the
forever territory.

In marriage, you need space interpersed with stimulating
conversation and romantic adventures. Though you initially
aren't so sure about children (you never completely leave
that realm yourself), if the marriage is going well, you get
curious about parenting. Actually adding little ones to the
entourage often depends on the spouse you choose.

Money and Career

There are many things you want to do and really resent
the nine-to-five job thing. This is why you head to college,
art school, or acting class—it allows you to tread a little
water. You take courses that interest you, and some that
don't, to confirm you don't want to be an accountant. Funny
thing is that if you learn how to handle credit and not give
away two nickels for every one you get, you can develop
the talent to turn a little money into a lot.

You could earn big bucks—it just takes focus and discipline (is that all?), and choosing how. Many Aquarius Threes
are happier running their own show. Because you enjoy
people and like to flex your creative muscles, you do best
working with the public. Whatever you choose—from chef
to professional psychic—it's your enthusiasm and warm personality that open doors—yes, that's *all* the doors.

The ≈≈3 Potential

To you, the world is even more beautiful than others see
it, even on an amazing summer day on Nantucket. You spin

a web of fascination with your tales of wonder and woes. No one tells a morality tale or a weepy romance better than you. Reality can be a tougher gig, but you aren't afraid to break a pattern and try a new one in your search to find the life you envision.

Use your gift of gab and creative vision to set the pace for others. Knowing you are often an example to others improves the quality of your life and is more rewarding than any other gradiose plan you might have. Determine the values that matter most to you and stay focused to achieve what you think you want. You can always use the invitation to Wimbledon as an excuse for not finishing the widget report on time, but it's a hollow excuse when you miss out on the pay raise that was tied to it. People naturally like you and want to see you succeed. And you are talented. For your own sake, go with it.

FAMOUS AQUARIUS THREES

Mia Farrow	2/9/1945	Richard Dean Anderson	1/23/1950
Jody Watley	1/30/1961	Charles Dickens	2/7/1812
Tina Louise	2/11/1934	John Travolta	2/18/1954

~~~ • 4

Aquarius Four
"The Conservative Rebel"

~~+	4+	~~~ -	4-
Innovative	Practical	Radical	Undemonstrative
Informative	Constructive	Secretive	Too Busy
Philosophical	Determined	Insecure	Contrary
Freedom-loving	Good-hearted		

One look at your desk is enough to make the heartiest boss cringe. One moment there are a dozen neatly stacked piles; an hour later, umpteen layers of files scattered about and littered with pink phone messages. Ah, the mark of a creative mind, and you *are* organized, thank you very much.

Just let anyone touch so much as a two-month-old memo and you know the paper has moved two centimeters. Free-style organization works for you, and anyone who lives with you can verify you have an uncanny knack of pulling Aunt Sue's address scrawled on the back of a used envelope out of an apparent pile of trash.

If you're lucky, you have a secretary and a housekeeper to match up the earrings and cuff links. If not, you lose a few items before getting a system together to hang on to important things while cogitating how to present a new idea to your honey, boss, mother, or teacher. You always have a new idea ready, keeping everything in a continual state of flux.—It may not be obvious, but you're always looking for a new desk, antique clock, seascape, etc. And heaven help those around you when you do find it, because you'll move everything around to make the room fit with the new prize.

You surprise people who think your head is so far in the clouds that you never accomplish anything. While it's true you ponder, theorize, and philosophize, you also gather facts. You adore information. "Knowledge is power" must have first been uttered by an Aquarius Four who then moved on to see how to make that concept work.

Whether you take giant steps or baby steps, with good humor for a cover and an endless supply of what-if questions, you march steadily towards your goal. Along the way you gather facts and inspire supporters as you place one brick on top of another. Before anyone else realizes what you're up to, you're there atop the tower you built and don't even have to stretch to touch the stars.

Love, Sex, and Marriage

Like a bee to honey, you draw prospects to you in droves. Many buzz around until you invite them in. But you appear too busy, too preoccupied, too worldly—the same generous laugh and enthusiasm that attracts them also keeps admirers at a cautious distance. If you want more than a buddy or be more than just ships that pass in the night, you've got to make the first move.

Marriage is complicated. While you believe in a collaborative approach to the relationship and your roles within it, there are certain aspects that aren't negotiable. If you've got to pack off to Croatia, or review a concert in London, you're going. Also, mutual respect, endless conversation, and the spark and sizzle of romance are necessary to consider the big "I do." Then there's absolute loyalty to confirm. Talk out all the quirky requirements beforehand too okay?

Money and Career

You're bursting with ideas. You have an artistic eye and intuitive grasp of what's important, and your opinion matters to the big boss. It's okay to *be* the Big Boss, too, as long as you're surrounded with a capable crew and expert advisers to translate your concepts into real events or products.

Money *is* important because it represents freedom and creates the platform from which you can launch humanitarian efforts and artistic projects, or play out those inventive surges. In addition to helping others and furthering your own plans, you want to own a piece of the planet and a home—maybe two. This is a good thing and keeps you grounded.

The ≈4 Potential

Your patient, steady manner comforts people. You know change is inevitable, and place yourself in the game to implement positive change. Because of your cosmopolitan air and voluminous education, you have a gift for explaining the past and possible future in a way that makes a good outcome appear achievable. A practical rebel, you sketch out an improvement map and send us down it in your no-nonsense, friendly way.

Take care of you, too. When ample money is available, you adore being pampered, but cut it out as an extravagance when time or money is in short supply. Even if you can't afford a trip to the spa, make an effort to effectively recharge your batteries. Many others depend on your merry eyes and the way you always seem to know when a pat on the shoulder or encouraging words are needed. Choose confidants carefully. Even you need a shoulder to lean on sometimes. Everyone does now and then. You say you know that, but where is that shoulder that's there for you right now?

FAMOUS AQUARIUS FOURS

Oprah Winfrey	*1/29/1954*	*Tom Brokaw*	*2/6/1940*
Mary Lou Retton	*1/24/1968*	*Neil Diamond*	*1/24/1941*
Kim Novack	*2/13/1933*	*LeVar Burton*	*2/16/1957*

≈ • 5

Aquarius Five
"The Big-Hearted Reformer"

≈+	5+	≈ -	5-
Congenial	*Resourceful*	*Radical*	*Impulsive*
Humane	*Adventurous*	*Gullible*	*Fickle*
Eloquent	*Progressive*	*Impetuous*	*Restless*
Scientific	*Curious*		

In private dreams, you're transported to a land where anything is possible if you can just hold on to Pegasus's back until he places you on the next lofty ledge. The image makes you smile as you scan the three dozen names on your phone list to find out who is delivering the blankets to the flood victims south of the city. You write a check or arrange transportation, but prefer to let someone else form the committee and hand them out. Hence you worry until you know these shivering folks have gotten the blue-wool comfort that you intended.

You are, in fact, loved by many for the generous yet practical way you point them in the right direction, offer an answer when they seem confused, or validate their decisions. You find solutions and implement unusual ideas, sometimes taking a lot of heat for, say, dumping the coffee machine for a fruit juice dispenser in the office. Nothing compared to the challenges of Aquarius Five presidents Abraham Lincoln, who had a broken nation to mend, or

Franklin Roosevelt, who dealt with a devastating economic depression.

When you withdraw to contemplate a problem's solution, you know your resolution might be unusual, but eventually you present it you always want to be helpful. So what if that makes you controversial! Even when you aren't at the center of the storm, you always get credit for being the activist element—your reputation does precede you.

While some people call you a godsend, just as many are apprehensive about what you might do. Then there are those (the majority) who are somewhere in between—wondering what marvelous new plan you have to lighten the load and brighten the day.

Love, Sex, and Marriage

Intelligent and studious, you have a keen interest in the mystery of intimate relationships. Marriage could be based either on friendship born of common interests and goals, or one of complete magic when you bumped into each other on the street and saw stars—a sure sign of an angel's blessing. If you're both carrying an Eddie Bauer bag and both love Thai food, the relationship is well on its way.

You think of life as a journey and consciously walk towards the stops you intend to make along the way. As much as you love zooming around the planet at Mach 3, you also crave a tranquil, comfy den with the latest stereo and computer equipment available. Children are a nice thought, as well as having a close-knit, loving family. The family gig works if you have a live-in spouse to share responsibilities so you can keep zooming around now and then.

Money and Career

Your public and private personalities are different but accurate faces of the real you. You have a wide array of concerns and talents to work with. For this reason, and because you get bored easily, you tend to dabble in anything that interests you. Paint watercolors, be a psychologist, a dancer, a writer, a doctor, a politician, or a scientist; you always pursue several interests that earn money at the same time.

Should you be born into money, you won't have to waste time building up the cash reserve you like to have. You don't think about the green stuff much, but you never underestimate its value either. Born poor, you earn your way and stash some away for tomorrow when you might need a vacation or want to follow up on a hunch instead of punching the clock. Boss or worker bee, you succeed with people who tell you what has to happen and the bottom line, and then get out of your way.

The ≈5 Potential

You help people achieve higher heights than they believed they could by helping them believe in themselves. Your unique perspective sometimes gets you into trouble with the establishment, but that doesn't stop you from making beneficial suggestions before moving on. Take care to include the people you care about in your schemes and dreams as well as your workaday world.

Protecting your individuality in a marriage, friendship, or team business environment is a worthy goal, but could backfire if interpreted as indifference or as an effort to avoid intimacy. It's difficult sometimes for others to realize that the big "I" word has a different meaning for you. You love just as deeply, but never want to hinder anyone from fulfilling their own potential. There is a fine line between encouraging personal freedom and appearing indifferent to loved ones. Think about it. You know the difference. And if you want to be happy, act as if you are!

FAMOUS AQUARIUS FIVES

Christie Brinkley	*2/2/1954*	*Charles Darwin*	*2/12/1809*
Natalie Cole	*2/6/1950*	*George Segal*	*2/13/1934*
Gloria Naylor	*1/25/1950*	*Burt Reynolds*	*2/11/1936*

≈ • 6

Aquarius Six
"The Loyal Liberal"

≈+	6+	≈ -	6-
Informative	*Responsible*	*Thoughtless*	*Outspoken*
Friendly	*Nurturer*	*Obsessive*	*Possessive*
Generous	*Seeks Harmony*	*Withdrawn*	*Self Sacrifices*
Diligent	*Idealist*		

When inventing the electric lightbulb, Thomas Edison was known to say, "We haven't failed seventeen times, we've found seventeen ways that won't work." What else could an Aquarius Six with a mission say to keep going to invent a revolutionary improvement for mankind? Okay, so all you want to do is find a way to make M&M's make you lose weight (an equal improvement for our times), or on a more modest scale, make sure that everything that finds its way into your kitchen cabinets is healthy, and actually good for you.

Your hunches have substance and you aren't afraid to dig around for a bona fide fact or two to get the funding, buy-in, or green light from the powers that be so you can get on with it. Whatever the vision, if there's a benefit involved, you make it happen. This is why you hide Grandpa's cigarettes, feed the cat brown rice, and encourage everyone to get married. So what if you haven't taken the plunge yourself. You tell everyone you're relentlessly searching for the perfect yin to your yang.

A loving friend, you expect every relationship to be a combination of give and take and are stunned when Grandpa goes berserk looking for his smokes, and your exercise chum at the gym blames you for his race to the altar. As for the cat looking down his nose at the rice, you aren't really surprised, but do rush to the health food store for upscale cat food for Fatima, the spoiled Manx. Peace and harmony are restored. Peace in the family is more important than your ideas; you frequently make sacrifices to calm troubled waters.

Love, Sex, and Marriage

Being all things to all people makes you an easy person to love, but it's not easy to find a mate capable of the same selfless love. Before getting to the kiss at the front door on the first date, you review your criteria. The marrying kind of love is friendship plus passion, though you have been known to settle for the skyrocketing passion of an occasional dalliance.

When you find a like-minded soul, you eagerly make the forever-and-ever promise without reservation. Don't forget to tell him that you expect a broad-minded but utterly faithful mate because you have lots of other friends, want children, and hope to have the whole group under your roof (maybe under his feet) whenever you want. In return, you are a jewel as a partner and an uninhibited lover when you know that in and out of the four-poster, you are appreciated—no, treasured.

Money and Career

In addition to that brilliant brain of yours, you have the foresight to choose a career that takes care of your worldly needs (or a partner who's an excellent provider). Because you are liberal-minded, you give everyone at the office the benefit of the doubt and find rolling with the punches fairly easy. That's because you have a private life that lets you be the artist, inventor, and cosmic parent.

When it comes to work, you keep it in perspective. Your only hot button in the office is unjust politics or outright prejudice. As a boss you are legendary—willing to help others move up or pull up stakes to pursue their dreams. As a counselor, you're top-notch, and while you can be too generous with your money, it's usually for a good cause, like shoes for the girls' soccer team, or an inspirational art print for a co-worker who's hit a rough patch.

The ♒6 Potential

With your excellent memory, you remember every kindness and slight. The kindnesses warm you and you minimize

the slights. Everyone has their bad days, you think, even if
the disappointment cuts deep. You give people every opportunity to figure out the error of their ways but can't forgive anyone for careless or hurtful behavior.

While opening minds to new ideas and motivating everyone to live life to the fullest, it's easy to lose sight of your
own dreams. But you won't "settle" forever, and when
enough is enough, you can leave a messy trail in your wake.
Try to keep communications open and honest to avoid
such trauma.

You may have financial success, but the most enduring
achievements happen when your beautiful spirit shines out
and beyond your beautiful physical appearance. Stay true to
your own ethical code and find out firsthand what this
means. You'll be glad you did.

FAMOUS AQUARIUS SIXES

Jane Seymour	2/15/1951	Lewis Carroll	1/27/1832
Vanessa Redgrave	1/30/1937	Clint Black	2/4/1962
Melissa Manchester	2/15/1951	John McEnroe	2/16/1959

≈ • 7
Aquarius Seven
"The Cosmopolitan Charmer"

≈+	7+	≈ -	7-
Generous	Analytical	Insecure	Secretive
Philosopher	Private	Detached	Suspicious
Independent	Articulate	Radical	Aloof
Diligent	Perfectionist		

Rocking the boat or developing a plan to put things back
together after a crash are what you do best. Farsighted with
visions swirling around in your head, you are always stretching the envelope. You never miss an opportunity to put one
of your novel ideas into play. It might start with talking
about taboo subjects such as how to seduce a man, and end

up with a product like *Cosmopolitan*—à la Helen Gurley Brown. Her sharp eye and willingness to push the boundaries produced a magazine used as a valuable resource by several generations of women. Aquarians are always thinking about doing something like that, but leave it to an Aquarius Seven to make it happen.

Instead of a Ms. Brown or Gertrude Stein, you may use the qualities of Aquarius Seven to strive to be an actress like, Cybill Shepherd with a polished glamorous side. One thing is certain: It's your flexible sense of humor that lets you take the considerable ups and downs in stride. That and your analytical talents make you a key player who's in the game long after others have dropped out. Confrontation is something you avoid, but when in a toe-to-toe position, do take pity on the opposition. Few are your match at fingering the truth, and others are astonished at what you know and the strength of your convictions.

Varied interests bring scores of friends from assorted backgrounds. You genuinely find everyone interesting and have no prejudicial barriers to hold you back. Whatever hesitation you might have comes from previous unpleasant personal experience. Though you move in diverse circles at will, you prefer some people to others but are courteous enough to never let those preferences be known.

Love, Sex, and Marriage

Falling in love is serious business. With your combination of psychic flashes and keen skills of observation, you immediately know if an encounter has potential. Courting you is sometimes a frustrating experience, so give any would-be suitor a break. Don't let your amazement that someone loves you as a reserved, charming intellectual who occasionally jumps off the deep end stop you from exploring the possibilities. Remember, your warts are as attractive as the smooth satin skin part.

You fall in love with a brain, but won't investigate its existence unless the package is attractive, when looking for a lifelong partner. Not that you would exclude anyone, but you might hold yourself at a distance for observation. Don't forget, even the most beautiful of butterflies needs a snort of nectar to stick around.

Money and Career

You have very definite ideas about spending money, which means you put the brakes on and spend as little as possible on anything not On The List. You invest a bit of cash here and there as you see fit, and undoubtedly have some accumulating interest in places that no one, not even a spouse of thirty years, knows about. You need surplus cash for your inventions and those trips to Tahiti that beckon from time to time.

You approach work in a practical and studious way. Whatever you decide to be—in creative or scientific fields—you will stick with it until you do what you set out to do. Earning a particular amount of money, getting to be an executive director, seeing your name in lights, conducting a symphony, or making the winning touchdown, you pay attention to every contributing factor and find a way to be where you want to be. Of course, after reaching the goal line and making a generous donation to your favorite charity, you might bail without notice to find a new place to fly.

The ≈7 Potential

Since you're an enigma of sorts, a friendship with you is confusing for mere mortals. You are not an open book, but are honest about the areas where you interact with others. There will be those who don't understand why you work where you do, or married the person you did, or are going to so-and-so's party. Not only do you not explain yourself, but you appreciate it when they don't ask these questions out loud.

You learned young that explaining your plans to improve your lot in life often falls on deaf ears or elicits a look that says, "What are you talking about?" Before kindergarten, you've tucked away the really good ideas to share later with a soul mate. Strive to find the right venue to blossom, get the education necessary, and cultivate the friendship of like-minded spirits. You may think intimacy is a risky rumba, but without those intimate interludes, you wouldn't have the security to be all you can be and find true happiness.

FAMOUS AQUARIUS SEVENS

Justine Bateman	2/19/1966	Robby Benson	1/21/1956
Farrah Fawcett	2/2/1947	Robert Wagner	2/10/1930
Roberta Flack	2/10/1939	Arsenio Hall	2/12/1955

≈ • 8

Aquarius Eight
"The Versatile Specialist"

≈+	8+	≈ -	8-
Cooperative	Global View	Thoughtless	Indecisive
Determined	Professional	Self-defeating	Workaholic
Unbiased	Ambitious	Detached	Aggressive
Eloquent	Enduring		

Never say never—you haven't, have you? Because at some time or another in this long life, you will try a multitude of angles to get results, including changing sides of the fence when it works to your advantage. From the first title of Jacks Champion Supreme in the school yard at PS 27, you know that when it comes to any game, someone has to win and someone has to lose. Though you are gracious in defeat, life is sweeter when you win. The win/lose thing might make you hesitate before accepting a job offer. You have a big-picture mind and have to see a winning angle, personal or professional, or you say thanks, but no thanks.

Getting to know you isn't as hard as people might think, and you warm up to people who love the same work and causes that you do. Communication poses no problem, whether it's to thank the travel agent for putting together a magnificent trip for you, or to express complex ideas to a group of strangers in a lecture hall. You do have an opinion about everything but usually keep it to yourself—unless your reputation is involved.

Underneath that busy, work-until-midnight-and-wow-'em-in-the-meeting-tomorrow exterior beats a heart of gold. You are happy to give advice and tell others how you got where you are. You honestly hope your experiences can help them reach their own particular heights. A natural mentor on everything from yummy sex to baking apple pie, you love to be needed, though hate to be tied down. A whirling dervish of activity, you never lack for friends or destinations.

Love, Sex, and Marriage

Falling in love and/or lust isn't the problem, and stepping up to the altar isn't either. The difficult part is wooing a partner as ambitious and loving as you are. Oh sure, you both like watching sunsets together, and never run out of things to discuss, but when you veer off to chase a dream, will he stick with you? That's the tough part in the partner search.

Home is important—the Monet print on one wall and the sparkling blue ocean view out the other are parts of the home you hope to share with a lover. A domestic homebody, you're not. You can combine career with a family, if you choose, but often find yourself too busy to think about it until later in life. Well, the same can happen with marriage, too.

Money and Career

Staff members consider themselves lucky to call you boss. You are respected in any field you choose to work because of the effort and energy, plus the foresight, you put into planning. They love you because you also help them be successful. You motivate everyone to evaluate their talents, get more training, and contemplate their personal future. In addition you do an outstanding job at separating the private from the professional parts of your life.

Your relationship with money is challenging until you bite the bullet and get reliable counseling/training in how to make it work for you. How to make money with other people's money is no problem, but when it comes to handling your own, the silver-spoon appetite and confidence in your abilities are sometimes the trigger for being far too generous with your own resources. Dwindling cash flow is a huge motivating factor in why you continue to earn money long after friends have retired.

The ≈≈8 Potential

Since you're a genius at getting ahead and playing the political game, little stops you in your campaign for joy and prosperity. Helping others is a genuine pleasure, and not only in the impersonal philanthropic way. Taking their needs into consideration one on one, you are always a willing mentor. Once you have the recognition and security you want, you look to enjoy the other things in life, such as a loving family—those things that make the whole game worthwhile.

You can swing from the top of the world to the bottom of the barrel in the blink of a Newt's eye, without someone to believe in you every step of the way. As independent as you can be, flying solo simply isn't very much fun. (It may take you several orbits to find that out.) You give everyone the benefit of the doubt, the compassionate hug, and the practical conversation to quell their self-doubts. Take your own advice. Everyone falls off the carousel horse now and then, and most of us need help to get back on. Why did you think you wouldn't?

FAMOUS AQUARIUS EIGHTS

Geena Davis	*1/21/1957*	*Wayne Gretzky*	*1/26/1961*
Laura Dern	*2/10/1967*	*General Douglas MacArthur*	*1/26/1880*
Molly Ringwald	*2/18/1968*	*Paul Newman*	*1/26/1925*

≋ • 9
Aquarius Nine
"The Magnetic Mover and Shaker"

≋+	9+	≋ -	9-
Inventive	*Worldly*	*Indecisive*	*Impersonal*
Sociable	*Compassionate*	*Outspoken*	*Careless*
Concentrates	*Performer*	*Thoughtless*	*Self-absorbed*
Expressive	*Charismatic*		

You've been known to live on the edge, even if it's just occasionally. You push the fringe because you believe in yourself. Well, at least you're a believer until a plan backfires and sends you off the ski jump headfirst into the woods. Up until that moment, you thought you could pull it off because you believe in any theory until you don't believe it anymore. Fickle? Not exactly, it's simply that you have an open mind that readily evaluates Actions vs. Results when the results fall short. Next time, you want to be better prepared when another opportunity falls in your lap, as they often do.

It's not as if you popped into the world filled with ambition to own half of it or anything like that. No, you envision a tranquil existence of painting landscapes and solving mystic mysteries. Maybe you'll teach people to solve problems à la Aquarius Nine Sir Francis Bacon's concept of deductive reasoning, or learn more about Copernicus, who told us the Earth revolved around the Sun instead of vice versa.

Experimenting and questioning, you wait until you reach maximum inspiration before you let the rest of us in on your latest revolutionary idea. As much as you love to give advice, the performer in you wants to put on a good show. Okay, so you might not think that you have a flair for the dramatic, but you have to admit that being the center of attention suits you, especially when you get the chance to show off your musical skills *and* make the audience smile.

Love, Sex, and Marriage

All the world loves a lover, which is why it's difficult to go through the selection process with any enthusiasm. You do so love to be that lover, and consider your performance as a playmate and a sweetheart a vital part of any relationship. You might not actually pop the big question to anyone (or say yes) until the last one of your college chums is already living in suburbia with a mortgage. And even then, you want a loving marriage, but not one quite so predictable as a white picket fence implies.

Tasteful art and interesting gadgets are found in the place you call home. You adore picking out new items with the love of your life to make it a perfect haven. Finding that first home for the two of you, whether married or not, is a painstaking process. You need room for books, art supplies, and multiple PCs, but if there isn't a wonderful view of green trees and water, you won't completely unpack.

Money and Career

You're a money magnet; figuring out how to make it stick around is the challenge. Generous to a fault, you can never turn away a friend in need or a particular charity even when you aren't that flush with funds. When considering the next job or promotion, you barely have to make a few phone calls to get the wheels in motion. Of course, without your careful orchestration, the job search might not get off the ground, or it could take you someplace you don't want to go.

You prefer to stick with your best talent and keep plugging away until kudos are offered for a job well done. But you recognize when you're spinning your wheels and make the necessary changes to get going again. You are happiest in entertainment, engineering, law, and education, but only if the position allows you to work with a large group. You thrive on group energy and cross-pollination to boost you to even greater success.

The ♒9 Potential

When you feel cut off or shut out from those you love the most, it bothers you, but you manage to pick yourself up and stay focused to get the job done. You were born a trouper, especially when you know others are depending on you. When your self-confidence is low, all you need do is remember the last shower of compliments you received and it revitalizes you.

Personal love is difficult. Somewhat naive, you assume that nothing is personal that anyone does or says to you. You know people "love" you but are stunned when they make it personal, such as Aaron following you to the kitchen to collect a kiss. You have difficulty accepting the Personal You, but don't be afraid of the wonderful person you are. Experience the full range of personal love as well as the impersonal, and you become even more adept at understanding all the people in every facet of your life.

FAMOUS AQUARIUS NINES

Brett Butler	1/30/1958	Norman Rockwell	2/3/1894
Lisa Marie Presley	2/1/1968	Garth Brooks	2/7/1962
Carole King	2/9/1942	Gregory Hines	2/14/1946

PISCES

●

)(• 1
Pisces One
"The Empathetic Executive"

)(+	1+	)(-	1-
Compassionate	*Direct*	*Careless*	*Myopic View*
Knowledgeable	*Courageous*	*Extremist*	*Inflexible*
Innovative	*Inventive*	*Procrastinates*	*Overbearing*
Focused	*Leader*		

A single red rose placed carefully atop your Filofax starts the day off with a sunny shot of enthusiasm. Later you can seductively—ahh, properly—thank the gift giver, but right now there are things to do. Love is every bit as important to you as friendship and business, and you like to have a full plate with a little of everything on it every day.

Routine is a big snooze, but you put up with it because there are certian things you want to accomplish. Technically you're not a rabble-rouser, which makes it all the more interesting to watch you zigzag around the planet asking impertinent, thought-provoking questions, pushing hot buttons, and urging everyone you meet to find a better way to run things. Seldom do you mean "*I* have a better way of running things," though you do such a good job mixing rhetoric with charm that your audience not only agrees with you, but puts you in charge of orchestrating the change. In zero to sixty seconds, you go from expressing an abstract ideal to having the responsibility to make it so. Whew!

Not only do you take your responsibilities seriously, but you genuinely want others to be happy. Whether leading a fledgling country like famous Pisces One George Washington, or charming generations of youth like Dr. Seuss, you endeavor to convince people to live better. Then you tell or show them how. In the process, you ruffle the feathers of the Keep the Status Quo Because I Get a Kickback Gang, but hey, what's a missing feather or two in the big picture?

Speaking of roosters and eagles, you do your fair share of being both the Big Man in the Barnyard and a Soaring Eagle at Large. Yet even when you get to soar, you're pragmatic enough to keep one eye on the folks at home and the other on your bank balance.

Love, Sex, and Marriage

Falling in love is as high an experience as you will ever have. Romance is the food of the gods, and you expect to get an ample helping of the "pinch me, I've gone to heaven" sort. This doesn't mean that you haven't sown a few (or maybe a bushelful of) wild oats in your day—the chemistry-motivated or romance kind.

A serious love match is a binding partnership, and you prefer defined ground rules before cleaning out a closet for the new roomie. You KNOW you try to be everything to your partner and want to minimize the adjustment time. Somehow when the front door opens with your lover, luggage, and taffy brown cocker spaniel ready to move in, you and your "can't believe a dog's moving in" cat are prepared to embrace the whole package.

Money and Career

Starting out, money is confusing. You understand that earning money funds your escapades and lets you dress in style, but it doesn't mean much beyond that. Once you know how to earn it, you learn that money and recognition are not the same thing, and that you need a bit of both. The employer who figures out that a hearty slap on the back and a deserved compliment go as far in keeping you happy as the annual raise does employs you indefinitely.

With the ability to focus that you have, you can figure out a zillion different ways to climb a tree. You do best when you specialize in a particular talent and profession. Of course, during your life you will also explore all sorts of detours and offshoots in the course of pushing on to the next level. You do so love using that creative mind of yours to improve, explore, and entertain.

The)(1 Potential

You figure it's okay if you take yourself too seriously when away from the prying eyes of the crowds. Behind closed doors you visualize how to implement your latest and greatest idea and keep everyone happy in the process. But when you are out with the crowd, you become a gracious coach and lively companion. As much as you love being alone, you love meeting new people and staying in touch with old friends.

For about a minute, you might let a "friend" walk all over you, but you bounce back and stand tall and firm to maintain your self-respect. This resiliency makes you a natural champion of others who don't seem able to stand up for themselves. You might not consider yourself one of the Pollyanna persuasion, but you'd be surprised to know how many others think you've made a noticeable difference in their lives.

FAMOUS PISCES ONES

Lynn Redgrave	3/8/1943	Shaquille O'Neal	3/6/1972
Drew Barrymore	2/22/1975	Rob Reiner	3/6/1945
Taylor Dayne	3/7/1962	Michael Bolton	2/26/1953

)(• 2
Pisces Two
"The Mystic Matchmaker"

)(+	2+	)(-	2-
Inspirational	*Diplomatic*	*Procrastinater*	*Argumentative*
Focused	*Conscientious*	*Extremist*	*Sensitive*
Good Humored	*Supportive*	*Cynical*	*Worries*
Compassionate	*Patient*		

When it comes to protecting your privacy, you are a master of the slight of hand. So careful are you to focus on the other person that an inquisitive acquaintance won't notice until hours later that you never answered a single personal question. Should an uncivilized cretin persist in posing impertinent questions, you pull another favorite trick—the Disappearing Act.

Even friends know how good at it you are. Now they see you—at the theater, at the Italian restaurant on the corner, shopping at your favorite store—and then poof! Now they don't! You disappear and messages pile up on your machine asking where you are. Chances are you've hit the road again for work, pleasure, or reflection, but unlike famous Pisces Two Jack Kerouac, when you're on the road, it's with a cell phone, laptop, and American Express.

You are somewhat of an enigma—a romantic touchy-feely creature with a fascination for gadgets and curiosity about the technical aspect of everything. Information matters. You want to know what's going on behind the scenes as well as on center stage. You not only want the truth, you want details.

Creative and chatty today, you change to a silent observer tomorrow for no apparent reason. There are many layers to you, from gregarious gadabout to serious competitor à la another Pisces Two, former world's chess best Bobby Fischer. You're surprised when someone says you've changed. You simply decided to try out a new look and express an unexpressed opinion. Since your preferences change continually, it probably is a good idea that you don't play out every new notion. It would be too much for friends to handle.

Love, Sex, and Marriage

Love is complicated for a Pisces Two. As much as you want your personal freedom, you want lots of attentive quality time and a mate to slip between the satin sheets with you for cuddling and fireworks. You wonder if there's an accomplished, handsome professional who would treat you like a lady in public and like the wench of his dreams in private.

Guess again! The toughest hurdle you climb in any intimate relationship is tuning the communication dial from Fantasy to Reality. You often connect with a lover through ESP and have an intuitive way of knowing what the other person is going to say. But real love doesn't flourish with psychic vibes alone. Not talking could be a fatal relationship flaw. SAY what you think and need, and discuss plans. Listen to each other. You might not agree, but it is the ONLY way to have the seamless, loving relationship you want.

Money and Career

Making money is a form of magic, and while you aren't anxious to own Microsoft, you never underplay the importance of the green stuff. You believe in stashing a bit in the bank for the inevitable drain on your resources that's sure to come. You would like to work only when you need the money, but also know precious few people are lucky enough to pull it off. Still, no nose to the grindstone 365 days a year for you! Unless it's in a field that lets you be as creative as you want and manipulate your daily schedule, you won't stick with it.

The honest goal of most Pisces Twos is to make a bundle and retire young, but instead of toasting your toes in front of the fireplace straight on into your golden years, it often turns out to be a vacation break between careers. Besides, you want to know what's happening out there and need the personal contact and discipline of the workaday world to stay grounded. Whatever you do will be noticed. Whether you're famous or infamous, people know your name. It's up to you to make sure that they remember it with a smile.

The)(2 Potential

You have considerable personal power, yet often submit to the whims and needs of others. Use your charisma and develop diplomatic skills to charm (or coerce) those who might otherwise overlook you because you don't speak up. Because you long for personal freedom and a genteel world, you hope we learn how to behave better and with more sensitivity towards each other.

With your devilish sense of humor and intuitive understanding of people, you are a joy to know. It's the whiplash changes and disappearing acts that are uncomfortable, so for goodness' sakes, tell someone when you head out to walk Big Sur. And remember we all make mistakes; even you for all your psychic powers. Allow time to grieve, debrief, and rework the plan after a setback before getting back to business, lest you lose that winning smile.

FAMOUS PISCES TWOS

Paula Prentiss	*3/4/1939*	*William Hurt*	*3/20/1950*
Nancy Wilson	*3/16/1954*	*Peter Fonda*	*2/23/1939*
Chelsea Clinton	*2/27/1980*	*Billy Crystal*	*3/14/1947*

)(• 3
Pisces Three
"The Sociable Statesman"

)(+	3+	)(-	3-
Intuitive	*Sociable*	*Frivolous*	*Easily Distracted*
Unbiased	*Creative*	*Lethargic*	*Gossipy*
Inspirational	*Expressive*	*Extremist*	*Extravagant*
Altruistic	*Romantic*		

It isn't as if you planned to leave the new building sketches at home, you were distracted with all this glorious sunshine and thoughts of the Hunt Ball coming up. A quick, sweet smile accompanies a more acceptable excuse for the boss as you proceed to produce ten hours' work in two. Amazingly, you pull it off, and the client is dutifully impressed. Impressed enough to sign on the dotted line? Sure, and you're not a bit stunned even if your boss is.

Duplicating your efforts isn't your forte, but bringing people together to solve common problems is. You use a dose of gentle persuasion and one of your many artistic talents to land the project. Not only do you make a top-notch pitch, you also land another project requiring a lot of work and a big stretch. Remember those pesky voices that keep telling you to look before you leap. Tut, tut, there you go—leaping again.

A glittering companion, you teeter between saint and scoundrel, landing somewhere in the middle. You embrace various philosophies out of personal curiosity and to confound the opposition. The tables are turning all the time, and you make important allies when you can. "Love your enemies as well as your friends" is a personal credo that has saved your bacon many times.

New horizons beckon, and while you're an adept juggler, it still galls you to deal with the dreck left behind by others. Finishing someone else's half-baked plan is a drag. Besides, you have a better vision of the future than many give you credit for. What other star/number combo besides this one can boast a Levi Strauss, who, some 170 years later, still has his name sewn on almost everyone's pants for all the world to see?

Love, Sex, and Marriage

The bedroom is one place you don't need to use persuasive charms. Quite the opposite as you have many more invitations to sample fragrant oils and steamy videos than you care to accept. Besides, you're a little choosy and prefer love, candlelight, tenderness—the whole dreamy enchilada, thank you, and nothing less.

Marriage provides a protective haven from which you venture out to build bridges and exchange smiles and beads with the other natives in foreign places. It's the breaks in a marriage, you believe, that keep chemistry bubbly and conversation lively. Together you pursue a myriad of interests, making every year a unique one. That's the real reason you get married. In addition to the romance and fun, it's to have an enduring friendship to counterbalance the normal craziness of life.

Money and Career

Business finds you to be a true original and welcomes you with open arms. You might prefer to while away the hours in your studio overlooking the park, but care too much about living a good life (not to be confused with THE good life, which is a different thing altogether) to settle for a constant diet of the mundane. A quick study with a perceptive mind, you can succeed when you decide to.

The money thing is something you would honestly like someone else to handle, but when forced to get your hands dirty with it, you can do a remarkable job. You instinctively understand the whys and the wherefores of people's motivations, which includes the movement of money and purchases on any scale. You might not ever stick your finger in the financial whirlpool, but it's that understanding (plus a dash of effervescent charm) that keeps you in the corner office as other workers come and go.

The)(3 Potential

You touch others with the merry twinkle in your eye, your unprejudiced compassion, and by being a perpetual fountain of inspiration. You know things have a way of working out, and encourage others to take comfort from that thought while doing everything they can on a practical level to make it happen. You teach how to combine logic with vision and to solve problems while charting a future course.

As your own worst enemy (and who isn't?), watch your tendency to go overboard, You are somewhat extravagant, particularly with praise and credit cards. One lands an unwanted suitor on your door, and the other makes trips to the beauty spa next month impossible. And when in doubt, stick to the facts. As much as you enjoy embellishing them, the cold, hard truth will keep you out of big trouble. You're needed to help us continue believing in our dreams. You can't do that if you don't separate fact from fiction or let mood swings color everything, but you knew that, didn't you?

FAMOUS PISCES THREES

Samantha Eggar	3/5/1939	Ted Kennedy	2/22/1932
Barbara Feldon	3/12/1941	Peter Graves	3/18/1926
Levi Strauss	2/26/1829	Fats Domino	2/26/1928

♓ • 4
Pisces Four
"The Capable Wizard"

♓+	4+	♓-	4-
Empathetic	Persistent	Gullible	Too Busy
Methodical	Thorough	Indecisive	Serious
Knowledgeable	Practical	Temperamental	Lazy
Creative	Constructive		

First there were the pair of Sister Ducks who lived in the closet and would only come out to play when no grown-ups were around. They attended your tea parties with Bonnie Bear and shouted, "You can do *that!*" Later the Discovery Channel informed you the Sister Ducks were penguins who lived in ice and snow (Santa's House?) and wouldn't know a teacup from a crumpet.

No matter, they listened while you in preschool overalls spun tales of wonder that formed the basis of a To-Do List for Life. Simple goals turn into sophisticated plans, and by the time you rent your first apartment, you're torn between shouting, "Look out, world, here I come!" and staying in bed with a raunchy novel and a box of popcorn. Those big dreams of yours take *mucho* sweat to make them come true. Not that sweating bothers you, and you don't mind working hard, especially when you're able to use your what-if skills to find a direct route to the finish line.

It's walking out the front door that's the hardest. It was easier to believe in yourself with the pudgy penguin audience. Now it's up to you to get up the gumption to show your stuff. Remember the encouragement you got at those tea parties? And you can always call Mom for a pull-yourself-up-by-your-bootstraps chat. All right then take a deep breath and prepare to join the throng of the productive crowd.

On the first day, wear your lucky ring, the one that looks like a crystal ball, and stick on that penguin pin Mom gave you. Whatever it takes, walk through that door and get to the office on time. Once you actually engage in the game, you see the lofty heights hovering over your head, almost within reach. Well, what *are* you going to do about that?

Love, Sex, and Marriage

When it comes to love, you prefer the straight-arrow, honest approach. This is one area where any game a pursuer plays is sure to backfire. Affection, poetry and lace, nachos and margaritas, and the right stage set work. Bonding has to happen before having sex, which is why it's not at the top of the Find a Mate list.

You function better if married because you weren't meant to go it alone. You have great fun setting up housekeeping with a heartthrob. From searching for the perfect flat to unpacking new dishes from Williams-Sonoma, you're happy nesting and have high hopes for your future together. Find a place to live with a fireplace and a room for a nursery, and you're no longer sorry to leave childhood behind.

Money and Career

Security rather than cold cash is what the whole work gig is to you. You prefer a flexible routine and are a hands-on manager. Your door is always open and you are reputed to have a heart of gold plus a passel of good advice to dish out. No, you're no wanna-be Dear Abby; it's just your way of helping others, which you do readily.

You have the versatility to succeed in countless endeavors. As long as the establishment is run with common sense and financial finesse, and you're amply rewarded, you stay put. Money isn't the end all and be all to you, but you do want a home of your own and do have those two kids to put through college—not to mention the ballet lessons and new computer. Oh, those are for you? Good for you!

The)(4 Potential

The picture in your head of who you are changes continually—faster than the weather and twice as dramatic. You strive for stability and in the process demonstrate how we can all build a strong foundation. Although somewhat of a nonconformist, you join in with many traditional celebrations with gusto. Why should the two conflict?

With the ability to intuitively link with friends, it's surprising that you seldom count on anyone but yourself. Doing that makes the responsibilities you carry grow into big burdens. This is an opportunity. You know, you aren't the only one who needs to be needed—ask friends to share the load. It's mutual love and respect that provide the elusive security you crave. To get it, surrender to a little give-and-take. Sure, the first time is a bit scary, but the rewards are exactly what you're looking for!

FAMOUS PISCES FOURS

Rob Lowe	*3/17/1964*	*Vanessa Williams*	*3/18/1963*
Roger Daltrey	*3/1/1944*	*Téa Leoni*	*2/25/1966*
Nat King Cole	*3/17/1919*	*Rue McClanahan*	*2/21/1952*

$)($ • 5

Pisces Five
"The Resourceful Dreamer"

$)($+	5+	$)($-	5-
Perceptive	Resourceful	Indecisive	Impulsive
Inspirational	Progressive	Trusting	Restless
Idealistic	Curious	Escapist	Fickle
Versatile	Adventurous		

Elephants don't have the corner on the not-forgetting thing. You, too, never forget a slight or a generous act, though you are much too cordial to mention the slight. Everyone has their off days, and every tomorrow brings a new sunrise and a new trail to try. On the next trail, roles could be reversed—a thought that keeps your tongue in check. Because yes, you always have a lot to say.

An eternal optimist, you believe what people say, and that naïveté is as charming to others as it is frustrating to you. When Donna says she wants to vacation together in the Greek islands, you believe her. Visions of azure seawater dance in your head, and she doesn't call. So you call her, leave a message, and then mark her name off the list—that mental one you keep of Inner Circle Friends. Does this mean you go through people like wet Kleenex? Nope—when the moon is right and there's a reason to reconnect with Donna (business or pleasure), you still may be smarting from the last encounter, but you make the call and hope for the best.

Relaxing under the stars of a crisp Rocky Mountain night, you let a mental reel rich in fantasy roll. All talented people have a library full of those technicolor dreams, don't they? Some folks think you're a drifty dreamer, but one look at your checkbook or calendar shows how busy you are earning a living and sharing your creative spirit. You not only know how to survive in this big, bad world, but also know how to be congenial about it.

A self-made idealist, you have an ingrained personal code of ethics and conduct to guide every step. Problems stay private; you solve them yourself, which earns the respect of friends and foes alike. When life *is* a bowl of cherries, you share. You pause, put the horse you always ride to the next adventure in the pasture and call one of those Inner Circle Friends lucky enough to have your unconditional love.

Love, Sex, and Marriage

The first love affair or two are easy-breezy, but you do expect to be loved forever by any lover—altar in view or no. Pisces do better with a partner, but fives like to come and go, free of any hint of a ball and chain. "Love me for who I am, not what I can do for you!" you cry to would-be wedding partners (and friends). Marriage is founded on friendship in your book, but it has to have its steamy side too in order to sparkle.

Your idea of chemistry is two-dimensional (at least). You want not only a physical reaction when the date of your dreams walks into the room, but also a psychic link and mutual fascination of the metaphysical realm. Your partner may have a very different sort of personality, but must value what you think is important and understand your quirks.

Pisces Fives never think they will be good parents because of their own needs and issues, which is exactly what makes them excellent parents. Besides, they love any excuse to play, and rambunctious tots certainly supply that.

Money and Career

When it comes to business, you are a genial networker and let wisdom direct your actions. A realist about work, when you go after a job you want, you know you can charm folks with your patter, even those you don't particularly admire. Everyone has an ego, and you put yours under wraps until the contract is signed.

Even if you have a punch-the-clock kind of job, you also have freelance activities going on the side. This side of you believes in what you're doing, paycheck or no (though having one is better). You recognize money is a necessary evil and you always manage to attract a job offer when it's needed.

Opportunist is just another word for knowing a break

when you see it. Not only do you have that down pat, but also how to seize an opening however small. You know that the best opprtunities are those you create.

The ♓5 Potential

Beautiful dreamer that you are, you also have much to say to the world, and the motivation to get out there and say it. Writer, actor, songwriter, explorer, director, painter—the work you do will be innovative and must be about a topic that fits your vision of a better quality of life.

Don't let the worries and broken dreams immobilize you or put a martyr's cap on your head. You are loved and there are people who will always be there for you. You have a unique connection to the realm of fantasy, today's reality, and visions of the future. With your tender heart and creativity you teach the rest of us about changing ourselves in order to change the world.

FAMOUS PISCES FIVES

Ursula Andress	*3/19/1936*	*Dirk Benedict*	*3/1/1945*
Catherine Bach	*3/1/1954*	*Jon Bon Jovi*	*3/2/1962*
Chastity Bono	*3/4/1969*	*Ron Howard*	*3/1/1954*

♓ • 6
Pisces Six
"The Visionary Teacher"

♓+	6+	♓-	6-
Altruistic	*Nurturing*	*Procrastinates*	*Jealous*
Versatile	*Idealistic*	*Gullible*	*Self-sacrificing*
Creative	*Responsible*	*Inconsistent*	*Overbearing*
Gracious	*Loyal*		

When you meet new people, you see them as they are, as well as recognize their potential. Even if you aren't a classroom teacher, you still encourage people to reach for the stars as you point them in the right direction. You also, nudge, kick, push, and pull, particularly if it's a family member or a good friend. You're adamant that they get their greatness off the ground. Lucky them! There is a risk of pushing the right buttons at the wrong time, but you have a gift for spotting talent in its early stages.

When people let you down, as they inevitably do, you take it personally. Why don't they listen? They hear you, and may recognize the truth in what you say, but if they aren't ready to take The Plunge, all the encouragement and wheedling in the world won't make them jump. Don't take it personally. Do everything you can do, then step back. Accept that you aren't responsible for anyone's life choices except your own.

The main reason you like to go away is to come home again—including long trips to faraway places. Sure, you adore meeting new people and photographing exotic locales, but you never fail to get a warm rush at the sight and smell of the living room you so carefully decorated with silver-framed pictures on the grand piano overlooking the snapdragons in the garden. Not only do you love beauty and music, you surround yourself with them.

You bring out the best in people but are chameleonlike even with close chums. You have an innate understanding of the human condition (and a whole lot more). Consider Pisces Sixes Albert Einstein and Donald Duck. Between them they cover all your states and moods, from brainy to zany, don't they?

Love, Sex, and Marriage

You're a dyed-in-the-wool romantic, but no one would guess your private passion for roses and champagne when you first meet. You are so gifted at concentrating on the other person that you might forget to find out the important things, like is this someone who revs up your engine? Hmmm.

You deftly deflect prying questions with the Turn the Tables ploy. But before his attention wanders, you start your own subtle twenty questions to decide about him. Whether to pursue or say good night becomes crystal-clear before the entrées arrive.

At heart, you're a domestic type (even if you don't cook) and want a partner who enjoys the home scene as much as you do (and maybe does cook). That's after the sex-and-sizzle test, of course, which happens just after the exchange of love promises, of course.

Money and Career

You're a soft touch for money, and for some reason feel responsible for everyone else. You have faith in people, and that's not a bad thing unless you sacrifice your rent money today so a friend can pay his Visa bill. Be discerning and set boundaries. There's no disgrace in sticking to those limits. If you haven't heard, martyrdom is out, and you're in charge of your cash flow.

A career in the entertainment field, medicine, art, cosmetics, public relations, or service of any kind is where you will be happiest. Music is an integral part of your life, and not just as a performer. You strive for the same harmony and balance in other endeavors, too. Since you detest the humdrum, meeting new and interesting people makes an otherwise ho-hum job just perfect for you.

The)(6 Potential

Happy at home writing or reading an intriguing novel, tossing together a primo salmon pesto, and napping on the couch with Mr. Periwinkle curled up beside you are classic scenes from the days of your life. Find what you do well and concentrate your efforts there: It inspires others to do the same. "Look at me," you say. "If I can do it (whatever it is), so can you!"

Don't be too possessive of the people you love and/or mentor. Keep an open mind about new opportunities and avoid the "I would have, should have, could have" trap. Keep at least one ball in the air even when you aren't too sure of the game. It prevents you from lapsing into Technicolor dreams and contemplating time travel so you stay sharp for the next genuine break that comes along. Be careful not to aim too low, because as we all know, you get what you expect to get.

FAMOUS PISCES SIXES

Joanne Woodward	*2/27/1930*	*Quincy Jones*	*3/14/1933*
Adelle Davis	*2/25/1905*	*Bruce Willis*	*3/19/1955*
Erma Bombeck	*2/21/1927*	*Michael Caine*	*3/14/1933*

⟩(• 7
Pisces Seven
"The Discerning Dream Weaver"

⟩(+	7+	⟩(-	7-
Perfectionist	*Analytical*	*Inconsistent*	*Aloof*
Charming	*Articulate*	*Shy*	*Suspicious*
Knowledgeable	*Intellectual*	*Escapist*	*Stingy*
Methodical	*Private*		

With a wizard for an imaginary friend, you don't need anyone else. At least not until you want to play *Lord of the Rings* and need someone to play the other parts. Basically you're shy and curious—smart, too. Develop a specialty—become an expert about something fascinating to give you a cover of sorts until you figure out who you are.

Mr. Rogers wasn't always in the neighborhood beaming in on your TV every day, but he is typical of the Pisces Seven energy, combining childlike whimsy, basic psychology, and technology to teach children about the nice and caring adults out there. Like him, you know how tough it can be on a little one with a head buzzing with questions, bursting with enthusiasm, and too timid to bounce and bubble.

Able to alter your appearance and personality in a flash, you have different circles of friends to pursue your varied interests. So you're a closet skydiver. Why worry the boss by telling him? And if you told him it's a solo sail to the island this weekend, he'd probably worry about that, too.

You just need alone time at the helm to recharge and refocus.

You have an unending stream of incongruous thoughts flowing from the left to the right side of your brain continually. No wonder you sound like the wizard Gandalf directing an action movie half the time—you don't know whether to weave spells, chant *om,* or reprogram all the computers you've encountered. Tough choices until the sexy redhead from the public-speaking class calls and inquires about your weekend plans. Toss the magic wand, laptop PC, and leather-bound book of chants. Pack the margarita mix, beach clothes, and George Winters for the boat. The trip has turned into a very different event. Is that a big grin on your face? Much better!

Love, Sex, and Marriage

Few would guess that you've got a technique for torrid tangos that would make the most experienced lover blush. Few people see that side of you, and as a lover-in-waiting, it might be "only fair" to warn anyone interested before he gets charged up, that you might be more uninhibited than they realize. But if they don't turn *you* on—physically, mentally, and with gusto—the trip to the water bed doesn't happen.

Marriage has an entirely different set of criteria for you. Romance and sex are hard to find, let alone keep. To consider the wedding-bell routine, you have a tough list: must love me in spite of myself, looks out for "us," and not have a sharp tongue. Everything else is workable, including the quiet time you need. Should children join the love nest, you become a fine parent with more understanding than most when little Brian takes the bathroom clock apart to see how it works and then blames the broken clock on the purple tiger who lives under his bed.

Money and Career

Bouncing back and forth, a Pisces Seven has to grip the earth tightly to not swing to one extreme or the other and get lost in the process of searching for the center. Money to tuck in the bank is a hollow trophy. Hence you spend it on a wood-paneled study lined with intriguing books, or a jewelry box holding select gems and twenty-four-karat gold. You're as likely to spend a bundle on camera equipment as on a T-bill. At least until you see the whole money-stock-security thing for the adult game it is.

A profession that allows you to set your own hours plus use your intellect and penchant for perfection is the one for you. You earn more money at it, too, than you thought you would. You spread a piece of it around—to the AIDS Foundation, drug rehabilitation centers—and never breathe a word. Money is only good for what you do with it, isn't it?

The ⟩(7 Potential

You have a relatively slow start in life, observing mankind, experimenting, and getting a formal education. Specialized training is essential to devleop your talents. You enjoy sharing your considerable knowledge and enchanting narratives with kindred spirits in and out of work.

It's fine to look to others for approval, but don't be so consumed with it that you toss out beliefs or veer too far away from the road that takes you where *you* want to go. Self-doubt can be turned to an asset when you use it to pinpoint areas of improvement, but never use it as an excuse to let yourself down. You have a gift of understanding complex concepts and quantum mysteries of life along with the ability to enrich the lives you touch.

FAMOUS PISCES SEVENS

Glenn Close	*3/19/1947*	*Johnny Cash*	*2/26/1932*
Bernadette Peters	*2/28/1948*	*Frédéric Chopin*	*2/22/1810*
Patrick Duffy	*3/17/1949*	*Mr. (Fred) Rogers*	*3/20/1928*

♓ • 8
Pisces Eight
"The Shrewd Sifter"

♓+	8+	♓-	8-
Inspirational	*Professional*	*Sensitive*	*Indecisive*
Romantic	*Open-minded*	*Critical*	*Workaholic*
Mystical	*Capable*	*Diffident*	*Overreacts*
Focused	*Global View*		

Now, let's see, what goes best with my new diamond (pavé, turquoise, silver, bold gold) bracelet? It's a dockside lunch for lobster in the rough, so don light denims and strappy sandals, and off you go. The original denim-and-diamonds sort, you always have a packed schedule without a precious playtime second to waste, so you hustle. Besides, you can't wait to hear the buzz about Jan's latest Greek god or Marilyn's shopping coup.

You bring along an envelope of facts and figures Joanne requested—much easier than bundling them up and mailing them. When it comes to creating a mood, picking an outfit, or researching the national debt and how it relates to the consumption of Java Chip ice cream, you're on top of it—see? Already done! Surfing the Net, sorting the vibes and political climate of every room you enter, and digging for facts to support your point of view, yes! Printing and collating a hundred copies and mailing to all the stockholders, no, not unless you absolutely have to.

For all the glitter and charm you lavish on the general population, the neurons are always firing in that brain of yours—filing away valuable information, adding sparkling comments, while worrying about meeting Lorenzo's plane tonight (what were you thinking when you invited him to visit?) or wondering if the papers arrived at the office for the Jones deal.

You always appear well put together, but you know what it's like to have the bottom fall out. After the first half dozen times, you get the hang of getting back up, but seldom chat

about it. Friends love you because you know when to keep
everything but the positive strokes to yourself.

Love, Sex, and Marriage

You're attracted to the diamond-in-the-rough type as a
fantasy companion. Though this is out of step with your
otherwise sharp scrutiny approach, it *is* the romantic you
who sometimes places too much credibility on the circumstances and chemistry of a first meeting. Who wouldn't fall
in love with an able-bodied man who swept you off your
feet seconds before the mannequin in Nordstrom's crashed
to the ground where you were standing?

Also attracted to powerful men, you seldom marry them.
They become friends, mentors, and occasionally lovers. And
there has to be room in the tie that binds for personal and
shared goals. For you, love is sweeter when you stop hearing or using the words *dependent* and *codependent*. Most of
all you need another adult player who doesn't want a parent, but a red-hot lover and true-blue friend who's got his
life in order and viable dreams for the future.

Money and Career

In the beginning of your foray into the How to Earn a
Living process, you enter quietly, in spite of your education
or financial background. After the bevy of dreams and
schemes that do little more than rattle around in your head,
you learn the language of money. Since it's an early lesson,
you would think it would stick, but you always pay attention
to what comes in and goes out.

You are a magician at helping friends and clients make
the most of their money. As for your own, keep a firm grip
on your checkbook and be sure you fully understand all the
fine print of any contract you sign. Friends can sometimes
cost you money, too, but you can control the depth of the
touch and still be a compassionate resource for them. You
will try a variety of careers, but do best when focusing on
one endeavor at a time, because you choose such challenging ones. Inventor, poet, teacher, musician, financier, actor—

whatever your preference, don't settle for second best or you won't be happy.

The)(8 Potential

Though you were forced to depend more on yourself than anyone else at a relatively early age and thought it was a bore, you got the jump on the rest of us in becoming an adult. Obligations and commitments get heavy, but you keep your perspective and strive to keep a balance between the Important Three: Family, Yourself, and Business.

Learn to say no when your body is screaming no; don't let logic or loyalty drown it out. As a young adult, you often feel like the only adult out there. Sometimes your mere presence inspires others to reach for greater heights. In your positive practical way, you teach others how to turn fantasy into reality—that and leave them feeling better for having met you.

FAMOUS PISCES EIGHTS

Edna St. Vincent Millay	2/22/1892	Kelsey Grammer	2/21/1956
Elizabeth Taylor	2/27/1932	Fabio	3/15/1961
Liza Minnelli	3/12/1946	Michelangelo	3/6/1475

)(• 9
Pisces Nine
"The Perceptive Performer"

)(+	9+	)(-	9-
Visionary	Performer	Lazy	Impersonal
Versatile	Charismatic	Extreme	Demanding
Perceptive	Artistic	Fickle	Perfectionistic
Creative	Worldly		

The sky is the limit? Ohhh! Is that as high as I can go? An innocent question from a three-year-old surrounded with finger-paint pictures he's drawn. Mom wanted to let you know you could paint like a pro if you wanted, but you have other ideas, such as winning a karate tournament, marrying royalty, and setting up the folks in a mansion. And then maybe rocketing off into the sky to, oh, beyond our sun to gaze at someone else's sky.

A few stubbed toes and noses later, you get serious. You know exactly how to make things happen even if it takes years of being a bumper car bouncing from one highway to another. As perceptive a perfectionist as you are, once you decide a vehicle will take you where you want to go, you stick with it. That focus and persistence gets you to the top with a scrapbook of memories.

So you win a trophy or two, marry an enchantress worthy to be a royal, and add on that family room with the slate fireplace to your parents' house that they've always wanted. You glance at the sky and know you can still get there if you keep going. Look how far you've come already!

Instinctively you know what others want. This is a great help as a child, because you always know what the adults expect of you. Of course, that also means some confusion later when you don't know what YOU really want. Thus starts the lifelong process of your education, and using the two talents together—what do I want to do that others really want to have, see, or do? The tools get sharper, and no matter how long it takes, you never doubt you're going to get there.

Love, Sex, and Marriage

As you tell everyone at the dinner table at the ski resort that you won't ever get married, your eyes scan the room looking for a likely candidate. Winning looks, a spirited laugh, and intelligent eyes grab your interest, and if he is dressed in an elegant/casual sort of way, you're hooked. At least for now.

Fantasy and romance play a big part in the relationship formula, and you've been disappointed before when the reality fell short of the promise, which is why you say no, no, but think, well, just maybe . . . A happy relationship means having a lover who not only delights in various bedroom games, but who also has the intellect and energy to keep up with you in the outside world, too. Compassion and self-motivation complete the package. Tall order? Maybe, but knowing you, if it's out there, you will find it—whether by psychic beacon or an intensive search.

Money and Career

You've got to spend money to make money, and that explains the huge swings in your net worth. As astute a businessperson as you are, get a second opinion from a reputable money man before signing over any huge sums. Sometimes what you think will be hot tomorrow is actually a few years into the future—you have a knack for being ahead of the crowd. And other times you just want to help someone or lots of someones. As a friend, you never forget a debt owed.

You prefer to be part of a working team, but this arrangement only works if you're the boss and calling the shots. Routine and you are not a good mixture; you prefer travel and variety. At some point you must express the creative side—athlete, actor, writer, dancer, or straight-arrow visionary. You have what it takes to push the limits; that is, of course, if that's what you want to do.

The)(9 Potential

You approach the great mysteries of life with the same fervor with which you do everything else, and have two immediate realizations. Being connected to the cosmos psychically is fascinating, and yes, we are all connected on that psychic wave, but without having tangible, physical contact with fellow earth-walkers, it isn't all that valuable.

You only publicize your good works enough to reach the people who can benefit from them. You always figure a way to have what you need, and hope to show others how to do the same. Dump ideas that don't work—be a bumper car bouncing through life. Let go of the past and embrace the new. Until you do, more heavy-duty rain fills your skies. You were meant for more. Develop self-compassion and flexibility and your car turns into a rocket ship to take you wherever you decide to go.

FAMOUS PISCES NINES

Sharon Stone	*3/10/1958*	*Spike Lee*	*3/20/1957*
Irene Cara	*3/18/1959*	*Kurt Russell*	*3/17/1951*
Chuck Norris	*3/10/1940*	*Jean Harlow*	*3/3/1911*